D1825887

BUILDING
YOUR BUSINESS
THROUGH EXPORT

STRATEGIC SUCCESS SERIES

BUILDING YOUR BUSINESS THROUGH EXPORT

JOHN WESTWOOD

KoganPage

LONDON PHILADELPHIA NEW DELHI

Publisher's note

Every possible effort has been made to ensure that the information contained in this book is accurate at the time of going to press, and the publishers and author cannot accept responsibility for any errors or omissions, however caused. No responsibility for loss or damage occasioned to any person acting, or refraining from action, as a result of the material in this publication can be accepted by the editor, the publisher or the author.

First published in Great Britain and the United States in 2012 by Kogan Page Limited

120 Pentonville Road	1518 Walnut Street, Suite 1100	4737/23 Ansari Road
London N1 9JN	Philadelphia PA 19102	Daryaganj
United Kingdom	USA	New Delhi 110002
www.koganpage.com		India

© John Westwood, 2012

ISBN   978 0 7494 6375 5
E-ISBN   978 0 7494 6376 2

British Library Cataloguing-in-Publication Data

A CIP record for this book is available from the British Library.

Library of Congress Cataloging-in-Publication Data

Westwood, John, 1947–
    Building your business through export / John Westwood. – 1st ed.
        p. cm.
    ISBN 978-0-7494-6375-5 – ISBN 978-0-7494-6376-2   1. Foreign trade promotion.
2. Exports.   I. Title.
    HF1417.5.W475 2012
    658.8'4–dc23
                                                                                    2011049145

Typeset by Graphicraft Limited, Hong Kong
Printed and bound in India by Replika Press Pvt Ltd

This book is for Louise

CONTENTS

Introduction 1

1 Why start exporting? 3

The export superpowers 3
Why start exporting? 6
The benefits of exporting 7
Is your company ready to start exporting? 8
Summary 13

2 How to get started 14

Types of exporter 14
Online or traditional exporting? 15
How to get started 16
Government support for exporters 17
Why do you want to start exporting? 17
Assessing whether you are ready to start exporting 20
The export audit 21
Making the decision 25
Summary 30

3 How to decide which markets to consider first 31

The world market 31
Regional trading agreements and trading blocs 33
Other economic groupings 36
Selecting potential export markets 37
Which country first? 38
Summary 46

4   Researching the market 47

How to plan your marketing research 47
Carrying out marketing research for overseas markets 49
Carrying out the research yourself 52
Desk research 54
Country (market) and industry (sector) reports 55
Other sources of market and sector reports 58
Company information 60
Product and statistical information 61
Field research 63
Using an agency to carry out market research 64
Summary 69

5   Developing an export strategy and preparing an export plan 70

Developing your export strategy 70
The marketing planning process 73
Research and analysis 74
Situation analysis 75
Pricing for export markets 81
Objectives and strategies 84
Tactics and action plans 89
Costs and budgets 91
The written plan 96
Summary 99

6   Entry strategies for overseas markets 100

Types of exporting 100
Market entry strategies 101
Deciding which entry strategy to use 112
Marketing channels 113
Summary 116

**7   Setting up and managing overseas
      distribution** 118

Finding and selecting overseas agents and distributors 120
Agent/distributor questionnaire 122
Legal aspects of dealing with agents and distributors 124
Agency and distributor contracts 128
Managing distributors 134
Summary 135

8   Sales promotion 136

Understanding your target market 136
Reviewing your sales promotion for overseas markets 139
Websites 140
Sales literature 142
Presentations 143
Advertising 144
Exhibitions and trade shows 145
Sector-focused trade missions/visits 148
Summary 151

9   Selling goods online 152

Websites for international e-commerce 152
Types of site 153
Web hosting 155
E-commerce sites 156
E-commerce regulations 159
Summary 164

10   Quoting for international business 165

Pricing for export business 165
Export contracts 169
Payment methods 170
Terms of sale (Incoterms) 174
Summary 180

11   Moving your goods 181

Modes of transport 181

Using freight forwarders 185

Export packaging 186

Labelling 190

Transport insurance 191

Export documentation 193

Classifying your goods 196

Reporting procedures 201

Summary 204

12   Managing the risks of exporting 205

Understanding the market 205

Country risks 206

Customer risks 207

Creditworthiness 208

The risks of currency and foreign exchange 210

Delivery delays and frustrated exports 216

Intellectual property rights in international trade 217

Avoiding litigation 221

Personal and company risk 221

Risk management and insurance services 222

Summary 224

13   Individual export markets 226

Europe 226

Other top export destinations 231

Brazil, Russia, India, China (the BRICs) 233

Summary 238

Government support organizations 239

Useful websites 243

Appendix 1: Types of government support services available 247

Appendix 2: Example of a complete export plan 253

Appendix 3: Example of an export marketing plan 261

Index 271

INTRODUCTION

Exporting is a fantastic way to grow your business. Any company with a good product that it is successfully selling in its domestic market should think about starting to develop an export business. Exporting is not just for large companies and major multinationals – the majority of exporters in most countries are small businesses.

There has never been a better time for companies to move into exporting. All countries want to persuade more of their companies to export their products and most governments provide assistance for their exporters. The support on offer ranges from straightforward advice to financial incentives or support.

There is a huge amount of information and assistance available to exporters, much of it on the internet. If anything, the problem is that there is so much information that it is difficult to sort the most important material from the rest. Hopefully the information and examples in this book will guide you in the right direction to start your journey into exporting, but it is your journey and every one is different.

The information that you will find is continually changing and websites are being continually updated, so what is current today may have changed in six months' time. But persevere, because it will have been replaced with updated information even if it has been moved to another part of the website.

Also bear in mind that our examples are just that. They show what should be the best way forward for some companies, but not for all. Always take appropriate advice as you develop your export business and where you need financial or legal advice make sure that you consult experts in that field.

I have tried to make as much as possible of the material in this book applicable to exporting worldwide, regardless of the country that you are based in. Most material is truly global: Incoterms for different terms of trade are universal and documents such as Letters of Credit are governed by internationally accepted rules. Much is used globally, but applied locally. This is particularly true of the countries within the European Union. Much EU legislation and regulation is the result of EU Directives. But although these directives apply to all EU countries, each individual country enacts the directive into its own laws and this results in differences in the statutes and regulations from country to country. Examples of this are HS commodity codes and laws relating to agency and distribution agreements.

Where possible we have tried to give examples of support services that are available to exporters in many countries, but on occasions I have had to give examples of a specific support service available in one particular country. In such cases, I have tended to use examples of services available to UK exporters from UK Trade & Investment or from the UK Chambers of Commerce. We should point out that similar government support services are usually available to exporters in other major developed economies. Even if your own government does not provide major amounts of support material for exporters on their own website, we will show you how you can still access free information on government websites in many countries.

Throughout this book we concentrate on helping you to make and implement the key strategic decisions: deciding whether exporting is for you, getting started and developing your export business. We have included information on topics such as export procedures/reporting and packing, labelling and shipping your goods, all of which are necessary for you to understand. But we have not included the detail of filling out forms and other tasks which will ultimately be carried out by the trained personnel that you will employ.

If you are new to exporting, this book will get you started on your export journey. But even if you are an experienced exporter, you will find a wealth of information to help you to take your export business to a higher level. Exporting is a team effort and will only succeed with the professional dedication of all of the members of your export team. It is also addictive – so once you start, you will never want to stop.

Additional resources to accompany the book are available on Kogan Page's *Strategic Success* website:
www.koganpage.com/strategicsuccess.

CHAPTER ONE

WHY START EXPORTING?

Any company that has good products and a steady level of business in its home market should logically consider exporting as a way of growing their business still further. The risks are greater, but the rewards can also be significant. Although expanding your sales abroad gives you major opportunities for growth, you need to be aware that the associated costs are higher than selling domestically – so margins will usually be lower. Language and cultural differences, political instability, currency and payment problems can all pose risks to inexperienced exporters too. These are reasons why your export sales should always supplement your domestic sales and not replace them.

The export superpowers

In recent years world trade has grown at a faster rate than world output. At the time of writing, world exports of merchandise and commercial services are worth around $18.5 trillion. World merchandise exports in the form of manufactured goods, minerals and agricultural commodities account for about 80 per cent of global trade, with services comprising the other 20 per cent. The proportion made up by services is continuing to increase year on year.

According to the World Trade Organization (WTO), (**www.wto.org**), China is the largest merchandise exporter, followed by the United States and Germany. The United States is the largest exporter of commercial services, followed by Germany and the UK. Figures 1.1 and 1.2 show the

10 largest merchandise exporters and the 10 largest exporters of commercial services in 2010 based on WTO figures. It is clear that exporting is very important to all major economies and in most developed economies governments actively encourage companies to export by providing expertise and a range of financial assistance packages.

FIGURE 1.1 Top merchandise exporters (2010)

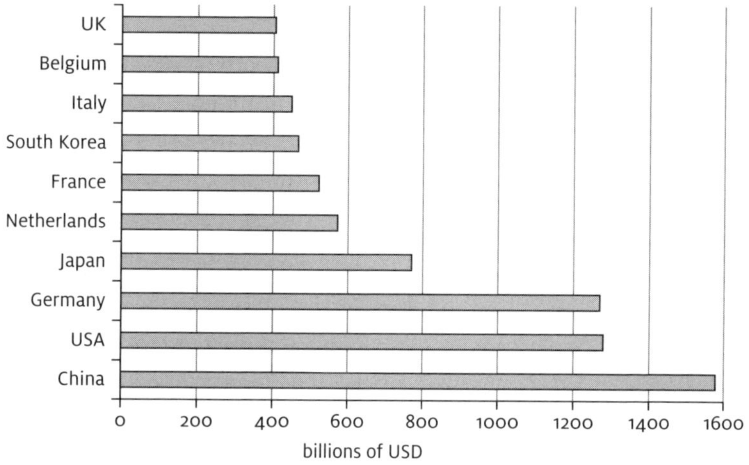

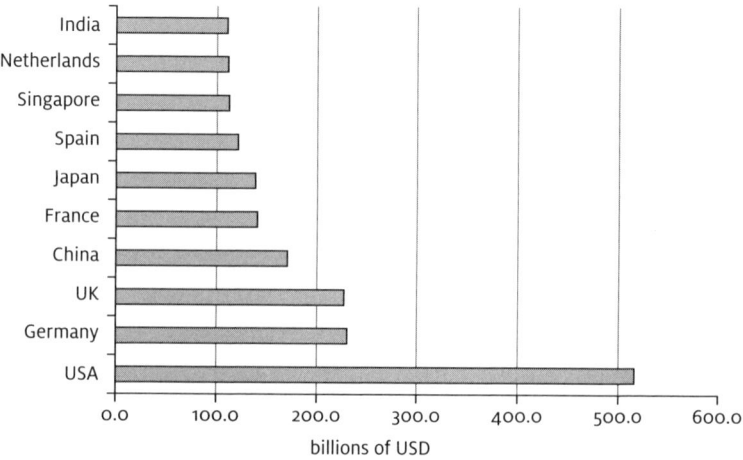

FIGURE 1.2 Top exporters of commercial services (2010)

- In the United States, many small companies find that they can develop and grow their businesses adequately, just selling domestically. Even so, many American companies make as much as a third of their profits outside the United States.
- Although the UK is the sixth largest manufacturing economy in the world and a major exporter, a survey of 500 businesses carried out by the British Chambers of Commerce in 2010 found that 27 per cent of UK manufacturers do not export at all and that a further 15 per cent of companies export less than 10 per cent of their turnover.
- The bulk of UK merchandise exports come from the 34 per cent of companies that export over half of their turnover.

If you look at the top 10 merchandise exporters you will see that some small countries such as Belgium and the Netherlands perform as well as much larger countries such as France, Italy and the UK, even though they have much smaller populations and a smaller manufacturing base. One of the main reasons for this is that these countries have a high degree of re-exports. As well as exporting their own goods, they have large ports (eg Rotterdam and Antwerp) that also import and export goods destined for Germany and beyond.

The example of Germany

Germany, with a population about one-third larger than the UK, Italy or France, is third only to China and the United States in its level of merchandise exports. It exports nearly three times as much as the UK and more than twice as much as France. Why is this? A large part of the reason is that, apart from well-known and very large exporting companies such as BMW and Mercedes, Germany has a wide range of medium to large companies (the 'Mittelstand') whose key strategy has been to focus on market niches and to develop their sales in these niches on a worldwide basis. Many of these companies are cutting edge in their field, but the field is more likely to be in areas such as mechanical engineering or building components than in computer graphics or iPods. Germany is a major worldwide supplier of machine tools, but it also has companies that make everything from vacuum furnaces and high-pressure cleaners to specialist doors or even pencils.

The strategy is simple – concentrate on one range of products and aim to become the world leader (or at least one of the top three companies) in that field. This way they avoid competing directly with many of the large multinationals that have much more diverse product portfolios.

So this is a lesson we can all learn from. If you are going to start exporting you should analyse your product ranges and the applications that you sell into. Do you have any particular market niches, where you are strong in your domestic market? If so, you should consider targeting the same market niches in your export markets. Remember that even a small market niche can be huge on a global scale.

Why start exporting?

If your company has been successful at selling its products in your domestic market, there is a good chance that it will also be successful in overseas markets – at least in those overseas markets where similar needs and conditions exist.

Any successful company will adopt a range of strategies to help to grow its business. Exporting can bring major benefits, but why should it be top of your list of strategies to adopt? There are two very good reasons:

- Exporting expands your available market.
- No other business activity receives so much encouragement and support.

The available market

According to the International Monetary Fund (IMF), the size of the world economy in 2011 was about $68 trillion. For any company any-where in the world the potential export market for their product is much larger than their potential domestic market.

Support for exporters

Virtually all governments provide support for their exporters. In major economies this includes providing vast amounts of information, advice to individual companies and even financial support for things such as market research, trade fairs and trade missions. Why do they do this?

Because they know that if they want to grow their economies, part of this growth has to come from exports. This is particularly true for the established economies of the developed world, and it is also becoming increasingly the case for developing countries. The increased growth rates over the past decade in countries in regions such as Africa and South America have been, in large part, fuelled by the growth in their exports of minerals and other commodities. See what official sources in some countries say themselves:

- Exports account for 30 per cent of UK GDP and contribute 60 per cent of UK productivity growth. One in four jobs in the UK is linked to business overseas and up to 3.5 million UK jobs are linked both directly and indirectly to the country's trade with the EU. Even so, just one in 25 UK companies currently exports their goods or services (UKTI 2010).

- Exports accounted for nearly 25 per cent of US economic growth during the past decade and are expected to grow by nearly 10 per cent per year for the next several years (US Department of Commerce 2008).

- Nearly 96 per cent of consumers live outside the United States, so even for a US company, two-thirds of the world's purchasing power is in foreign countries (US Small Business Administration 2011).

- It is estimated that exports provide more than 20 per cent of Australia's gross national income and that more than 1.7 million jobs nationally are dependent on the export sector (Austrade 2011).

The benefits of exporting

Exporting can help you to increase your potential market, increase your turnover, improve your business's reputation, avoid being overdependent on your domestic sales and provide a buffer to any cyclical deterioration in your domestic economy. Exporting companies can utilize their capacity more efficiently and gain economies of scale. By finding export markets in different hemispheres, agricultural suppliers can even out seasonal fluctuations in the demand for their products.

According to UK Trade & Investment (UKTI), **www.ukti.gov.uk**, companies that export:

- improve their productivity;
- achieve levels of growth not possible domestically;
- increase the resilience of their revenues and profits;
- achieve economies of scale not possible domestically;
- increase the commercial lifespan of their products and services;
- increase the returns on their investment in R&D;
- improve their financial performance;
- feel the benefit.

Academic research confirms that exporting companies are more productive than non-exporters, achieve stronger financial performance and are more likely to stay in business. A study of UK companies by Harris and Cher Li showed that firms beginning to export gained a 34 per cent productivity uplift and that those that exported were 11.4 per cent more likely to survive.

Recent surveys by UKTI show that doing business overseas also gives companies increased exposure to new ideas. By working with international clients and partners, companies gain knowledge of different cultural environments and get a better insight into customers' requirements. They gain exposure to new technologies and ideas and also experience a wider range of competitors. This gives them the opportunity to develop new and improved products and services, which can help them to gain and retain competitiveness at home as well as overseas. In the longer term they can also improve their return on investment (ROI), because competing in world markets helps companies improve their efficiency and performance.

Is your company ready to start exporting?

Developing new export markets takes time and money. There are many new challenges – from identifying the best markets and potential customers to making sure your product complies with local standards and regulations. Exporting isn't just an add-on to your existing business – it should be part of your overall business development strategy.

In developing your business, you may have concluded that you need to increase the volume of sales of particular products to make them more viable. If you already have a reasonable level of sales of these products in your domestic market it is unlikely that you could achieve something like a 100 per cent increase in sales in your domestic market alone. But such an increase in sales may well be possible in markets where you are currently not selling, ie overseas.

But you can't just say: 'OK, that seems a good idea. Let's do it!' Before you start exporting you need to carry out an export audit, develop an export strategy and prepare a complete export plan, which includes looking at all the costs and risks involved. (We will look at export audits in Chapter 2 and show you how to develop an export strategy and prepare an export plan in Chapter 5.)

Potential risks involved in exporting include:

- Greater complexity:
  - Exporting involves all the usual marketing challenges. You have to find customers and persuade them to buy from you. You have to research the market so that you understand what the customers want and how the market operates – both may be different from what you have found in your domestic market.
  - You will need to cope with extra logistical problems, paperwork and contractual issues. You will probably need to get standard contracts prepared for selling directly, through agents and through distributors.
  - You will need to comply with regulations in both your domestic and overseas markets and these may not be the same.
  - The protection of intellectual property can be difficult and more complex in overseas markets and in some it may not be 100 per cent effective.
- Increased pressure on your resources:
  - You will need additional resources, in terms of both skilled personnel and financing. You will need additional personnel and these personnel will need to possess or learn the skills required in dealing with export markets.

- Exporting may impact on your company's domestic activities. It may reveal capacity and productivity constraints.
● Increased financial exposure:
  - Exporting will initially involve expenditure which may impact on your company's cash flow.
  - Payment terms will usually be longer than for domestic sales. Customers often want credit from the time they receive the goods. This could be weeks after you have produced and shipped the goods, so you get paid later than you would be by a domestic customer.
  - There could be export financing and/or currency issues and the additional risk of potential non-payment for goods and services supplied to overseas customers.
  - At the same time you may have to meet extra costs for transport and insurance.

Dealing with these issues means additional costs for your business. Equally importantly, you may find that you just can't compete with local suppliers in some overseas markets. If the market only offers low margins or you don't have the extra resources that you need, you may decide that exporting is not for you. But if you have good products and efficient manufacturing, there will certainly be opportunities for you in overseas markets.

The extra costs of exporting

To support an export operation your company will need to train existing personnel and add additional personnel with new skills. As existing personnel start to support your export business they will no longer have the time to handle all of their original responsibilities. So whether you train up existing staff or recruit new staff for your export operations, you will still have additional personnel costs. The key areas that you have to consider are:

● Development. You will have to research and develop new markets, including putting the necessary distribution in place.
● Sales support. You will need to support the new distribution that you set up and you will need to provide training, make quotations, process orders, etc.

- Logistics. Your shipping department will need to learn to pack, label, document and ship goods abroad.
- Finance. Your finance department will need to learn the skills to allow them to assess risks, decide on credit arrangements, manage accounts and, where necessary, manage currency risks.

You can start an export operation with your existing staff, but very quickly you will need additional resources to manage the day-to-day business. Even a small ongoing export operation will require a minimum of one dedicated internal sales person and one outside sales person. You also have to add in their travelling costs and other expenses.

That is the investment that you can easily see. But then you need to consider the fact that you may not be able to make the same level of margins in your export business that you do on your domestic sales. You have to be sure that your top management accept this and that they recognize that your export sales are additional sales.

The exchange rate factor

Exporting is a continually changing ball game and one of the main change factors that is completely outside your control is the movement of currency exchange rates. When you put together your budget for domestic sales for next year, in addition to sales and margins, you will also include a number of assumptions, such as the estimated inflation rate, the rate of economic growth and the rate of value added tax. If you put together a budget for export sales, you also need to include assumptions for key exchange rates. If you are a UK company and your main export sales are to the eurozone, you may have included an assumption that the exchange rate will be €1.2 : £1. If you are selling in euros, then you will have calculated your sales back to pounds using this exchange rate. If the average actual exchange rate over the year is €1.15 : £1 you will make a slightly higher margin on your export business than you budgeted for. If the average exchange rate over the year is €1.25 : £1 you will make a slightly lower margin than budget. If you want to avoid even this risk, you may have taken out a level of forward exchange contracts to cover most of your business. You can take out forward exchange contracts for a year or even up to two years ahead. But what you cannot do is cover for the wider medium-term movements in exchange rates that often occur.

In 2010 the $: £ exchange rate moved between $1.43 : £1 and $1.64 : £1. That in itself is more than a 10 per cent range. But over the last twenty years or so the exchange rate has ranged from about $1 : £1 to as high as $2.4 : £1. When a major currency moves against other currencies, it tends to overcompensate and may never move back to its original rate – or if it does it may take several years. So you need to be certain that your top management understand that this type of situation can arise. If it does happen your only choice is to try to ride it out.

Getting top management on your side

If you have decided that selling your products overseas is a good expansion policy for your company and that the time is right to start now, you need to prepare justifications and make sure that top management, both in your own company and at head office (if you are part of a larger group), are behind you. Depending on the culture in your company you may only need to prepare a simple export plan including details of the opportunities, the costs and the risks, or you may need to prepare a complete marketing plan for your export venture, including a partial profit and loss account for the additional sales. A common problem in many companies is that although management accept a plan they will suggest that you try to grow the sales first and then invest in the extra people to support the new business afterwards. This will not work with export sales. Of course you need to be sensible about staffing levels and you may start by just taking on an export sales manager or export salesperson and getting proper training in export procedures for some of your other staff. But if you want to expand your overseas business you just cannot afford to be under-resourced. Whether in your domestic market or overseas, customers will not wait for quotations if they want to buy a product now. There is nothing more demoralizing for an export salesperson who has spent time and effort finding a new customer and getting an enquiry to be told by that customer that they have already placed the order elsewhere, when their own company still has not made a quotation.

Summary

Any company that has good products and a steady level of business in its home market should consider exporting as a way of growing their business. Exporting can help a company to increase its potential market, increase its turnover, improve its business reputation and avoid being overdependent on sales in its domestic market. Exporting companies are more productive than non-exporters, achieve stronger financial performance and are more likely to stay in business. However, exporting isn't just an add-on to a company's existing business and it should be part of its overall business strategy with the full support of top management. Exporting involves all the usual marketing challenges of having to find customers and persuade them to buy a product, but there are extra logistical problems, paperwork and contractual issues to cope with and this requires additional resources, in terms of both skilled personnel and financing.

CHAPTER TWO

HOW TO GET STARTED

Moving into export is a large step for any business – so it's important that you honestly assess if you are ready and able to take on the challenge. Before you start you need to prepare a list of the reasons why you want to export and you also need to assess whether your company is actually fit and ready to do so. You need to carry out an export audit and analyse the results.

If you then decide that you do want to move into exporting, you don't have to do it alone. There is plenty of assistance available and most of it is free. Nowadays almost every country, large or small, provides government support to their exporters, so it is unlikely that your country will not have a government agency that supports export trade and inward investment.

Types of exporter

In exporting, size is no obstacle. Small companies or even sole traders can expand their business by exporting, just as easily as large companies. The spread of company size in the UK is fairly similar to that of any other developed economy. About 70 per cent of companies employ less than 50 people and have a turnover of up to £5 million. Only about 5 or 6 per cent of companies employ more than 250 people or have a turnover of more than £50 million. So most companies that are just starting to export will be small and medium-sized enterprises (SMEs).

There are different ways of categorizing exporters. Risk management companies categorize exporters using factors such as the type of product that they sell, the typical size of contract that they receive and the frequency of the orders that they receive. From a marketing point of view, exporters can more easily be categorized by their approach to exporting. According to Robin Godfrey, manager of the Export Marketing Research Scheme, the British Chambers of Commerce categorize exporting companies as one of four different types:

1 Strategists: companies that see exporting as part of their business strategy. They are clear where the business is going financially and have a clear plan of how to get there.
2 Adaptives: companies that are starting to formulate a plan for export but have no clear picture of which markets they will target. They are willing to adapt their marketing materials, products and services as required.
3 Reactives: companies that develop their exports in response to opportunities that arise. Their overseas trade is uncertain and it changes rapidly.
4 Passives: companies that do not have exporting as a part of their business plan. Overseas orders may come to them unsolicited, but this type of company is unwilling to provide anything that is not on their product list.

Any company wanting to develop and expand its export business should, at the very least, become an adaptive exporter and should aim to develop its export skills further until it becomes a strategist.

Online or traditional exporting?

If your company is well promoted and your website attracts attention from search engines, there is no reason why you cannot pick up some business from anywhere in the world. However, you must be aware that there are additional national and international regulations relating to e-commerce that companies that sell or market products or services online must comply with, and in most countries you are not exempt from the normal obligations to report export sales to government and tax authorities just because you are trading online. When you take orders online you still need to get paid and your goods still need to be safely delivered. So unless you make sure that you get payment by credit card online, getting payment could be difficult. The risk of fraud or of goods being returned is also higher than with traditional methods of conducting export business.

Using your e-commerce site to generate some export sales is perhaps a first step and for some companies it may be the perfect way to proceed. The 2010 'Doing business overseas' survey carried out by the Institute of Directors and UKTI found that 4 per cent of companies relied on the internet for most of their overseas sales. But for the other 96 per cent of companies the internet is only one of many channels to market.

How to get started

We have said that moving into export is a big step for any business and by no means an easy option. So it's important that you honestly assess if you are ready and able to take on the challenge and move ahead.

In the guide, 'Exporting – an overview', UKTI advises that there are 10 key steps to successful exporting:

1 Research your market.
2 Implement an export strategy.
3 Construct an export plan.
4 Choose your sales presence.
5 Promote your product.
6 Get the customs side right.
7 Get paid on time.
8 Choose your distribution methods.
9 Transport goods effectively.
10 Have a good after-sales policy.

But where do you actually start and what should you do first?

Starting and progressing with exporting are iterative processes. Even though some things will happen in parallel I would suggest that you try to take one step at a time and work through the following list:

1 Prepare a list of the reasons why you want to start exporting and decide whether it would be the right thing to do.
2 Carry out an export audit of:
    – your company;
    – your internal organization;
    – your products.

3 Assess whether you are ready to start exporting.
4 Develop your export strategy.

Only then should you start to prepare your detailed export plan.

Even at this stage, it is worthwhile contacting your government support organization and speaking to a local adviser.

Government support for exporters

Trade is the lifeblood of economic growth, so all governments do their best to promote both exporting and inward investment. It can be a difficult sell and that is why many governments have organizations that provide advice, support and in many cases even financial support to companies that export. Twenty years ago only large exporting countries, mainly in the developed world, had government agencies to support their exporters. Nowadays almost every country, large or small, has a government agency that supports export trade and inward investment.

If you want to expand your export business you need to adopt a planned and structured approach. You need to get professional export advice. Details of government support organizations for a number of major exporting nations are given at the end of this book. To show how extensive and helpful the tools and services offered by these government organizations can be, Appendix 1 gives an example providing an outline of the services available to UK exporters from UKTI. Similar and equivalent support services are available to exporters in many countries from their local government support agencies, so this is a really essential avenue to investigate.

Why do you want to start exporting?

If you are having problems with declining sales, a tired product range and limited resources, then exporting is not for you. Exporting is a way of growing a successful business and not a way of getting out of trouble. It is very important to consider why you want to export and what the benefits would be for your company before you start your export activities. You must be sure that exporting fits in with your company's short-, medium- and long-term goals. You also need to have a clear definition of what your export product would be.

The reasons that you may decide to start exporting could include any of the following:

- It will increase the size of the potential market for our products and give us a wider and more stable customer base.
- The increase in sales should give us economies of scale in our manufacturing.
- It could increase the lifetime of some of our products.
- In addition to overall economies of scale, increased sales of some products with limited sales at present could make these products viable in the long term.
- For some products there will never be a large enough market just in one country and exporting could provide a justification for developing a new product that would not be viable if we had to rely on our domestic market alone.
- With our type of product we can take advantage of seasonal demand in other areas of the world. (This is particularly the case with seasonal food products such as high-range fruit and vegetables that can be shipped cost effectively by air.)
- We have identified a good opportunity to sell our product in a particular market.
- We have been contacted by an overseas company who believe that there are good opportunities to sell our products in their country.
- Our main competitors have made significant increases in their turnover by selling their products in overseas markets.

The following reasons would not justify moving into exporting:

- Head office think it would be a good idea.
- We are losing money and need to increase our level of sales.

To help make your decision, you should ask yourself the following questions:

- What does our company expect to gain from exporting? What are our objectives?
- Is exporting consistent with the company's goals?

- How committed is top management to the idea of moving into exporting? Will they be prepared to live with low profitability or even losses in the early stages?
- Do we have the necessary financial and personnel resources to start exporting?
- If we put a major effort into exporting, will our domestic business suffer?
- Are our current products or services suitable for export markets, or would major modifications be required?
- Are the benefits we expect to get from exporting worth the cost and investment involved?
- Would we be better off using our resources to develop new domestic business?

In fact, for many companies the decision will not be made from a zero base. Many companies find that they are starting to get enquiries from overseas, either directly or through their website, and some of these enquiries may have already turned into some orders.

Example

A South African company manufactures specialist safety equipment that is used in mines. The South African mining industry has historically sourced this type of equipment from Europe or the USA. Over the last 10 years the company has developed a number of products and now has a significant share of the market for these products in South Africa. They have been approached by a Chinese company that is interested in selling the company's products into the Chinese coal mining industry. Although they have no experience of exporting their products, they see this as an opportunity to significantly increase their turnover and to generate increased profits that can be used to develop additional products.

Assessing whether you are ready to start exporting

The export readiness checklist

There are a number of key issues that a company's management needs to consider that will help to determine if the company is ready to commence exporting or if alternative strategies are better suited to its current position.

Business Victoria, the business support organization for the State of Victoria, Australia, has produced an excellent export readiness checklist, available to download from their website, **http://export.business.vic.gov.au/getting-started/export-readiness-checklist**. The key issues to be considered are defined as:

- Commitment. Is the business prepared to devote the necessary time, effort and resources required for export success? Will the board and CEO give their full backing to exporting as a core business activity?
- Product/service. Will the business be able to identify and exploit market niches based on unique product or service features and qualities? Can the product design be modified if necessary to accommodate market requirements?
- Marketing. Does the business have strong marketing skills and a proven track record in its domestic market? Is there high-quality marketing material which could be translated if necessary?
- Management. Does the business have sufficient management capabilities to develop and service export markets or could skills be acquired if necessary?
- Production. Does the business have adequate surplus capacity or the flexibility to expand production quickly to service exports? Would the business consider alternative forms of market entry?
- Finance. Does the business have sufficient financial strength and resources to develop new overseas markets? Initial items of expenditure may include advertising, promotional material, training and the cost of market visits.

There are also a number of government websites with online question-naires to assess your 'export readiness'. These include the UKTI/Business Link interactive tool 'Are you ready to export?' at **www.businesslink.gov. uk**, and the US Department of Commerce online readiness assessment at **www.export.gov/begin/assessment.asp**. These useful free resources can be accessed and completed by anyone – not just UK or US citizens. When you complete the questionnaire you get an immediate assess-ment. It is no surprise that the conclusion of the assessment is never going to be that your company is not ready to export. It will tell you that you are 'ready to export', 'almost there', 'well on the way', 'have made a good beginning' or are 'on the right track'. But it will also give you a lot of useful information and explain how you can get assist-ance to address some of the areas of weakness highlighted by the assessment.

The export audit

Just because you can see an opportunity to expand your business by exporting does not mean that you are ready to do so. You may not have the resources to take on the extra work. Even if you have the financial resources, you may well not have the people in place to do the work. Nothing turns a potential customer off more than having to wait a long time for a quotation or not getting their goods delivered on time. To properly assess whether you are ready to start exporting you need to carry out an export audit.

The areas of your business that you should look at are:

- export sales history (if any);
- potential overseas markets;
- applicable products;
- sales staffing levels and experience;
- finance experience and requirements;
- logistics experience and requirements.

A useful way to proceed is to prepare a simple checklist that you can work through and complete. The exact detail will vary, depending on your business, but a typical example is given below:

Audit Checklist

Sales history

Give details of any overseas sales received over the last three years by value (including margins where available) by:

- country;
- customer;
- product.

Potential overseas markets

List any potential overseas markets that you are considering and give reasons why. For example, have you been contacted by potential customers from these markets? Do you know of competitor activity?

Applicable products

Which of your products would you consider selling overseas? Do you think that they are suitable without modification?

Sales personnel

- Do any of your sales personnel (either internal or external) have experience of dealing with overseas sales either with your company or with previous employers?
- Do any of your sales personnel speak any foreign language? If so, which language and what is their level of competence

Finance

For any of the above overseas orders, how have you handled finance/payment?

- Did you always receive payment in advance?
- If not, do your personnel have experience of chasing overseas payments?
- Do any personnel have experience of dealing with Letters of Credit?
- Do you have any foreign currency accounts?

Logistics

Do any personnel have experience of:

- export packing?
- export shipping?
- export paperwork?

Example

A US company based in Illinois manufactures industrial lawnmowers and lawn-treating equipment. Their main business is around the Great Lakes and throughout the Midwest. They have some contacts and are considering moving into exporting. They prepared a checklist and have now completed an initial audit. The results are given below.

Sales

We have received a small number of orders from outside the USA over the last few years. Details are:

Country	20X1 $k	20X2 $k	20X3 $k
Canada	30	60	40
Mexico		12	6
Total	30	72	46

We have received several orders from the Ontario Municipal Parks Department and one order from the Quebec Parks Department. The only customer that we have in Mexico is Parco Municipal Monterrey.

Virtually all orders have been for our mid-size 'Sneaker' range of ride-on mowers. Some orders have included mechanical lawn-spiking attachments and one included our 'Injectoram' liquid fertilizer injector.

Potential overseas markets

Canada. This is our main target market, both because of its proximity to our factory and also because of the ease of doing business there. We have been contacted by Park Services of Toronto, which is interested in representing us in Canada. We have not yet had the chance to evaluate them.

Mexico. Although we want to continue to sell to Mexico, it is not our main target market, both because of distance and language. This may change as we become more confident.

Applicable products

We see the 'Sneaker' range as the most applicable product. It is more suited to the wider range of smaller parks and municipal gardens that are found in Canada and Mexico. The range includes a wide range of accessories, including lawn spikers, injectors and selective treatment systems. Also, most of the accessories are available with both imperial and metric connections.

Sales personnel

Our district sales manager for Wisconsin and Michigan has experience of dealing with Canada from his previous employment with Ace Machinery and we will initially extend his territory to cover Ontario and Quebec.

Michelle has been handling the export orders that we have received so far and is becoming quite proficient. She also speaks Spanish reasonably well. If we expand the export business significantly we would need to recruit a replacement for domestic sales so that Michelle can handle the export business full time. We are intending to send Michelle for export training with the consultancy Frank Lynn in Chicago.

Finance

For the initial orders from all customers we insisted on payment before shipping the goods. We have now established a good relationship with Ontario Municipal Parks and the last two orders have been shipped on payment terms of net 30 days. So far we have not had any problems with payments. Our financial controller has experience of dealing with customers in Canada, but has no experience of dealing with shipments by Letter of Credit, which we understand is the prefered method of payment for shipments to smaller municipalities in Mexico.

Logistics

Our shipping manager has handled all of the packing, paperwork and shipping requirements for the orders we have received so far. If we want to expand this business, we will need to send him for more specialist training.

Making the decision

So you understand why you, your company management and key personnel want to start exporting. You have carried out an export audit and now have a clear idea of the additional resources that you will require to start exporting and have an estimate of the extra costs to your business. You also have an idea as to whether your product is going to be suitable for export markets. Is it just a yes/no decision? The answer is no. Nowadays there are number of ways that you can start exporting. Your choices are:

- Domestic exporting. Many companies are already selling products that are being exported, although they may not be aware of it. If you are supplying components or ancillary products to a major domestic manufacturer, your products may already be being exported in complete units or plant that that manufacturer is supplying to their overseas customers. If a company becomes aware that this is happening, the next step would be to actively seek out companies that could include their products in equipment that they export and to also look for domestic buyers who represent or purchase on behalf of foreign companies.

- Online or e-commerce exporting. Exporting your products by selling them online is another option that many companies use, particularly as an initial export strategy. But selling goods online to overseas markets is not as straightforward as selling online in your domestic market and you need to understand the rules and regulations that apply to international online sales. This is covered in detail in Chapter 9.

- Indirect exporting. This involves entering into a contractual relationship with an intermediary. The intermediary could be an agent who represents a number of indirect exporters who are not in direct competition with each other, an export management company that will export products on your behalf and also gather market information and arrange shipping and documentation, or an export trading company which will handle all the aspects handled by an export management company, but in addition may also provide distribution and storage facilities in the overseas market itself.

- Direct exporting. This is what most people understand as exporting. It involves selling your product or service to overseas customers either directly or through agents or distributors in the overseas market. This is the best way for most companies to export their products, but it also requires the most additional resources.

These different approaches to exporting are explained in much more detail in Chapter 6.

Once you have made your decision to start exporting, you will need to develop your export strategy, from which your export plan will be developed. We will look at this in Chapter 5.

Example of a UK company

Simply Solar Ltd manufactures solar tube systems used for domestic and commercial building water heating. The company is based in Brighton and employs 50 people. It was founded five years ago and sales have grown rapidly. Annual turnover is now £6 million.

They have not made any real attempt to sell their products overseas, but they are now getting an increasing number of enquiries and a few orders from overseas – mainly from other EU countries. The company management has decided that if they want to export, they need to adopt a professional approach. They contact their local Chamber of Commerce, who advise them to speak to their local UK Trade & Investment trade team. They go to the UKTI website, **www.ukti.gov.uk/export**, and under 'Contacts in your region' they enter their postcode and find contact details for the UKTI South East International Trade Team. They phone and speak with an International Trade Adviser. The adviser suggests that they download some basic information and then arranges to meet them. They go to the Business Link website, **www.businesslink.gov.uk**, and in the section 'International trade', they find a list of export topics beginning with 'Getting started – export basics'. Under 'Export basics' the first two topics are:

- Exporting – an overview: What's involved in selling goods or services to another country.
- Preparing to export: Assessing whether you are ready to export and planning your approach.

On both of these web pages they access useful guides, which they print.

With the International Trade Adviser they use the UKTI's online interactive tool to complete an export readiness questionnaire called 'Are you ready to export?' After discussing the results, they sign up for UKTI's 'Passport to export' programme. They are given help in developing an export strategy and preparing an export plan. With the help of their International Trade Adviser they analyse the enquiries and orders that they have received over the last year and conclude that their type of product will not be able to compete on price with the much simpler combined 'tank plus heat exchanger' solar systems that are common in southern Europe (Greece, Portugal and Spain) and that they should concentrate on countries such as Germany, Austria, Switzerland, the Benelux countries and countries in Scandinavia.

Having decided to look at Germany in much more detail, they decide to use the Export Marketing Research Scheme (for which they can get a 50 per cent government grant) to look at the market, distribution channels and competitors and to take it further by using the Overseas Market Introduction Service to look for potential distributors. Once this research is complete and a list of potential distributors has been prepared, they discuss the reports with their International Trade Adviser. They then arrange to visit Germany and the British consulate staff who carried out the work arrange meetings for them with a number of the potential distributors from the list.

Example of a US company

The Gym Equipment Company is a manufacturer of specialist exercise machines used in gyms and leisure centres. The company is based in Springfield, Missouri, and employs about 100 people. Until now virtually all of their business has been with customers within the United States, although for the last few years they have been selling some equipment to a few customers in Canada.

The company management decide that to expand their business further, they need to look at overseas markets in parallel to their domestic marketing initiatives. They contact their local Export Assistance Center in St Louis for professional advice. The trade specialist suggests that they use the US Department of Commerce online readiness assessment at **www.export.gov/begin/ assessment.asp** to assess their export readiness and understand what additional resources they are likely to need if they want to develop export business. The company is already intending to exhibit at the international trade show, Leisureworld 20X3, in Kansas City that summer and the trade specialist suggests that they use this show as an opportunity to do some research and make some contacts. At the show they see a number of overseas visitors on their booth and they also visit a number of booths. There are a number of booths from overseas manufacturers, including one for Salud y Felicidad from Mexico. From their sales director they learn that the Mexican market for leisure products is expanding rapidly with the expanding middle class, but that the biggest and fastest-growing market by far is Brazil. They decide to target Brazil.

They get more advice from their local trade specialist and download information on the Brazilian market from **www.buyusa.gov/brazil**, the website of the US Commercial Service in Brazil (CS Brazil). They are able to download a 96-page document entitled 'Doing business in Brazil' and another document entitled 'Top US export prospects'. They download a list of trade shows in Brazil over the following 12 months and find that there is one called Expo Lazer taking place in São Paulo in six months' time. The website gives a contact person for that trade show and they find that this person is also the contact person in CS Brazil for their industry, so they are able to make e-mail contact with them. They find that CS Brazil has published a number of market research reports on Brazilian market sectors, including leisure. CS Brazil also offers customized market research and they decide to use this service, because the price also includes a free online promotion on the CS Brazil website. The company has to provide a summary of the company and the products that it offers and CS Brazil translate it into Portuguese and post it on their website, together with a link to the company website. The next thing that the company does is to start to plan a visit to Brazil to coincide with the Expo Lazer exhibition.

Example of an Australian company

Water Valves and Fittings Pty Ltd is a manufacturer of innovative small-bore valves and fittings used in dosing and filtration systems in water-treatment plants. The company is based in Newcastle, New South Wales, and employs 30 people. It only started up five years ago, but in that time it has built up sales of 5 million Australian dollars. Although some of their sales are directly to water companies, the bulk are to engineering and contracting companies supplying systems that include their valves. Although all of their sales are to customers in Australia, they know that nearly half of all the valves and fittings that they supply are for equipment that is exported from Australia.

Although their sales are still buoyant, they believe that they will soon reach the limit of what they can achieve through just domestic sales. Their managing director has decided that he needs to start looking at export markets. He contacts the NSW Business Chamber in Sydney, and is given the contact details of his local export adviser based in Newcastle.

The adviser explains the 'Getting into export' programme and suggests that he and his sales manager attend a 'Getting started in exports' workshop in Sydney later that month. After attending that, the export adviser helps them to start developing their export strategy and an export plan. They conclude that one of the most likely markets to take up their innovative valve designs is the USA. They download information on the US market from the Austrade website and also sign up for the NSW Export Lab Event – USA. At this event they are able to collect further information on the US market and they also meet people from other companies interested in exporting to the USA and also some who are already successfully exporting there.

They are given details of the G'day USA programme. As part of this they decide to participate in a two-week trade mission to the west coast of the USA through the USA Water Tour Series. The Water Tour is managed by Austrade with funding for NSW companies covered by Industry & Investment NSW.

Summary

Exporting is very important to all major economies and nowadays almost every country, large or small, provides government support to their exporters. Export trade advisers working for government support agencies have a wealth of their own experience on exporting as well as access to other experts and to staff at embassies and consulates around the world. Much government support for exporters is free and services that must be paid for are usually charged at very competitive rates.

Moving into export is a big step for any company and you need to be clear as to why exporting should be a priority for your business and what the real benefits would be. Carrying out an export audit of your company, your internal organization and your products will give you a clear idea of the extra resources that you require and the extra costs to your business. You will also need to have a clear idea of whether your product will be suitable for export markets without modification and whether your cost structure will allow you to sell your product profitably overseas.

CHAPTER THREE

HOW TO DECIDE WHICH MARKETS TO CONSIDER FIRST

When you consider selling to export markets, it is important to consider the cost-effectiveness of building up sales in one market rather than another. Different markets have different requirements and your products may be perfectly suitable for some markets, but require modifications to be suitable for other markets. Trying to export to a number of widely different markets can be expensive in both time and money. For some companies, choosing their first export market can be difficult, whereas for others there is an immediate and logical choice. As with many things in exporting, you should take professional advice and also look at what companies that are already exporting successfully did, to see if you can learn from their experience.

The world market

According to the International Monetary Fund (IMF), the size of the world economy was about $68 trillion in 2011 and 12 economies account for more than two-thirds of the world's output. The measure of a country's wealth is its gross domestic product (GDP). Figures 3.1 to 3.3 show the International Monetary Fund's estimated figures for GDP at market exchange rates for 2011 for major countries and the EU.

FIGURE 3.1 Top 10 economies by GDP (2011)

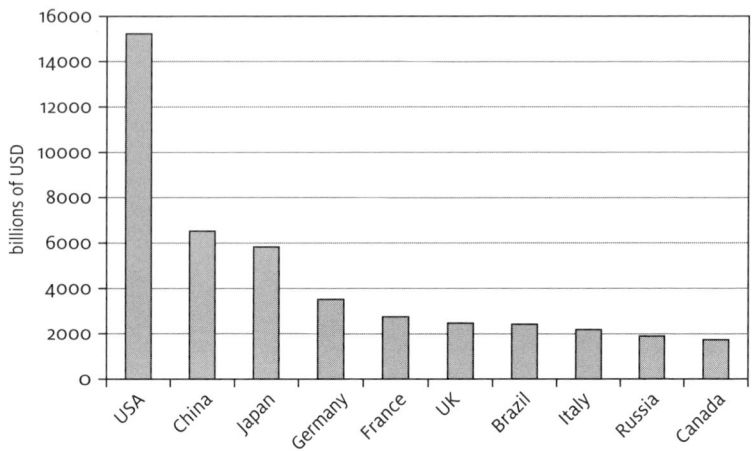

FIGURE 3.2 Next 10 economies by GDP (2011)

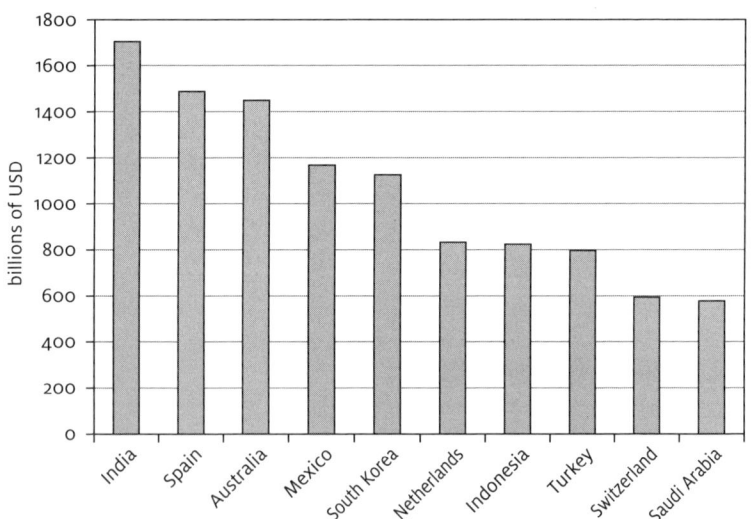

FIGURE 3.3 Comparison of GDPs of EU and USA (2011)

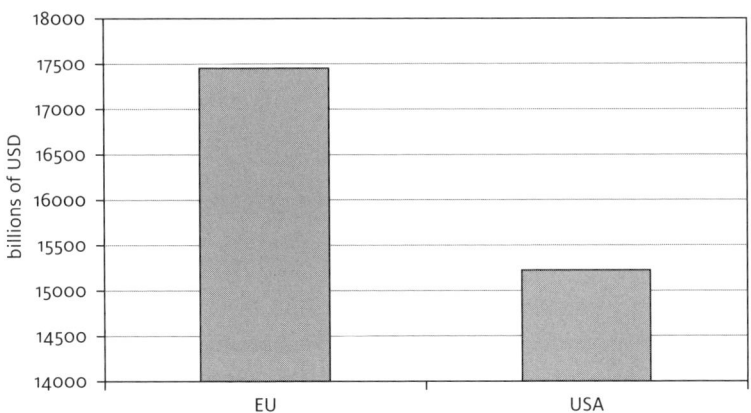

Regional trading agreements and trading blocs

The world is becoming increasingly divided into trade blocs. The purpose of trade blocs is to increase regional trade by reducing or eliminating customs tariffs. Regional Trade Agreements (RTAs) have become a major feature of the Multilateral Trading System (MTS). According to the World Trade Organization (WTO), **www.wto.org**, as of July 2010, some 474 RTAs had been notified to GATT/WTO and 283 of these were in force.

Of these RTAs, 90 per cent are Free Trade Agreements (FTAs) or partial scope agreements and 10 per cent are customs unions. Modern RTAs tend to go far beyond just tariff-cutting exercises. Many provide for the increasingly complex regulations governing intra-country trade, including such things as standards, safeguard provisions and customs administration, and they often also provide for a preferential regulatory framework for mutual services trade. The most sophisticated RTAs go beyond traditional trade policy mechanisms, to include regional rules on investment, competition, the environment and labour.

There are three major trading blocs in the world that together account for more than half of world trade. These are the European Union (EU), NAFTA in North America and the Association of South-East Asian Nations (ASEAN) in Asia-Pacific. The best-known examples of regional trade agreements are as follows.

The European Union (EU)

The European Union (EU) has become the most powerful trading bloc in the world, with a population and a GDP larger than those of the United States. Britain now does more trade within the EU than with any other trading bloc. Nearly three-quarters of the EU's trade is between member states.

The EU has a population of over half a billion people in 27 countries, 17 of which belong to the euro area. The EU is now the 'home market' for every company operating within it. Companies based in England can sell directly to customers in Rome or Frankfurt and French companies can bid for refuse collection contracts in London. There are still some obstacles, but there is an ever-increasing move towards European rather than national standards throughout the EU.

The European Free Trade Association (EFTA)

The European Free Trade Association (EFTA) is an intergovernmental organization set up for the promotion of free trade and economic integration for the benefit of its four member states: Iceland, Liechtenstein, Norway and Switzerland. The Association manages the EFTA Convention; EFTA's worldwide network of free trade partnership agreements and the European Economic Area (EEA) Agreement.

European Economic Area (EEA)

The European Economic Area (EEA) unites the 27 EU member states and three of the EFTA states (Iceland, Liechtenstein and Norway) into an internal market governed by the same rules. (Switzerland rejected the EEA in a referendum and instead signed a set of bilateral agreements with the EU.) The EEA Agreement provides for the inclusion of EU legislation covering the four freedoms – the free movement of goods, services, persons and capital – throughout the 30 EEA States. It also states that when any country becomes a member of the EU, they should also apply to become party to the EEA Agreement.

The North American Free Trade Agreement (NAFTA)

The North American Free Trade Agreement (NAFTA) is less comprehensive than the EU treaties. It links the United States, Canada and Mexico to form a free trade zone. It covers environmental and labour issues as well as trade and investment. NAFTA now accounts for about 50 per cent of North American trade.

The Southern Common Market (MERCOSUR)

Mercosur is a regional free trade pact between Brazil, Argentina, Uruguay, Paraguay and Venezuela.

The Association of South-East Asian Nations (ASEAN)

The ASEAN free trade area is a grouping of 10 countries in South-East Asia. In 2010 a free trade agreement linking China and ASEAN came into force. They have also agreed a trade deal with India and separate agreements with Australia and New Zealand.

The Asia-Pacific Economic Cooperation forum (APEC)

This is a loose grouping of 21 countries bordering the Pacific Ocean that have pledged to facilitate free trade. They have pledged to liberalize trade among themselves by 2010 for developed countries and by 2015 for developing countries.

The Common Market of Eastern and Southern Africa (COMESA)

COMESA has 19 member states with a total population of 430 million. It forms a major marketplace for both internal and external trading throughout Africa. Its mission is to 'endeavour to achieve sustainable economic and social progress in all Member States through increased cooperation and integration in all fields of development, particularly trade, customs and monetary affairs, transport, communication and information, technology, industry and energy, gender, agriculture, environment and natural resources'. In 2000 it set up the COMESA Free Trade Area and nine member states initially joined. South Africa is not a member of COMESA, having opted for membership of the Southern African Development Community (SADC).

The Southern African Development Community (SADC)

The Southern African Development Community has 15 member states including South Africa and surrounding countries. It aims 'to promote sustainable and equitable economic growth and socio-economic development so that the region emerges as a competitive and effective player in international relations and the world economy'.

Although there is talk of widening free trade areas between NAFTA and South and Central America and even between the EU and NAFTA, the real trend is towards regionalization of trade and extending bilateral agreements. With rapid growth forecast in intra-regional trade, many companies are responding by regionalizing their sales and marketing approach into the three areas of the Americas, Europe and Asia Pacific.

Other economic groupings

BRICs

The term BRIC was first used by Jim O'Neill of Goldman Sachs to encompass the rapidly expanding economies of Brazil, Russia, India and China. They are not a trading bloc, but they are the four largest economies outside the OECD (Organisation for Economic Co-operation and Development). They are also the only developing economies with annual GDPs of over $1 trillion. By the second quarter of 2010 China's GDP had not only overtaken that of all individual European countries, but also that of Japan. A recent report by Goldman Sachs projects that China's GDP will overtake the USA's by 2041. Over the same period it is projected that the Indian economy will overtake those of the European countries, putting it fourth in size after the USA, China and Japan by 2030.

The E7

PricewaterhouseCoopers (PwC) added Indonesia, Mexico and Turkey to Brazil, Russia, India and China as the seven largest emerging market economies, which they refer to as the 'E7'. In their report 'The world in 2050 – beyond the BRICs: a broader look at emerging market growth prospects', they project that by 2050 the E7 emerging economies will be around 50 per cent larger than the current G7 (USA, Japan, Germany, UK, France, Italy and Canada). PwC are even more optimistic about the Chinese economy and estimate that it will overtake the USA's to become the world's largest in around 2025.

Selecting potential export markets

Depending on which definition you use, there are between 180 and 200 separate countries in the world. When you consider exporting, it is important to consider the cost-effectiveness of building up sales in one market rather than another. If you are only getting started in export, you need very good reasons for developing the African or South American markets before you develop your sales in Western Europe or the USA (unless, of course, you are an African or South American company, in which case it would be your logical choice).

But if you are already an established exporter, you should bear in mind that although emerging markets account for only one-third of the world economy, they account for two-thirds of its growth. China is powering ahead and India is opening up. Intra-Asian trade is growing and an increasing number of countries within Africa and within Latin America are increasing their exports to each other. The biggest growth markets for established exporters are in Asia, where populations are growing and getting richer, with an expanding middle class.

Before looking at potential export markets you need to understand why you are successful in your domestic market. A clear understanding of your existing market and the reasons that you are successful there can help you to eliminate some countries that are clearly inappropriate for you. So ask yourself:

● Why do your domestic customers choose your product? Is it because of the quality? The price? Or is it because of the reputation of your company and your product? Or is it the quality of your after-sales service?

- What type of product do you supply and what do your customers do with it? Is it an end product in its own right? Is it incorporated into the customer's equipment or product? Is it a service?
- What alternatives exist that your customers could buy instead of your product?
- Are any of your major competitors overseas companies? If so, they will almost certainly be very strong in their own domestic market, so you may want to eliminate this from your list of potential target markets.

Which country first?

When you consider potential export markets, an important factor to consider is their 'similarity' to your existing market. If they exhibit many of the same characteristics that your own market exhibits, your product is more likely to be accepted and the channels to market would probably also be similar. You need to consider potential export markets, in terms of both their size and the ease of doing business there. Size is not just related to the size of the population. The size of the potentially available market is the most important thing.

Some of the factors that would determine the likely demand for your product in a target country include:

- The size of market for your type of product or similar products (if they are available).
- The population and its structure. The size of the 'economically available' population. Does it have a large middle class with higher levels of disposable income?
- The economic climate. Is it favourable?
- Cultural or climatic issues which may drive the market.
- The level of development, measured by such things as education and literacy, computer literacy and IT readiness.
- The infrastructure – both the transport infrastructure and the IT infrastructure.

Remember that you cannot define the size of the market in purely geographic terms. You need to segment the market and identify the segments of the market that contain your potential customers. The segmentation could be by size of a particular industry or type of customer.

Factors that can help you to determine how easy it may be for your company to enter the market could include:

- Language. This will affect your sales literature and advertising as well as contact with customers in the market.
- Political stability. Is the country stable? Are there any risks?
- Legal and regulatory issues. Are there any legal or regulatory barriers to entry? Does your product comply with local standards?
- Import duties/tariffs. Is there a preferential tariff arrangement between your country and the target market? Are there any barriers to trade?
- Distance to the market. This will certainly be a factor if your products are low value/high volume.
- Competition. Is there strong local competition for your type of product? If a company from your target market is one of your major competitors in your domestic market, you need to consider whether you will be able to compete with them in their own market.

It is frequently not possible to decide whether a particular export market is right for your company and your products until you have carried out a certain amount of research into the market. For this reason it is usual for a company to select a number of potential target markets and to research these markets in parallel. You need to establish selection criteria and score each potential target market against these criteria. Once sufficient research has been carried out, you will be able to score each market against your criteria on the basis of the likely demand for your product and the relative ease of entering the market for your company. The markets that score the highest against your selection criteria will be the ones that you select for further, more detailed, market research.

Rating charts

If you have no experience of selecting markets, I strongly recommend that you have a discussion with your local trade adviser and they will help you to decide on the criteria that are most important to your

TABLE 3.1 Country selection chart – Part 1

	Yes	No
Political: Is the country stable?	☐	☐
Economic: Is the economic climate favourable? Is it likely to remain so?	☐	☐
Non-tariff barriers: Are there any major trade barriers – quotas, import restrictions?	☐	☐
Tariffs: Are import tariffs or taxes so high as to make our local pricing uncompetitive?	☐	☐
Local standards: Do we need to get any local testing certification for our product?	☐	☐
Product protection: Do we need to get patent/ trade mark protection before proceeding?	☐	☐
Safety: Is the country safe to visit?	☐	☐

business and your type of product and will also guide you towards selecting sensible initial target markets.

If you are putting a selection chart together yourself, I would suggest that you keep the list of selection criteria to fewer than 20 and that you split the chart into two sections. An inexperienced exporter does not want to have to deal with difficult markets and the criteria in section one would allow you to decide if it is worth moving down to section two of the chart for that particular target market. The criteria in this section would require a simple yes or no answer and would include such things as political stability, import restrictions or barriers, and legal issues or regulations (see Table 3.1).

A negative answer to any of the above criteria would almost certainly eliminate the country from the list of potential target markets. Part two of the selection chart would be used to compare the countries that have not been eliminated in part one. Each of the questions would be answered by using a score of between 1 and 5 (5 being the most positive; see Table 3.2).

TABLE 3.2 Country selection chart – Part 2

Country	A	B	C	D	E
Size of market					
Market demand/growth potential					
Population/structure					
Level of development					
Transportation to market					
Transport infrastructure					
Product acceptability					
Level of competition					
Language					
Local business practices					
Cultural issues					

Most new exporters start with markets that are relatively easy to deal with. In fact, many companies begin exporting by selling their products to customers in neighbouring countries, countries within their own trading bloc or countries with a common language. There is a high level of trade between countries within the European Union (EU), between the USA and Canada, between Australia and New Zealand. Within the EU, there is a very high level of trade between the UK and the Republic of Ireland and the same is true of trade between Austria and Germany and between the Scandinavian countries. Although there may be some differences, the things that make these markets easier to deal with in each case are common languages, common standards and historical traditions. Developing countries are riskier to deal with and are probably best left until you have more experience.

The US Department of Commerce report for 2005 showed that more than half of all US exporters only exported to Canada. Figures from the Office for National Statistics showed that in 2009 exports from the UK to its neighbour Ireland, with a population of less than five million, were more than its exports to China, India, Russia and Brazil combined.

If you are an Australian company you may begin with New Zealand or target one of the more developed economies in Asia. African countries are also likely to choose another African country as their first export market. This is not surprising when you consider the recent high growth rates in sub-Saharan Africa. An analysis by *The Economist* magazine in January 2011 found that over the 10 years to 2010, no fewer than six of the world's 10 fastest-growing economies were in sub-Saharan Africa, and according to IMF forecasts, Ethiopia, Mozambique, Tanzania, Congo, Ghana, Zambia and Nigeria will all be in the world's top 10 fastest-growing economies (excluding countries with a population of less than 10 million) for 2011 to 2015, with annual growth rates of between 6.8 and 8.1 per cent.

If you want to find out what countries have special trading arrangements with your own, you can usually get this information from your own government export support website. You can also look on the WTO website, **www.wto.org**. The WTO has an RTA database which contains summary tables for 371 of these RTAs (counting goods and services together), of which 193 are currently in force. You can download this information as either a PDF or an Excel file.

How many countries should you initially target?

Different markets have different requirements and your products may require additional certification or modifications to be suitable for some markets, whereas they may be perfectly suitable for other markets as they are. Trying to export to a number of widely different markets can be expensive in both time and money. Most companies that are starting in exporting focus on one or two individual markets. In a large country like Germany or the USA you may even decide to concentrate initially on one region. This is borne out by surveys of exporters carried out in both the USA and the UK. These showed that:

- 58 per cent of US exporters sold to only one country, 25.8 per cent sold to between two and four countries and only 7.3 per cent sold to 10 countries or more.
- 80 per cent of the UK exporters responding had done business in more than one country, 32 per cent were trading with two to five countries and 15 per cent with six to 10 countries. Only 7 per cent of companies were trading with 50 countries or more and these were the larger companies.

So the advice is clear. Start exporting to one or two target countries and develop your sales in these. Make sure that you have the resources in place to continue to service and develop these markets before you move on to others.

Industry sectors and clusters

You may also choose to target a particular export market, because that country has an industry sector that uses your type of product. A country such as Norway, although only number 24 in the world in terms of the size of its economy, could be a very good choice for you if you manufacture and sell equipment to the offshore oil and gas industry.

In fact, many governments target as much of their export support by industry sectors as by country or region. UKTI in the UK takes this approach (most UK trade missions are sector specific), as does The Australia Trade Commission (Austrade) in Australia and the Department of Trade and Industry (DTI) in South Africa.

Austrade's Global Opportunities programme provides export and investment facilitation services and funding support over a three-year period to eight industry clusters to help them expand their international business. Two of the clusters are in the automobile industry – Australian Automotive Aftermarket Export Network and Automotive Interior Systems.

The DTI in South Africa believe that the sector strategy offers a framework within which exports are encouraged and incentivized. They have chosen sectors with the greatest growth potential and marketability, including: agroprocessing, automotive industries, chemicals, pharmaceuticals and biotechnology, cultural industries, IT and electronics, mining, textiles and tourism.

So consider the industry sector you are in and contact your industry trade association to find out what industry-specific export support is available either from them or from government sources.

Product considerations

Although exporting can be a catalyst for innovation and developing new or modified products, clearly it would be ideal if you could sell your existing products, with minimum modification, into your initial target markets. In deciding which country to target as your first export market, your product is crucial. Some products may sell anywhere, but you will be surprised not just at the range of local rules and regulations, but also at local or cultural preferences that decide whether your existing product will sell or even whether it may be legally offered for sale in some overseas markets. Local regulations can affect everything from the labelling and the certification of foodstuffs and medical products to regulations for machinery and electrical goods.

The product requirements for emerging markets can be even more difficult for inexperienced exporters to understand. Although completely new products may be required, it is often the case that a product will need re-engineering or redesigning for some of the more mundane requirements that specific local conditions dictate.

An example of this is fridges. Any manufacturer of fridges will know that most US fridges are much larger than those used in Europe. So most multinational fridge manufacturers will have one range for the USA and one range for Europe. But Panasonic looked at local conditions around Asia and realized that they also needed a separate version for the Indonesian market, with big compartments to store lots of two-litre bottles. Indonesians boil water to purify it in the morning and then put it in the fridge to cool. But they need less space for vegetables, because they tend to buy them fresh and use them the same day.

There are of course, many other examples. Consider mobile phones. In Europe and the USA we are used to having a contacts list on our mobiles. But mobile phone providers have had to develop modified ranges of handsets for use in poorer developing countries. These handsets have the facility to set up multiple contacts lists, because in these countries it is not uncommon for one village to have only one mobile phone and for several people to use it, each with their own separate contacts list.

Example

In Chapter 2 we looked at examples of exporters from different countries using their government support organizations to get started and in some cases to help them decide which export markets to look at. In selecting target markets, it's not so much a matter of eliminating countries as making a shortlist. No new exporter (or even experienced exporter) is going to look at any countries with major stability problems.

The north–south divide in Europe shown in the example of the company selling solar water heating systems is not unusual. This two-tier level for products is particularly common in industrialized countries that have a lower level of GDP. I could give many examples that I have encountered over the years. When selling specialized industrial products such as pumps, I found that it is not uncommon for there to be two levels of product available. I found this to be the case with gear pumps in Turkey and with vacuum pumps in Russia. The market for our vacuum products manufactured in the UK and the USA turned out to be much smaller than we expected. In Russia there were two separate markets for vacuum pumps. There was a small market, consisting mainly of multinational companies now manufacturing in Russia, who insisted on only using the same international specification of product that they used in their plants in Western Europe and the USA, and there was a much larger market (in terms of the number of units) for old-fashioned designs of vacuum pumps, manufactured in old factories in Russia or the Ukraine. These local pumps were selling at prices that were less than half of our selling price, and in fact below our cost price. So we had to accept that although it was a much larger country with a much larger industrial base, we would be better off concentrating on theoretically smaller markets such as Norway and Sweden.

I have recommended that new exporters should look at a small number of initial target markets, but I should perhaps say that there is one exception to that rule. That is if your product is so revolutionary and innovative that people everywhere want to buy it. Unfortunately such products are usually things like the iPad being launched by huge multinational corporations like Apple. But every so often there is an exception.

There has been much in the press in recent months about the company Dusky Moon. The company was set up by two young mothers in 2009. Their invention was the 'Dream Tube'. This consists of a fitted sheet with side pockets containing long inflatable tubes and is designed to stop young children from falling out of bed in their sleep. After passing UK safety tests and going into full-scale production the company won its first major order from the children's retailer JoJoMaman Bébé. In their first year of trading the company achieved a turnover of £250,000 with 15 per cent of sales coming from exports. By the end of 2010 after only 19 months in business, the company was exporting to no less than 35 countries.

Summary

Before looking at potential export markets, you need to understand why you are successful in your domestic market. A clear understanding of your existing market and the reasons that you are successful there can help you to eliminate some countries that are clearly inappropriate to you.

It is usual for a company to select a number of 'potential target' markets and to research these markets in parallel. You should consider potential export markets in terms of both their size and also the ease of doing business there. Most new exporters start with markets that are relatively easy to deal with, selling their products to customers in neighbouring countries or countries with a common language. Many countries have built up a high level of trade with their neighbours or with other countries within their own trading region or trading bloc. Companies that are starting in exporting usually focus initially on one or two individual markets.

CHAPTER FOUR

RESEARCHING THE MARKET

Every overseas market is different and it is essential to research your target markets before you start to promote and sell your products or services within them. To give yourself the best possible chance of successfully entering a market you need to understand both the market itself and how your product will fit into it.

To do this, you need to carry out both market research and marketing research. Market research is research about markets. Marketing research involves not just collecting information about your markets but also analysing it in the context of the marketing of your products. Market research data consists of primary data and secondary data. Primary data is data obtained from primary sources, ie directly in the marketplace, either by carrying out field research directly yourself or by commissioning a consultant or market research company to carry out the fieldwork for you. Secondary data is not obtained directly from fieldwork, and market research based on secondary data sources is referred to as desk research.

How to plan your marketing research

Before you start to collect any information, you need to decide on your objectives and put together a plan for your market research. It is important to plan how you will do it to make sure that you obtain all of the information that you need. Much time, effort and cost can be wasted by starting an export market research project without defining the objectives.

The key steps to carrying out the marketing research are as follows:

- Define the objectives.
- Decide what information needs to be obtained.
- Decide the best way of obtaining it.
- Collect the data.
- Analyse the data.

The objectives

The objectives must be clearly defined and should explain why the research is being conducted. An objective could be:

- to obtain information that will enable us to decide whether or not to enter a new overseas market.

But you could also have a more specific objective related to one or more aspects of market entry, such as:

- to find out whether our product/service is suitable for the new market as it is, or whether it will require modification or further development;
- to find and evaluate suitable distribution for our product/service in the new market;
- to find out how best to promote our product/service in the new market.

You should also include the timescale that is necessary for completion of the work.

The information required

A list should be prepared, detailing all of the information required. This needs to be thorough and complete, as it is extremely costly to have to go back later to collect additional information because it was not considered in the first place.

How to obtain the information

You can obtain a lot of basic information about your target market by carrying out desk research. But in most cases this will need to be supplemented by carrying out some fieldwork in the market itself. You need to use someone who fully understands the business and will be able to understand the methods of marketing research and the full objectives of the project.

Collecting the data

Collecting the data involves using the methods and the data sources detailed later in this chapter. Some key sources of information are listed at the end of this book in the Useful websites section.

Analysing the data

Where specific projects such as customer surveys, market analysis or competitor analysis have been carried out, the data that has been collected needs to be verified and analysed. The assumptions used in interpreting the data must be stated. The analysis of the data will only be as good as the understanding of the person carrying it out, so it needs to be carried out by your marketing professional (this may be you personally).

Once all of the material has been analysed the key information needs to be put into a research report that can be used as a reference document for preparing your export plan.

Carrying out marketing research for overseas markets

The principles of carrying out marketing research for export markets are the same as those applicable in your domestic market. But the market and the marketing environment will almost certainly be different. In your domestic market you might carry out field research directly yourself or you might commission a consultant or market research company to do it for you. The same is true for overseas markets, but it is advantageous if this is supplemented by visiting the market personally.

You will need to look at and consider the following:

- the country type and population structure;
- the infrastructure;

- legal and regulatory issues;
- the market size;
- the industry structure within the market;
- the major customers for your type of product and their needs, usage and attitudes;
- the suitability of your product for the market;
- the way you will market the product;
- distribution channels;
- competition.

Country type

When researching target countries you need to consider a number of factors:

- The size of your potential market could be limited by the size of the population or by the size of the 'economically available' population in your target country.
- Political situation – is the country stable? What type of government does it have and could political changes adversely affect the local business climate?
- Economic climate – is this favourable and likely to remain so?
- Safety – how safe is it to visit, stay in or live in the target country? Are there high levels of crime? Is there a risk of terrorist activity?
- Legal issues – are there any local standards or regulations that would affect your existing or future products?

The infrastructure

- Communications – does your target market have widespread access to telephones or the internet?
- Internal travel – how good is the internal transport system within the country?
- Transportation – are there good transport links to the target market by ship? by air?

Legal and regulatory issues

- Are there any barriers with regard to access to the market, eg import duties, taxes, quotas, language, other government legislation?

- Does your product comply with local standards?
  Is any local testing or certification required?
- What is the patent situation? Do you have local trademark
  protection? Are there any other risks to your intellectual
  property?
- Is new legislation or new regulation likely?

The market size

- How big is it in value or volume terms?
- Will it be affected by future trends, eg population moving
  from the land to cities, a growing middle class, an aging
  population?
- The state of the market – is it a new market? A mature market?
  A saturated market?
- Are new areas of the market developing?

The industry structure within the market

- How is the market segmented/structured?
- How is the target industry geographically distributed?
  What are the key areas/regions?
- Are there a few large players, many small ones or a mixture?
- Are the target companies private or public sector?
- Is the market more or less advanced than your domestic market?

The major customers for your type of product and their needs, usage and attitudes

- Who are the main customers?
- Where are they located?
- Who are the main suppliers and what do the customers think of
  them?
- Why will they buy from you? Do they see a need for your product/
  service?
- What influences their purchasing decisions?
- How much are customers prepared to pay for your type of
  product?

The suitability of your product

- Is your product/service acceptable to this market in its current form or are modifications required?
- What are the main competing products? Are they directly comparable?
- Could cultural influences affect the way that your product will be perceived in this marketplace? A basic product in some markets may be a luxury item in another. A different perception of your product will mean that your marketing approach will need to be different.

The way you will market the product

- What methods of sales promotion are used in the marketplace?
- What methods of communication are used? Press, TV, internet, e-mail, direct mail?

Distribution channels

- How is the market supplied?
- What channels of distribution are available?
- Are agents or distributors used within the market?
- Is there local legislation relating to agents or distributors?
- What are the costs of distribution?

Competition

- Who are the key competitors?
- Are they local suppliers or international competitors?
- What products do they manufacture/sell?
- Are they more or less sophisticated than your company?
- What are their strengths and weaknesses?
- What are their marketing and pricing strategies?

Carrying out the research yourself

The first thing that you need to do is to prepare a checklist. This is important for two reasons. First, it can be extremely costly to have to go back later to collect additional information. Second, the problem for exporters is not that there is too little information available, but that there is so much that it is difficult to pinpoint the data that is really relevant. A checklist helps you to avoid collecting large amounts of irrelevant information. Ask yourself why you need specific information and what you will do with it; if you do not know, then you do not need it.

Your checklist should detail all of the information that you need to obtain and the headings would form the main headings in the final report. A typical checklist for a target market could include the following main headings:

- Market size
- Market structure and segmentation
- Market trends
- Market share
- Selling and distribution methods
- Marketing communication methods
- Product requirements
- Company/industry image
- User attitudes and behaviour
- Local pricing
- Competition.

Under each of these headings would be a list of the information required or the questions that your research needs to answer. Under 'Market structure and segmentation' a typical list of questions could be:

- Which are the main user industries?
- How large are these industries?
- What is the total number of factories that could use our product in its present application?
- Could this number be increased if our product were used for all possible applications?
- Are there geographical variations in the domestic market in the target country?
- Is the potential market for our products concentrated in particular geographic areas of the target market?
- Who/what would be our main competition in this market?
- Are there important domestic competitors?
- How much of the market is taken by imported products?

- Are our main international competitors present in the target market?
- If so, how well are they performing?
- How saturated is the market? What factors would favour new competitors coming into the market?

There could of course be many other questions on this list.

Desk research

Desk research involves the collection of data that is already available from existing sources. Huge amounts of information are available on most markets and much of this information is free or relatively inexpensive. Trips into the market can be expensive, so it is important that you obtain as much from published information as you can, before you actually visit your target market.

It is clearly a waste of money to carry out or commission research to obtain information that is already available and can be purchased in the form of a ready-made report. Many reports, particularly those produced by government departments or non-profit-making organizations are available free of charge.

The importance of desk research into export markets is that you can often find enough information to make an initial decision as to whether a particular target market looks promising or is just not suitable for your company or your product. If your product is sold into a particular industry sector, you can often find enough information by desk research to decide if that industry sector is large enough in one target market to justify entry into that market rather than another. A company selling products for industrial winemaking could easily find details of wine production in different countries of the world and decide which markets were large enough and developed enough to target. Further desk research would probably show if most production in the target country was on an industrial scale or just small local and family producers.

For general summary information on individual countries, I would recommend that you purchase a simple book such as those published by *The Economist*. They have two publications that are updated each year. The 'Pocket world in figures' gives a wealth of information, including world rankings for everything from population and economic growth to education and life expectancy. 'The world in...' also gives information and projections for the coming year for a number of countries and a number of industries. The latest versions at the time of writing are 'Pocket world in figures 2012 edition' and 'The world in 2012'. You can also access up-to-date information on the Central Intelligence Agency website, **www.cia.gov**. The CIA publish useful summary information on individual countries in their *World Factbook* in the Library & Reference section of their website.

Types of data and reports

There are a number of types of published data that can be used to provide you with information relating to markets and industry sectors as well as statistical information on exports and imports of specific types of products for different markets. The main types are described below.

Country (market) and industry (sector) reports

Before you start your desk research, I should perhaps point out that nomenclature can sometimes be a bit confusing. The descriptions 'market reports', 'sector reports' and 'industry reports' are sometimes used to mean different things by different organizations. Government support organizations tend to separate their reports into 'market reports' – reports on individual export markets and 'sector reports' (or 'sector in country' reports) – reports on individual industry sectors (usually for just one export market). Many companies that publish commercial reports often use the same term, 'market reports', for their reports on a particular market sector, usually in a single country or area. So whereas UKTI would refer to its report on 'The aerospace industry in Brazil' as a sector report, the company Euromonitor would refer to its report 'Healthfoods in France' as a market report. Similarly, a trade organization such as the British Pump Manufacturers Association may refer to a report entitled 'The UK pump industry in 2010' as an industry report.

General reports on specific overseas markets

Many government support organizations provide basic information on individual export markets. Much of this information can be printed or downloaded as PDF files from individual websites for free. Although for some services you have to register on the site, much of the information can be accessed by anyone from any country. A list of websites is included in the section, Useful websites, at the end of this book.

UKTI have a huge amount of information and reports available on export markets on their website, **www.ukti.gov.uk**, including market information from over 200 locations across the world. Their individual country reports, called 'A guide to doing business', vary in size and content ('A guide to doing business in Italy' is 16 pages, but 'The China business guide' is 103 pages!). The general format for these country guides includes information under the following headings:

● Introduction
● Preparing to export to the country
● How to do business in the country
● Business etiquette, language and culture
● What are the challenges?
● How to invest in the country
● Contacts
● Resources/useful links.

The Introduction includes basic economic and political information on the country, together with such things as details of major cities, industrial centres and key industries that would be of interest to potential exporters.

The US government also provides a wealth of market information and reports on its website, **www.export.gov**. This includes country commercial guides, industry reports and trade data. You can get more detailed information on individual markets by accessing the website of one of the US Commercial Service international offices. If there is a website for the country you are interested in you can access it by entering **www.buyusa.gov/country**. So to access the site for Germany, enter **www.buyusa.gov/germany**.

There are over 100 US country commercial guides. These are very comprehensive (many are at least 100 pages long) and are downloadable in PDF format. The standard contents include information on doing business in the country, the political and economic environment, trade regulations, investment, financing, travel and market research, with information specifically geared towards US exporters of products and services. Dates given for each report allow you to see how current the information is likely to be.

Similar information is provided for Australian exporters on the Austrade website, **www.austrade.gov.au**.

Sector or industry reports

The same types of government support organizations also supply reports on industry sectors. These are usually specific to that industry in one country and are often referred to as 'sector briefings' or 'industry within country profiles'.

'Sector in country' reports ('briefings') can be downloaded as PDF files from the UKTI website, **www.ukti.gov.uk** (you may need to register on the site to gain access to some of the reports). There are over 600 sector and market briefings on the UKTI website covering subjects as diverse as 'The aerospace sector in India', 'The food and drink sector in Brazil' and 'Renewable energy in Peru'. There is a standard format for the sector briefings, which usually include the following sections:

● Why you should look at this industry in this market
● Characteristics of the market
● Opportunities for exporters
● Major events and activities
● Contacts.

The US Commercial Service Market Research Library contains more than 100,000 industry and country-specific market reports that have been compiled by their specialists working in their overseas posts. Some of these reports are only available to US companies or US students or researchers, and to gain access to these, you would need to register on the **www.export.gov** website.

The market sector/industry reports available from commercial companies are the most comprehensive types of market research information. They look at all aspects of the market, including companies, products, customers and trends. They present an overview of the whole market.

The key areas covered are:

- history of the market;
- structure of the market;
- size of the market;
- data on major companies in the market;
- market trends;
- distribution channels;
- recent market developments;
- future market developments.

Reports may be on a single market, a single market sector or on a number of related markets.

Other sources of market and sector reports

One starting point for regional or global published market research reports is the specialist website Market Research.com, **www.market-research.com**. They claim to have access to the world's largest collection of market research, and registration on the site is free. But there are also a number of specialist companies that carry out research and publish reports. The most prominent are Euromonitor, **www.euromonitor.com**, Mintel, **www.mintel.co.uk**, Keynote, **www.keynote.co.uk** and Frost and Sullivan, **www.frost.com**. These organizations publish lists of reports that they have available on their websites. Euromonitor has about 25 business reference handbooks and hundreds of reports covering 26 different industry sectors. Reports have titles as diverse as 'Healthfoods in France' and 'The market for disposable paper products in Asia-Pacific'. The reports include information on the market, its segmentation, the products, competition, distribution systems and the consumer.

Trade associations

An easy way to find out if there are any specific websites relating to your industry is to contact your trade association. Details of trade associations can be found on the website of the Trade Association Forum, **www.taforum.org**. The advantage of your trade association is that they will already have information on your industry and will be able to direct you to sites that they think will have the information that you are looking for. They may also have links with their equivalent organization in your target country.

Industry websites

There are many specific websites for individual industries, eg **www.sugarinfo.co.uk** for the sugar industry, Leatherhead Food International, **www.lfra.co.uk**, for the food industry, and Jaakko Pöyry Group, **www.poyry.com**, for the pulp and paper industry.

Obviously, you can also just use your internet search engine to carry out general web searches and see what they bring in. If you want information on the dairy industry, you could initially just type in 'dairy industry', or for the chemical industry just type in 'chemical industry'. This will bring up a long list of websites and you will certainly find that they will include companies offering reports.

Chambers of Commerce

Your local Chamber of Commerce can provide a wide range of advice on market research and Chambers of Commerce in many countries can provide valuable market research material including reports on overseas markets. You can also use the World Chambers Network, **www.worldchambers.com**, which is the official global portal of Chambers of Commerce. On their website they have a 'Chamber directory' with details of over 14,000 Chambers of Commerce representing more than 40 million companies worldwide. You can use this directory to find details of local and national chambers of commerce in your target country. In many cases you will find that there is a bilateral chamber of commerce promoting trade between your country and that country and that they may well provide useful information such as contacts and relevant industry sector information relating to your target country via their website. (An example of this is the UK India Business Council (UKIBC), **www.ukibc.com**).

Company information

We need information on other companies in order to investigate potential customers and distributors and also to monitor our competitors and potential competitors.

Company information is of two types:

- directory information;
- financial information.

Directory information gives key data on companies. This includes names, addresses, telephone numbers, trademarks, details of directors and who owns whom. Directories usually list companies operating in particular markets.

The main trade directories such as Kompass Directories, **www.kompass.co.uk**, and Kelly's Directories, **www.kellysearch.com**, cover all of the larger companies and include a great deal of information with a detailed analysis of activities and products. Kompass have a wide range of directories covering many foreign countries as well as their UK directories. There is a business-to-business search engine on their website which can be used to search their database of 2.7 million companies in more than 60 countries worldwide. Their classification system lists over 57,000 products and services in all sectors of industry and economic activity.

Another useful website is Net Resources International (NRI), **www.nridigital.com**, which has separate sections for 25 different industries. They cover 85 countries and provide a range of information on their website, including details of companies and projects. You can also sign up for a monthly industry e-newsletter giving news of developments in that particular industry.

There is also a wide range of more specialized directories covering single industries or industry sectors (such as the chemical industry, offshore oil and gas, and the textile industry). These directories are often not as detailed as the main trade directories and only show the name, address and telephone numbers of companies, with a brief list of products, but they do have the advantage of being specific to their industry.

Product and statistical information

Government statistics are a useful source of information. These relate to business activity, as well as to details of imports and exports of products and commodities. International trade and production statistics are collected and made available by individual governments and also by wider-ranging organizations like the Food and Agriculture Organization (FAO), **www.fao.org** (a United Nations organization), and Eurostat, **http://epp.eurostat.ec.europa.eu**. Eurostat consolidates data collected by the statistical authorities in the member states of the EU and ensures that all data are comparable using harmonized methodology. Eurostat is the only provider of statistics at a European level. If you are involved in exporting or in the sale of industrial goods, you can find useful information from these sources to assist you. Having said that, the various product coding systems in use are not simple and some have been frequently revised and changed. So you may feel that collecting and analysing such data is a job best left to a professional who is familiar with the systems and the changes.

The Harmonized Commodity Description and Coding System (HS)

At an international level, the United Nations has the Central Product Classification (CPC), which provides a general framework for international comparisons of product statistics. The UN documentation of the CPC provides direct links to the Harmonized Commodity Description and Coding System (HS). The HS, known generally as 'tariff numbers', is the coding system used for trade worldwide. Care needs to be taken when making comparisons of products based on the HS coding system, because only the first six digits of the classification number are uniform among countries that use the HS. The other digits may differ from country to country. More detail of the HS System is given in Chapter 11.

The SIC coding system

The SIC coding system is the system that is most commonly used by directories or financial reports to classify companies into industries by relating their main activities to the official standard industrial classification (SIC) codes. The codes in use in the UK are the SIC codes (revised 2007). (Care should be taken to differentiate from the US SIC codes which are different and are still in use, although they in turn are now being replaced by the NAICS system.)

The latest updated version of the 'UK Standard Industrial Classification of Economic Activities 2007' (SIC 2007) was published in 2010 by the Office for National Statistics, the official UK statistics organization. You can download a copy of this guide as a PDF file free from the Office for National Statistics website: **www.ons.gov.uk**. On the website homepage, go to 'Virtual bookshelf' and then to 'Commerce, energy and industry' and then to 'Standard Industrial Classification' and you will find a number of free guides to SIC codings.

The UK SIC codes are based on the Eurostat System NACE Rev 2 (effective from 1 January 2008), which is an EU regulation requiring the use of common codes throughout the EU. The UK SIC is a hierarchical five-digit system where a fifth digit has been added to form subclasses of the NACE Rev 2 four-digit classes. The UK SIC (2007) and the NACE Rev 2 are completely consistent with the fourth revision of the UN's International Standard Industrial Classification of all economic activities (ISIC Rev 4).

Over the years the SIC codings have been expanded and changed to reflect the changes in the structure of industry and the new industries and products that have come into being. There have been seven re-classifications of SIC codings since they were first introduced in 1948. Although this is logical, it does mean that you have to be careful. The result is that the SIC (2007) coding for a product will probably be different from the SIC (2003) coding, which in turn may well be different from the SIC (1992) coding. So if you are using statistical information based on SIC codes, I suggest that you confine it to recently produced information unless you are prepared to acquaint yourself with the details of the earlier versions of the system.

Prodcom – statistics by product

Prodcom is a harmonized system used across the European Union for the collection and publication of statistics on the production of manufactured goods. Prodcom stands for 'Products of the European Community'. All EU countries are now using this system. The Prodcom statistics cover sections B and C of NACE Rev 2. The EU decided to use a product classification that was more akin to the industrial activity classification and devised the Classification of Products by Activity (CPA). Prodcom uses the product codes specified on the Prodcom list, which contains about 4,500 different types of manufactured products. The products are identified by an eight-digit code. The first four digits are the classification of the producing enterprise given by the NACE code and the first six digits correspond to the CPA coding. The remaining digits specify the product in more detail. Most product codes correspond to one or more of the Combined Nomenclature (CN) codes, although some (mostly industrial services) do not.

The information is in the form of reports, most of which are updated annually.

The various modifications to the Prodcom system were finalized in 2007 in order to tie in with the 2007 revision of the SIC codes. That does mean that it can be difficult to directly compare Prodcom statistics from reports prior to 2008 with those originating after that date unless you know both the old and new codes.

Prodcom reports are available from national statistics organizations in EU member states and provide total market data on a wide range of products. This means that the UK reports provide details of UK production, or, more precisely, UK manufacturer sales, exports, imports and net supply to the UK market in both value and volume terms as well as average price. The Prodcom reports are published online by the Office for National Statistics, **www.ons.gov.uk**, and can be found in the same way as the SIC coding guide. Not only can you read the summaries of the reports, but you can also view or download the entire documents free of charge.

Field research

Once you have obtained all of the material that you can get from desk research, you must decide whether you also need to carry out field research in your target market. Field research involves visiting the target market and can involve carrying out face-to-face interviews with potential customers, agents or distributors. You can of course visit your target market on your own, but if you have limited experience of doing business overseas, you would gain more from visiting as part of an organized group as part of a trade mission or to visit or take part in an exhibition.

Sector-focused trade missions

Sector-focused trade missions typically last between three and eight days and are usually organized by a government agency such as a Chamber of Commerce. Missions are often specific to a particular industry or event. They are an ideal way to visit a market that you are unfamiliar with and you can gain from the experience of the mission leader and others on the mission as well as from the local contacts that you make.

Tradeshows and exhibitions

Visiting or taking part in a tradeshow or overseas exhibition specific to your industry is an ideal way of finding out a lot about that industry in your target country. Although just by visiting the exhibition you can get an idea of the products being sold in the market and the competition, if you actually take part in an exhibition you have much more opportunity to meet and talk with potential customers. Many governments provide support for participants in overseas exhibitions and seminars. The participation is usually as part of a group, which is a big advantage for inexperienced businesses. The group is often on a country stand, which is split into individual sub-stands for the participating companies.

Using an agency to carry out market research

Using a professional market research agency to carry out market research will obviously be more expensive than doing the work yourself. But if you and your staff are inexperienced in doing market research it may well prove to be more cost-effective. The agency will probably complete the task more quickly and will have the skills to make sure that all parts of the task are completed properly. They can research the market anonymously and they may already have secondary data (or access to secondary data) from previous work that they have carried out in the target market. If they are locally based or use local personnel in the target market, they will bring local knowledge to the task, and since they do not work for your company, respondents in interviews may be more open in their replies. Additionally, less time is required to be spent on the project by your own company personnel, so they can get on with their normal jobs.

As with any work that you commission, unless you are already familiar with the agency and have used them before, you should get quotations from a number of different agencies before deciding which one to go with (though in some overseas markets there may only be one agency with a good reputation and experience in the field that interests you).

The marketing research brief

If you are commissioning market research you need to prepare a marketing research brief to inform the potential agencies of the aims and objectives of your research project. The brief should explain why you want the research to be carried out and detail the information that you need to obtain from it. It is important that everything is clearly stated in the brief to ensure that the final report will provide the information and recommendations that will help you to take your final decisions.

The brief should include the following:

1 Introduction
2 Scope
3 Purpose
4 Information required
5 Timescales
6 Progress reporting
7 Reporting requirements
8 Notes.

The research brief should be discussed with the agencies, who may make suggestions based on their own experience. They may see areas of research or information that you have omitted and may suggest extending or reducing the scope of the project or changing its emphasis in some way.

Choosing the agency to work with

The agencies will put together their proposals for your evaluation. You need to be sure that you understand exactly what they are offering and that their proposal shows that they have clearly understood your brief. Generally, you want to be sure that the project will be carried out in accordance with the Market Research Society's Code of Conduct. You can find this on the Market Research Society's website, **www.marketresearch.org.uk**.

The proposal

There are a number of key points that you would expect to see or confirm in the proposal. The most important is that they demonstrate that they clearly understand your brief and exactly what you expect to get out of their research. You should make sure that the following are also included in their proposal:

- a detailed list of the information that their research will provide;
- the proposed methodology – how much desk research will be carried out; the number and type of interviews that will be carried out in the target market; other techniques that will be used – such as sending out letters/literature and following up with a phone call, etc;
- the scope of the study – target companies, target industries, geographical area to be covered;
- the qualifications and experience of the researchers who will carry out the work;
- the timescale of the project, including both the time allocated for each stage of the project and the overall time from commissioning to the presentation of findings;
- the total cost of the project, including a detailed split between fees and expenses;
- whether there will be any progress reports or interim meetings and if so how many and how often;
- any specific areas where they expect to be able to make recommendations as a result of their research;
- the number of copies of the final report included in the price and their format;
- written assurances of both exclusivity and confidentiality.

The report

Although individual meeting reports or reports of telephone conversations may be added to the main report as appendices, the overall report that you receive should bring all of the information together in a clear and concise form. A suggested format for a research report is shown below:

1 Background
2 Scope
3 Project objectives
4 Methodology

5 Main findings
6 Summary of findings and conclusions
7 Recommendations
8 Appendix.

Using companies based in the target market

Depending on the type of market that you are looking at, you may decide to commission research with a company based in the target market itself. A local company clearly has advantages because they are actually in the market themselves and you would expect them to know how the market functions. But it can be more difficult to get a sensible proposal put together and it can be more difficult to judge the quality of the personnel who will carry out the work, because you will not want to go to the expense of visiting them and they will also not want the cost of visiting you before they have a contract. My suggestion is that you should consider local companies, but make sure that you can get a sensible recommendation, either from other companies who have used them before or through your local embassy in the target market.

Government support for market research

Apart from compiling market and sector reports, some governments also offer their exporters assistance for export market research projects. Some also provide financial support, particularly for small businesses. UK Trade & Investment, the US Department of Commerce and Austrade all have such schemes. In the UK, the Export Marketing Research Scheme (EMRS) is administered by the British Chambers of Commerce on behalf of UK Trade & Investment. Companies with fewer than 250 employees may be eligible for a grant of up to 50 per cent of the agreed cost of an approved marketing research project. This service helps companies carry out export marketing research on all major aspects of any export venture and offers free independent advice on how to get the most out of a marketing research project. The support can cover projects carried out in house or by an agency, including both field projects and desk research, and can also be put towards the cost of purchasing published market reports.

Example

A UK company used the Export Marketing Research Scheme (EMRS) to help it to investigate a potential export market and within three years they had generated more than £1 million in additional export sales.

The company designs, manufactures and supplies DC electrical systems for electro-refining applications. Its customer base has, traditionally, consisted of a number of large chlorine refiners who use electricity as a catalyst in the refining process. However, the company was keen to diversify away from chlorine refining into the base metals market and had identified Zambia as a potentially lucrative market.

Zambia has huge reserves of copper, and after years of decline as a nationalized industry, the copper mines and refineries are now largely under private ownership and there is a major programme of refurbishment and rebuilding. The company needed to find out about the market so that they could capitalize on the potential opportunities. They had no experience of commissioning a marketing research study and relied on advice from their Export Marketing Research Adviser for guidance. The research adviser acted as project manager and put together the brief. She identified four or five potential consultants and helped with the analysis of the responses. She advised the company to use a Zambian consultancy. Even though the consultancy had no direct experience of the company's particular industry, they had plenty of local knowledge and produced a comprehensive report with many good recommendations. They were able to identify the fact that there were two key markets for the company in Zambia – the spares market for businesses refurbishing old refineries and the new-build market, which uses engineering procurement and construction firms. The company rapidly made significant inroads into both and quickly generated additional export sales in excess of £1 million. The use of the EMRS with its expert advice helped the company to develop the right specification and identify the best research consultant to work with. This was key to their success.

Summary

It is essential to research your target markets before you start to promote and sell your products or services within them. To give yourself the best possible chance of successfully entering a market you need to understand both the market itself and how your product will fit into it. You need to learn about the customers who will buy your product and how they currently buy equivalent products. You need to understand who the competition is and how they operate within the market.

The principles of carrying out market research for export markets are the same as those applicable in your domestic market. But the market and the marketing environment will almost certainly be different. In your domestic market you might carry out field research directly yourself or you might commission a consultant or market research company to do it for you. The same is true for overseas markets, but it is advantageous if this is supplemented by visiting the market personally. Before you start to collect any information it is important to decide on your objectives and put together a plan to make sure that you obtain all of the information that you need. These days you can carry out the bulk of your initial research on the internet.

Government statistics are a useful source of information and Chambers of Commerce in many countries can provide valuable market research material, including reports on overseas markets. Many government support organizations also provide basic information on individual export markets. Apart from compiling market and sector reports, some governments also provide financial support to small businesses for market research projects.

CHAPTER FIVE

DEVELOPING AN EXPORT STRATEGY AND PREPARING AN EXPORT PLAN

Any company that decides to start exporting needs to develop its own export strategy. This should be easily understood by all company personnel and should provide a clear idea of why you are exporting and what you expect to achieve. From your export strategy you can develop your export plan – that is, a marketing plan for export markets that will define how entry into export markets will be made. It needs to include your specific marketing objectives and the marketing strategies and tactics to achieve them. It should also include details of the resources that will be required – both personnel and financial resources as well as an adequate budget to cover the export start-up costs. A company that is already exporting should prepare an export marketing plan every year as part of their planning and budgetary process. In addition to this, as companies expand their export sales they will normally prepare individual plans to support their strategies of developing sales in a particular existing export market.

Developing your export strategy

Successful exporters always know exactly why they are exporting and the results and benefits that they expect to achieve. A sound export strategy:

- shows that your company is developing its business in a professional way;
- provides direction to your staff;
- ensures that those who were involved in developing the strategy will buy into it and support it;
- is a useful tool when dealing with your bank and with government support agencies.

The starting point in developing your export strategy is to identify the key factors that influenced your decision to start exporting. You need to make a list of all the issues that made you decide to export, discuss them with key members of staff and rank them in order of importance to the success of your business. Choose the five most important factors from this list and develop your export strategy around them. Your full written strategy document should be clear, concise and relatively short.

Example

Precision Vacuum Products (PVP) is a company based in the south of England. The company was founded 10 years ago and manufactures specialist components such as valves and measuring equipment that are used in vacuum systems. Its main customers are two large UK manufacturers of vacuum pumps and systems and a number of companies that operate large vacuum systems in the food packaging and metallurgy industries. It employs 50 people and its annual turnover is £5 million. The company has decided that growth prospects in its domestic market are limited and has therefore decided to look at exporting as a way to grow its business further.

The managing director set up a brainstorming session with the sales director, production director, finance director and the sales team. They produced a list of all the reasons why the company should begin exporting. This list was discussed and debated and everyone was asked to rank the issues in terms of their importance to the business. After further discussion the top five factors were listed as follows:

1 to widen our customer base and reduce our reliance on our domestic market;
2 to increase turnover and profits;
3 to increase production levels to gain economies of scale;

4   to increase the viability of electronic pressure switch/controllers;
5   our main competitor (German) has increased turnover by exporting.

From the limited market research that they have carried out, they have concluded that the most interesting potential export markets are Germany, Austria and Italy. These countries all have major domestic vacuum pump manufacturers and a range of original equipment manufacturers (OEMs) selling vacuum systems on a worldwide basis. Local component manufacturers are strong in the supply of vacuum valves, but none has such a sophisticated combined pressure switch/controller as PVP. These countries are all part of the EU, which means that shipping and paperwork arrangements will be straightforward. Although there are also manufacturers in Poland and Russia, these manufacturers produce cheaper systems for the lower end of the market. The USA is also of interest, but they consider it to be a secondary target because they would need to modify their products which are all fully metric and would also need to have their products tested in order to get technical approvals required for the US market.

From their export audit, they have concluded that they could not be competitive with their simple products such as vacuum valves and they will concentrate instead on developing sales of their electronic pressure switches and controllers.

Their export strategy is as follows:

We have decided to grow our business by exporting our electronic pressure switches and controllers. We have expanded rapidly in the last five years, but further growth in our domestic market is difficult, because we are already supplying most of the large users and exporting offers us much better opportunities. We intend to:

- expand company turnover from £5 million in 20X3 to £6.5 million in 20X6;
- this will double our production of pressure switches and controllers and increase the utilization of the Xonor machine from 45 per cent to 90 per cent;
- concentrate on developing sales in Germany, Austria and Italy;
- appoint distributors in Germany/Austria in the first year and in Italy in the second year;
- at the same time targeting key OEMs in all three countries;
- develop export sales of at least £1.25 million by 20X6.

This strategy will be reviewed every 12 months or more frequently as conditions require.

The marketing planning process

The principles of marketing planning are used in the process of developing an export plan. Depending on where you are in terms of developing your overseas business, the process can be used to:

- prepare the justification for starting to export;
- prepare a basic export plan;
- put together a complete company export plan to be included in the business plan;
- prepare an export plan for an individual target market;
- prepare an argument for introducing a new product in certain overseas markets;
- revamp the marketing approach for existing products for overseas markets.

There are differences in the way that you use the marketing planning process to prepare an export plan compared to preparing a normal marketing plan for your domestic market. It is easier to split the process into a number of individual phases and to work on these consecutively. These are: research and analysis, preparing objectives and strategies, calculating costs and budgets, preparing the written plan, presenting and implementing it.

Research and situation analysis

- Evaluate and select the target markets.
- Carry out marketing research within the company and in the target markets.
- Look at the company's strengths and weaknesses with regard to exporting to the target markets.
- Look at the product's or service's strengths and weaknesses with regard to exporting.
- Select and price the products/services for the target markets.

Objectives and strategies

- Make relevant assumptions.
- Set specific marketing objectives for each target market.
- Define changes to internal organization and procedures.

- Generate marketing strategies and tactics.
- Decide market entry strategies and distribution methods.
- Forecast sales to be achieved in the target markets together with the timescale for achieving them.
- Define programmes to be carried out.

Costs and budgets

- Cost up resource requirements and programmes.
- Set budgets and prepare a partial profit and loss account.
- Review the results and revise the objectives, strategies or programmes.

The written plan

- Write the plan.
- Present the plan.

Implementation schedule

- Master schedule.
- Review and update procedures.

Marketing planning is an iterative process and the export plan should be reviewed and updated as it is implemented.

Research and analysis

Carry out marketing research

Marketing research involves not just collecting information about your markets, but also analysing it in the context of the marketing of your products. In your market research you need to look at the target markets, the potential customers and the competitors, as well as the overall economic and political environment. The main aim is to allow you to differentiate potential markets in terms of critical factors such as market size, the competitive environment and the availability of suitable distribution channels. The information that you collect should allow you to decide which markets have the most potential and which products are best suited to your customer's requirements.

Situation analysis

In previous chapters, we have explained how to evaluate and select target markets and how to research them. But marketing research involves not just collecting information about your markets, but also analysing it in the context of marketing your products. Situation analysis is the process that helps you to analyse information and to present it in a way that you can use for planning. It can be used to:

- review the economic and business climate in target markets;
- look at the strengths and weaknesses of your company – its organization, its performance and its key products;
- compare the company with its competitors;
- identify opportunities and threats.

You should carry out an internal review, an external review and also review your product or service. In your internal review you should examine your company structure, processes and objectives and identify both strengths and weaknesses as they relate to your readiness and ability to export. Assess your management, marketing, logistics and financial functions in the same way. The external review will look first at any domestic external factors that may impact on your ability to export. You should then look at your target markets to see which offer the best prospects for your company and its products. You should also carry out a review of your key competitors that will be present in your target markets. Finally, you should look at your existing products or services and assess whether they can be marketed in the target markets as they are or whether they would require modification or additional certification.

The key process used in situation analysis is SWOT analysis. It is a simple tool that can be used to analyse the information that you have gathered in your internal, external and product reviews. SWOT stands for:

- Strengths and Weaknesses as they relate to our Opportunities and Threats in the marketplace.

The strengths and weaknesses refer to your company and its products and should be identified from the internal and product reviews, whereas the opportunities and threats are usually taken to be external factors over which your company has no control and these should become clear from the external review. The strengths and opportunities support the objective and the weaknesses and threats are detrimental to the objective.

In carrying out SWOT analysis it is usual to list the strengths, weaknesses, opportunities and threats on the same page. This is done by segmenting the page into four squares and entering strengths and weaknesses in the top squares and opportunities and threats in the bottom squares, as shown in Table 5.1.

TABLE 5.1 SWOT analysis

STRENGTHS	WEAKNESSES

OPPORTUNITIES	THREATS

Example

Precision Vacuum Products have carried out an internal export audit in which they analysed and reviewed their sales and marketing, finance and logistics functions, and assessed their products for their suitability for exporting to their target markets. They have carried out desk research on their three primary target markets and their one secondary target market. The managing director made a visit to the Metaltech 20X2 exhibition in Düsseldorf, Germany in June 20X2 and was able to visit the stands of a number of competitors, potential customers and possible distributors. In talking to contacts at the exhibition, he was able to get a reasonable idea of how the vacuum market works in Germany and the strengths of the main competitors.

Based on this information PVP have had a further session and the management and sales team have prepared SWOTs on their organization and resources, products, main competitors and target markets. The SWOTs are prepared from the point of view of moving into export sales. Some of the SWOTs are shown below:

TABLE 5.2 Organization SWOT analysis

STRENGTHS	WEAKNESSES
Sales Director has considerable export sales experience We have industry specialists We have a new modern factory	No other staff have export experience
OPPORTUNITIES	**THREATS**
Recruit export sales manager Organize export training for key internal staff	Only one person in company with export experience Exporting will increase load on IT and finance departments

TABLE 5.3 SWOT analysis for product – combined pressure switch/controller

STRENGTHS	WEAKNESSES
Good range of sizes Quality product	Limited range of materials Limited production (high cost)
OPPORTUNITIES	**THREATS**
Economies of scale if increased level of sales through exports Developing complementary products	Initial cost means minimal margin initially Product not well known

TABLE 5.4 SWOT analysis for target market – Germany

STRENGTHS	WEAKNESSES
Largest market in Europe Good transport infrastructure EU country, so shipping and paperwork easy	Industry widely spread, so need countrywide distribution Customers prefer German products
OPPORTUNITIES	**THREATS**
Expanding market Large export sector	Competition – both local and from Italy

TABLE 5.5 SWOT analysis for market segment – vacuum coating systems

STRENGTHS	WEAKNESSES
A quality high-price market Some major OEMs Market is expanding	Customers standardize on equipment Limited number of customers
OPPORTUNITIES	**THREATS**
Our main UK customer has an alliance with V-Systeme Many major German exporters of vacuum equipment	New systems using nanotechnology

TABLE 5.6 SWOT analysis for a competitor in the target market – VaQu Ventile

THEIR STRENGTHS	THEIR WEAKNESSES
Wide-ranging distribution Wide range of products and accessories Strong brand, good quality Short lead times	Old-fashioned design No combined switch/controller Their service is subcontracted
OPPORTUNITIES FOR US	**THREATS TO US**
We have combination units We have ATEX certification They have high-cost factory in Germany	New product under development Their new factory in China

Evaluating and selecting target markets

The general principles for evaluating and selecting target markets are shown in Chapter 3. These include the market characteristics and competitive conditions, as well as cultural and political factors and the prevailing financial and economic conditions.

Example

Precision Vacuum Products have evaluated their three target markets and the results are shown below:

Target market	Germany	Austria	Italy
Market characteristics	5	3	3
Competitive conditions	3	3	3
Product suitability	4	4	3
Financial/economic	4	4	3
Cultural/political	5	4	3
Score	21	18	15

(score from 1 to 5; 5 is highest/best)

Comments: Germany is by far the largest of the target markets for our products, being nearly twice as large as the Italian market. There are more potential customers in Germany than in either of the other two markets. German and Italian competitors are active in all of the markets, but we have a specific advantage with our combined pressure switch/controllers, which none of our competitors possesses. We feel that there are more barriers to entry into the Italian market, because there are fewer potentially qualified distributors and because the market in Italy is led more by price than quality (when compared to the German and Austrian markets).

Pricing for export markets

You cannot assume that the pricing levels that you have for your product/service in your domestic market will be the right levels for overseas markets. You may sell direct to your customers in your domestic market, but will probably have to consider selling through an importer or distributor in overseas markets. There will also be additional costs to ship your product to your overseas markets and for some markets there will also be import duties to pay. Setting export prices for products and services is a key issue for all exporters and in some cases it will be the factor that decides whether exporting is viable for the company or not.

The most common methods of setting export prices are:

- cost-plus pricing;
- top-down pricing;
- marginal costing/pricing.

Cost-plus pricing

This is the traditional method of pricing exports. The export price is determined by adding the extra costs of exporting to the domestic manufacturing cost. The extra costs would include such things as export packaging, freight and documentation costs, customs duties and distribution costs. An example is given below:

	£
Ex-works price:	50.00
Domestic freight:	1.25
Export documentation:	0.75
Ocean freight and insurance:	2.00
Import duty (10% of landed cost):	5.40
Distributor margin (30%):	25.45
Final selling price to customer:	84.85

For industrial goods a 30 per cent distributor margin is quite normal. For consumer goods it may well be split between an importer/distributor mark-up of say 15 per cent and a retail mark-up of 30 per cent. Remember that a 30 per cent distributor margin is 30 per cent of the selling price, so this will be the largest 'cost-plus' in the whole equation. You may say that a distributor should be prepared to take less margin, but I can assure you that they won't. Like any business, if they cannot make what they consider to be an acceptable margin on your business they will find other products to sell. So while cost-plus pricing is simple to use, the resulting prices could easily make your product or service uncompetitive.

Top-down pricing

With top-down pricing the prices are calculated by working back from the market price that you believe you will have to meet in order to be competitive. An example is given below:

	£
Final selling price to customer:	75.00
Less distributor margin (30%):	52.50
Less import duty (10%):	47.25
Less ocean freight and insurance:	45.25
Less export documentation:	44.50
Less domestic freight:	43.25 = ex-works price

If you use top-down pricing, the most important issue is whether your ex-works price will cover your production costs and also give you an acceptable profit margin. It can sometimes result in a calculated price level that would be difficult to sell to top management. This is particularly the case with industrial or capital goods. In such cases, companies need to be realistic and this is where marginal costing comes in.

Marginal costing/pricing

Differential pricing is frequently used to set a sensible and acceptable price for products that are to be sold overseas. It uses the technique of marginal costing and treats export sales as additional business which makes a reduced contribution to a company's fixed costs. The same product is sold at a lower ex-works price when it is exported than when it is being sold in the domestic market. To avoid the risk of being accused of 'dumping' the product, it is important that this does not result in the end selling price of the product in your overseas markets being below the end selling price in your domestic market. (International agreements prohibit exports from being sold at a price that is below their actual cost.)

Marginal costing is based on separating your costs into fixed and variable costs and only allocating those costs which vary directly with the level of activity to the product or service. Fixed costs are not allocated to units of sales or production, but are treated collectively as costs for the period of time being considered. Fixed costs include items such as rent, rates, interest charges, depreciation and administration costs. Variable costs include the raw materials, labour and energy costs involved in the production process. In marginal costing, the technique of break-even analysis is used to evaluate the relationship between sales revenues, fixed costs and variable costs. As sales volumes increase, unit costs decrease. Fixed costs do not increase as production increases, so spreading the fixed costs over more units results in a reduction in the unit cost. The break-even point is the point at which the actual sales (or units of production) is equal to the total costs. As long as a company is operating above the break-even point, it will be making a profit on its sales. An example of break-even analysis is shown in Figure 5.1.

FIGURE 5.1 Example of break-even analysis

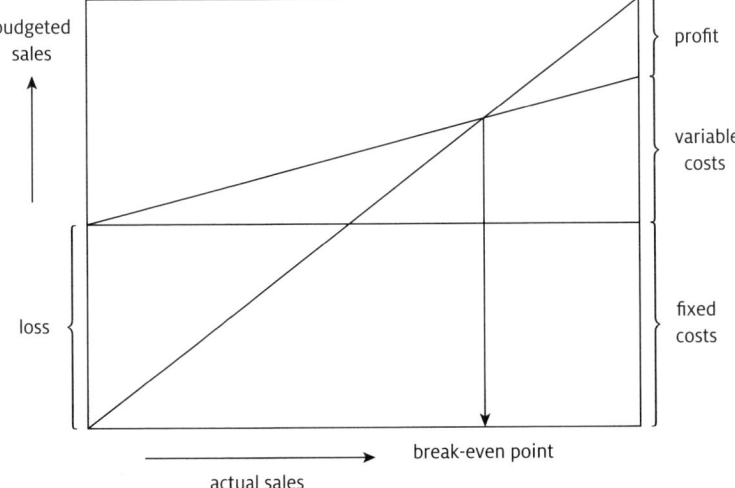

For differential pricing to work, your domestic sales need to already exceed the level of production that makes the product profitable. The initial budgeted level of export sales should be based on a minimum selling price that should at the very least ensure that when you sell your product you are covering your costs and making a reasonable return on investment.

Objectives and strategies

Assumptions

These are key facts and assumptions that you make when putting the plan together. They should be few in number and should relate only to the key issues which would significantly affect the likelihood of the plan's objectives being achieved. For example:

- The $: £ exchange rate will remain in the range $1.50 to $1.70 : £1 for the next 12 months.
- Interest rates will not increase by more than 1 per cent over the next three years.
- Company wage increases will not exceed inflation over the next three years.

Example

Precision Vacuum Products has made the following assumptions with regard to its export plan:

- UK inflation will remain below 3 per cent over the next three years.
- The pound sterling will not strengthen against the euro during the timescale of the plan.
- Company wage increases will not exceed inflation over the next three years.

Setting your marketing objectives

Objectives are what you want to achieve; strategies are how you get there.

Expanding your sales into overseas markets will involve you selling your existing products into your new export markets, but could also include modifying some of your existing products to make them suitable for those markets. Marketing objectives must be definable and quantifiable so that there is an achievable target to aim towards. 'Achievable' is the key word – an objective that is clearly impossible to achieve will be seen as a disincentive by your sales team. Marketing objectives should be defined in such a way that actual performance can be compared with the objective.

Objectives should always be SMART:

- Specific – they should be expressed in terms of values or market shares, and vague terms such as increase, improve or maximize should not be used.
- Measurable – you should be able to confirm whether you have achieved them or not.
- Achievable – are you putting in the resources, in terms of people and investment, to achieve them?
- Realistic – although targets should stretch you, if they are clearly unreasonable, they will just be demotivating.
- Time-bound – there should be a set timescale for achieving every objective.

The following are examples of marketing objectives:

- to increase sales of the product in the USA by 10 per cent per annum in real terms, each year for the next three years;
- to increase market share for the product in Germany from 5 per cent to 10 per cent over three years;
- to increase our export sales of the product by 30 per cent in real terms within five years.

You need to have short-term as well as long-term objectives. Increasing sales by 30 per cent over five years may seem a huge rise, but if you redefine it as increasing sales by 5 or 6 percent a year, it will appear to be much more achievable. Your marketing objectives will also translate into sales forecasts for your target markets.

Example

Precision Vacuum Products has set the following objectives for its export plan:

- to increase export sales from zero in 20X3 to £1.25 million in 20X6;
- to increase sales to Germany to £800,000 by 20X6;
- to increase sales to Austria to £200,000 by 20X6;
- to increase sales to Italy to £250,000 by 20X6;
- to gain annual sales to export OEMs of £700,000 by 20X6;
- to increase export sales of combined pressure switch/controllers to 400 units a year within three years.

Based on these objectives the company has prepared the following sales forecasts:

TABLE 5.7 Total export sales forecast

Year (all values in £k)	20X1	20X2	20X3	Forecast 20X4	20X5	20X6
Germany				150	300	800
Austria				50	100	200
Italy					100	250
Total				250	500	1250

TABLE 5.8 Sales forecast for Germany

Year (all values in £k)	20X1	20X2	20X3	Forecast 20X4	20X5	20X6
Distributor sales				100	200	400
OEM sales				50	100	400
Total				150	300	800

Devising marketing strategies

Strategies are the broad methods chosen to achieve specific objectives. They describe the means of achieving the objectives in the timescale required, but they do not include the detail of the individual courses of action that will be followed on a day-by-day or month-by-month basis. These are *tactics*, and will be discussed later.

In devising strategies for your export plan it is helpful to think in terms of the 'four Ps':

● Product – the benefits that your product offers your potential customers in your target market; whether it needs to be modified or changed to better meet the requirements of the customers.
● Pricing – will you aim to match the local competition? Will you try to beat them on price? Or will you sell at a higher price on the basis of additional benefits that your product offers?
● Place – how will you sell your product? Online? Direct to large end users? Through distribution or agents?
● Promotion – will you use advertising? Exhibitions? If the local language in your target country is different from yours you will need to have sales literature translated into the local language.

In looking at strategies it can be useful to expand the four Ps and add:

● People – do you need additional staff resources and do they and existing employees need specialist training?
● Processes – do you need to modify your processes and systems to make them more suitable for the requirements of exporting?

Strategies can come from many different sources and it is wise to consider all possible ways of generating potential strategies. All of the strategies should be consistent with each other and with the objectives that they are expected to achieve. You should also determine which strategies can be best implemented with the resources and capabilities that your company has or will have over the timescale of the plan.

Example

Precision Vacuum Products has set as the objective for its main target market, Germany:

● to increase sales to Germany to £800,000 by 20X6.

To help it achieve this objective it has decided to adopt the following set of strategies:

● Product:
  – Apply for ATEX certification for combined pressure switch/ controller with attached vacuum valve.
● Pricing:
  – Determine sensible list price level for target markets.
  – Produce euro price list and enter pricing into system.
● Promotion:
  – Produce German version of main sales brochure and data sheets for pressure switches and controllers.
  – Take part in Metaltech 20X4 exhibition in Düsseldorf in June 20X4 as part of the UK stand.
● Place:
  – Use the Overseas Market Introduction Service to find and evaluate potential distributors.
  – Use participation in Metaltech 20X4 to further evaluate potential distributors.

- People:
  - Recruit export sales manager (ideally German speaking).
  - Organize export training for key internal staff in sales, shipping and finance.
- Processes:
  - Enter HS codes into the system for all standard items and modify order-handling system to make sure that orders can only be entered onto the system for items with a valid HS code.

Tactics and action plans

Your strategies give a broad definition of how an objective is to be achieved, but the action steps are tactics and the action plans contain the detail of the individual actions, their timing and who will carry them out.

If your strategy for pricing was to change price, terms or conditions for particular product groups for particular markets, the tactics could be:

- Reduce price of product to maximize sales.
- Calculate price levels to meet specific pricing policies of competitors.
- Set price at 10 per cent below market leader.
- Price product high where we have technical advantage over competitors' products.

Similarly, if your strategy for promotion was to increase advertising/ sales promotion, the tactics could be:

- Increase advertising for the product in specific markets.
- Start new advertising campaign.
- Offer incentive scheme to distributors.
- Carry out e-mail shot.
- Increase company image advertising.

Example

Precision Vacuum Products has a strategy for pricing:

- Determine sensible list price level for target markets.

One of the company's new sales engineers used to work for the local distributor of their main German competitor and brought with him some knowledge of competitor pricing. The tactics the company is adopting to implement its pricing strategy are:

- Analyse all in-house competitor pricing information that we have for both the domestic market and overseas markets.
- Use industry contacts to obtain further pricing information.
- Talk to key domestic customers who also operate in our target overseas markets.

They have also adopted a strategy for promotion:

- Produce foreign-language versions of our main sales literature.

The tactics for this are:

- Use agency to produce German version of our main sales brochure.
- Prepare German versions of our data sheets for our pressure switches and controllers in house.
- Use agency to prepare German version of our key sales advert.
- Use agency to produce Italian version of our main sales brochure.
- Prepare Italian versions of our data sheets for our pressure switches and controllers in house.

Next your strategies and tactics will need to be turned into programmes or action plans that will enable you to give clear instructions to your staff.

Each action plan should include:

- aims – what you want to do and where you want to go;
- action – what you need to do to get there;
- person responsible – who will do it;
- start date;
- finish date;
- budgeted cost.

Each action plan would need to be broken down into its component parts.

Example

For the tactic 'Use agency to produce German version of our main sales brochure', Precision Vacuum Products have prepared the following action plan.

Aim	Action	By	Start	Finish	Cost
Produce German brochure	Meet with agency for kick-off meeting	AHF/IGT	15.9.X3	15.9.X3	£200
	Prepare text – UK text with changes for German market	IGT	15.9.X3	31.10.X3	£100
	Get text translated by Ace Translations	IGT	31.10.X3	22.11.X3	£850
	Check initial artwork	AHF/IGT	1.12.X3	1.1.X4	£500
	Check final artwork	AHF/IGT	15.1.X4	30.1.X4	£2500
	Print	AHF	15.2.X4	30.2.X4	£2500

Costs and budgets

To implement your export plan you will incur additional costs. These will include additional salary costs for sales personnel, travel costs for business-related travel and marketing costs for sales promotional materials and activities. Most companies starting to export set a sensible target for the amount of additional sales that they intend to achieve initially. So if you are expecting to increase your turnover by 10 to 15 per cent over a three-year period, you are unlikely initially to need to take on additional staff for functions such as logistics and finance. Equally, unless you are a manufacturing company operating with machines that are near to 100 per cent capacity, you are unlikely to need to include new investment in machinery and other equipment in your initial export plan. As your overall level of sales grows, including the contribution coming from export, you will need to look at making further investments as part of your overall business planning and budgeting processes. But for the purpose of an initial export plan, most companies will only need to prepare an additional profit and loss account to cover the additional sales included in the plan.

You should prepare an operating expenses budget to cover the export function in the same way that you would prepare your operating expenses budget for your domestic operations in your annual budgeting process. This should include the salaries of those who are now allocated to the export function, their travel costs and other expenses, as well as the cost of all export literature, advertising and exhibitions.

Example

Precision Vacuum Products plans to recruit an export sales manager to manage their export operations. The new manager will be supported by one full-time internal sales person. Functions such as logistics and finance will be handled by existing staff and it is not envisaged that any additional resources will be required during the next three years.

The operating expenses budget for their export operations is shown in Table 5.9.

TABLE 5.9 Operating expenses budget for 20X4 to 20X6

£k	20X4	20X5	20X6
Salaries	45.0	62.0	65.0
Recruitment	10.0		
Travel costs	10.0	15.0	20.0
Mobile phone	5.0	6.0	7.0
Literature	8.0	14.0	10.0
Exhibitions	30.0	35.0	40.0
Advertising	15.0	20.0	20.0
Sundry items	10.0	10.0	10.0
Total	130.0	162.0	172.0

These additional operating costs will be used to prepare a partial profit and loss account covering the additional business due to the export sales resulting from the plan. If the sales are based on marginal costing of the products, two versions of the profit and loss account can be prepared – one showing the profitability of the additional business if fixed costs are included and one without.

Example

Partial profit and loss account for Precision Vacuum Products including fixed cost allocation is shown in Table 5.10.

TABLE 5.10 Partial profit and loss account including fixed cost allocation

	20X4 £k	20X5 £k	20X6 £k
Invoiced sales	250.0	500.0	1250.0
Cost of sales	100.0	200.0	500.0
Gross profit	250.0	300.0	750.0
Sales and marketing costs			
Salaries	45.0	62.0	65.0
Recruitment	10.0		
Travel costs	10.0	15.0	20.0
Mobile phone	5.0	6.0	7.0
Literature	8.0	14.0	10.0

TABLE 5.10 *Continued*

	20X4 £k	20X5 £k	20X6 £k
Exhibitions	30.0	35.0	40.0
Advertising	15.0	20.0	20.0
Sundry items	10.0	10.0	10.0
Total sales costs	130.0	162.0	172.0
Administration costs	30.0	32.0	35.0
IT costs	10.0	12.0	15.0
Distribution costs	7.5	15.0	37.5
Total operating expenses (relating to plan)	177.5	221.0	259.5
Operating profit (relating to plan)	72.5	79.0	490.5

Partial profit and loss account for Precision Vacuum Products based on marginal costing (excluding fixed cost allocation) is shown in Tables 5.11.

TABLE 5.11 Partial profit and loss account based on marginal costing (excluding fixed cost allocation)

	20X4 £k	20X5 £k	20X6 £k
Invoiced sales	250.0	500.0	1250.0
Cost of sales	100.0	200.0	500.0
Gross profit	250.0	300.0	750.0
Sales and marketing costs			
Salaries	45.0	62.0	65.0
Recruitment	10.0		
Travel costs	10.0	15.0	20.0
Mobile phone	5.0	6.0	7.0
Literature	8.0	14.0	10.0
Exhibitions	30.0	35.0	40.0
Advertising	15.0	20.0	20.0
Sundry items	10.0	10.0	10.0
Total sales costs	130.0	162.0	172.0
Distribution costs	7.5	15.0	37.5
Total operating expenses (relating to plan)	137.5	177.0	209.5
Operating profit (relating to plan)	112.5	123.0	540.5

The written plan

The written plan should be clear and concise and should only contain the key information that needs to be communicated. It should include summary information resulting from the marketing research that you have carried out relating to your company and your target markets, but the bulk of the detail should be excluded from the written document, to avoid confusing the reader. A summary of the key action plans should be included, but not smaller sub-plans. A four- or five-page document will suffice for most plans, although a full plan including profit and loss accounts and justifications for capital investment as well as additional revenue expenditure could be longer.

Formats for export marketing plans

There are many different formats that can be adopted for export plans. There are two main types of situation where you need to prepare an export plan and these two types of situation lend themselves to a different format for the written plan. I differentiate these two types of plan by referring to them as the Complete Export Plan and the Export Marketing Plan.

● The Complete Export Plan. If you are a company that is completely new to exporting or not very experienced, you need to prepare a document that shows why you have decided that you want to export, what your export strategy is, the resources that you have and the new resources that you will add to achieve your new export sales goals. You need to confirm why you have selected your target markets, what changes (if any) need to be made to your product and what you expect to achieve.

● The Export Marketing Plan. As you become more experienced as an exporter, your export planning will become an integral part of your annual planning and budgeting process, so the plans that you prepare will take on the more traditional format of a marketing plan. Your marketing plan for your domestic market and your marketing plan for export markets will become two parallel parts of your annual business plan and your annual budget. Additionally as you get more experienced you will start to prepare export marketing plans for entering individual target markets or for introducing new products into some of your existing export markets.

The Complete Export Plan

For this type of plan I favour using the type of format developed many years ago by the US Department of Commerce. This format is now in use throughout the world and is also promoted by various support organizations in Australia and Canada. Details can be obtained by going to the US government website, **www.export.gov**. Click on 'Export basics' and 'Develop your export plan' and you will find 'Outline for an export plan'.

The outline of this plan format is as follows (source: US Department of Commerce):

- Table of contents.
- Executive summary (one or two pages maximum).
- Introduction: why this company should export.
- Part 1 – export policy commitment statement.
- Part 2 – situation/background analysis:
  - product or service;
  - operations;
  - personnel and export organization;
  - resources of the firm;
  - industry structure, competition and demand.
- Part 3 – marketing component:
  - identifying, evaluating and selecting target markets;
  - product selection and pricing;
  - distribution methods;
  - terms and conditions;
  - internal organization and procedures;
  - sales goals: profit and loss forecasts.
- Part 4 – tactics: action steps:
  - primary target countries;
  - secondary target countries;
  - indirect marketing efforts.
- Part 5 – export budget:
  - pro forma financial statements.
- Part 6 – implementation schedule:
  - follow-up;
  - periodic and management review (measuring results against plan).

- Addenda:
  - background data on target countries and market;
  - basic market statistics: historical and projected;
  - background facts;
  - competitive environment.

This format may look rather complicated, but it follows a logical progression of ideas. Not every company will need to complete information for every one of the individual subheadings and under other subheadings a sentence or two will suffice. The important thing is that your written plan is easy to understand, both for your own sales team and for others in your company or group who will need to help you to implement it.

The export marketing plan

This is the format that I have developed for marketing plans. (More detail on this can be found in my book *How to Write a Marketing Plan*, also published by Kogan Page.)

The outline of this plan format is shown below:

- Introduction;
- Executive summary;
- Situation analysis:
  - assumptions;
  - sales (history/budget);
  - key products;
  - strategic markets/industries;
  - key sales areas.
- Marketing objectives;
- Marketing strategies;
- Schedules;
- Sales promotion;
- Budgets;
- Profit and loss account;
- Controls;
- Update procedures;
- Appendices.

Depending on the scope of your plan you may need to omit or combine certain sections.

I have prepared sample plans based on these two formats. A Complete Export Plan for the company Precision Vacuum Products, that we have been following throughout this chapter, is shown in Appendix 2 at the end of this book and an Export Marketing Plan for The Pure Fruit Jam Company for their entry into the Japanese market is shown in Appendix 3.

Summary

Successful exporters always know exactly why they are exporting and the results and benefits that they expect to achieve. A sound export strategy shows that your company is developing its business in a professional way, provides direction to your staff and is a useful tool when dealing with your bank and government support agencies.

From your export strategy you can develop your export plan – a marketing plan for export markets that will define how entry into these markets will be achieved. Your export plan needs to include your specific marketing objectives and the marketing strategies and tactics to achieve them. It should also include details of the resources required – both human and financial – as well as a budget to cover start-up costs.

The principles of marketing planning are used in the process of developing an export plan, but there are differences in the way that you use the process compared with preparing a marketing plan for your domestic market. You should carry out an internal review, an external review and also review your product and service. SWOT analysis is a simple tool that can be used to analyse the information that you have gathered in your internal, external and product reviews.

As you implement your export plan you will incur additional costs. You should prepare an operating expenses budget to cover the export function in the same way that you would prepare your operating expenses budget for your domestic operations. There are many different formats that can be adopted for export plans, but the two main types are the Complete Export Plan and the Export Marketing Plan.

CHAPTER SIX

ENTRY STRATEGIES FOR OVERSEAS MARKETS

Having made the decision to enter an overseas market, you need to consider the ways you can go about it and decide which entry strategy is right for your business. It is not easy to manage overseas business completely from your home base, so most exporters set up a local presence in their target export markets. But the most suitable entry strategy for you will depend on your product and will be influenced by a number of factors including the size of your business and your willingness to accept risk. The entry strategy that you adopt may be different for different markets, and depending on your product and the target market, you may need to adopt a combination of entry strategies.

Types of exporting

There are a number of different types of export entry strategies that companies can employ.

FIGURE 6.1 Export market entry strategies

Market entry strategies

Passive or 'domestic' exporting

Most companies making a conscious decision to move into exporting are thinking about direct exporting, whether this is from their home base or by means of an intermediary based in the target country itself. In fact, although they may not be aware of it, many companies are already selling products that are being exported in complete units or plant that a domestic manufacturer is supplying to its overseas customers. This is called passive exporting. If a company becomes aware that it is passively exporting, the next step would be to actively seek out companies that could include their products in equipment that they export and to also look for domestic buyers who represent or purchase on behalf of foreign companies. This 'domestic' exporting is low risk because you are selling your product to a domestic buyer or customer who then ships the product abroad and handles all of the documentation and transportation. Apart from Original Equipment Manufacturers (OEMs), examples of this type of domestic customer include civil and mechanical engineering contractors and major multinational companies.

Example

Many large or multinational companies have a global purchasing network. This often means that although they have a local purchasing office in all markets where they are present, they often have a centralized purchasing organization at their home base or regional purchasing offices on different continents for the purchase of larger or more complicated items. These purchasing offices will be buying materials and equipment not only for the market in which they are situated, but also on behalf of their companies in other markets in the region.

For many years companies like Unilever and Shell have had central purchasing offices in London and the Netherlands. Other global companies like Procter & Gamble and Coca-Cola have regional purchasing offices in the USA, Europe and Asia. So if one of these large multinational companies has a purchasing unit in your country, there is a good possibility that you could sell them your product, not only for their factories in your own country, but also for export to their factories in other countries in the region.

Some major companies have central purchasing in major countries where they are not actually active themselves. The Saudi Arabian Oil Company Aramco is a good example. Aramco has purchasing offices in The Hague (Netherlands) and in Houston, Texas. European suppliers can register as a supplier with Aramco Overseas Company BV, and US (and other North American) companies can register as a supplier with Aramco Services Company. This means that they can supply their products locally for export to Aramco plants throughout the world.

Exporting online

Nowadays, any company with an e-commerce website can generate some overseas sales. As long as you have a product to ship, you have no limits to your business area. The requirements for order handling and after-sales service for export business are similar when you are dealing with them on and offline, but there are additional national and international regulations relating to e-commerce. If you want to start exporting by selling your goods online, you need to know what you are doing. This is covered in detail in chapter 9.

Example

When small companies decide to sell to overseas customers online they often do not realize the additional complications of exporting compared to selling the same products in their domestic market. An example of the difficulties that can arise is given by the case of a small US manufacturer of upmarket doll's house furniture. The company had been expanding its sales in the USA for several years and found that it was starting to receive enquiries from Canada. Not thinking anything of it, they decided to accept the orders from Canadian customers and ship the goods to them. Initially, their shipping clerk found it just as easy as selling to US customers. But a few weeks later the company started receiving bills from its shipping companies for arranging customs clearance into Canada and also bills for tariffs and Canadian taxes. They had not realized that they would have to pay these fees and had therefore not passed them on to their Canadian customers. They had to accept the costs themselves and this reduced their margins on these sales, so that many of the orders ended up being sold at a loss. Once this became clear the company decided to stop accepting orders from Canada. As a result of their bad experience, it was several years before the company decided to try exporting again. When they did, they decided to take an indirect approach to exporting so that they could continue to focus on their core domestic business.

Indirect approaches to exporting

Indirect exporting provides companies with a way of entering overseas markets without all of the costs and the risks of direct exporting. It involves working completely through an intermediary and not actually handling your export business yourself. The type of intermediary is determined by the level of resource that the company is prepared to commit to their export activity. Some types of intermediary will not only obtain orders on your behalf, but will also handle all of the export documentation and even shipping arrangements. Others will only obtain the orders, so that you still have to have your own staff who can handle the documentation and logistics. But by engaging in indirect exporting, a company does not have to invest in sales personnel experienced in travelling and selling abroad or in the cost of export travel. The main forms of indirect exporting are through export agents, export management companies or export trading companies. Although there are differences, the terms export management company and export trading company are often used interchangeably. The intermediary company is normally either based in your own country or has an office in your own country that deals with your business.

- Export agents usually operate by representing a number of indirect exporters who are not in direct competition with each other. Some types of export agent purchase products direct from the manufacturer, repackage them and sell them overseas in their own name. Others sell the products through their own contacts overseas and are paid a commission on the sales that they generate.
- Export management companies act as either agents or distributors and provide additional services on a commission or a retainer basis. Some export management companies offer their client companies the facilities of a complete export department and some of the larger export management companies will even take title to the goods and export on their own account. The services offered include organizing shipping and handling export documentation.
- Export trading companies may also offer access to distribution channels and storage facilities. Much trade with Korea and Japan is conducted through export trading houses such as Hyundai, Samsung, Mitsubishi and Mitsui. Some export trading companies are set up to market the products of a group of producers overseas. This is common with agricultural products and products such as wine.

It is quite common for a company to adopt a strategy by which they develop direct export business with markets that are easier to manage and use indirect methods for selling to other more difficult markets. So a European company may start by selling directly and through distribution to customers within the European Union and to countries such as the USA and Australia, but use an export agent or export management company for sales to Africa and the Middle East. Similarly a US company may start by exporting directly to Canada and Mexico and use an export trading company based in Miami to develop sales to South America. Much of Australia's trade with South Korea and Japan is through export trading companies.

Example

A few years later the US supplier of doll's house furniture was still receiving a few enquiries daily from prospective overseas customers. They did not feel that they wanted to devote their scarce resources to managing international trade and so they decided to look at indirect exporting using an export management company that could handle their export business for them. They found a service provider that was able to offer a seamless approach to the marketplace. This export management company was able to integrate its system with the company's shopping cart and provided overseas buyers with a US address for order shipment. When the orders arrive at this US address, the goods are packed, the export documentation is prepared and the goods are then shipped to the overseas customer. The service provider also verifies the overseas buyer's credit information and card details and analyses each order for potential fraud, thus reducing the credit risk to the company. The company now sees export sales as a valuable additional source of income. They know that with their type of product, their domestic sales will always be their bread and butter, but using an export management company means that they can handle any overseas sales professionally, whether the level of export business grows or not.

Direct approaches to exporting

Most companies embarking on exporting decide to engage in some form of direct exporting. There are four main ways that companies can sell direct to customers in overseas markets. These are:

- selling direct from your home base;
- setting up an overseas operation;
- using a sales agent in the target market;
- using a distributor in the target market.

Selling direct

Selling direct from your home base is an easy way to start selling into overseas markets. You can start by using your existing sales team or you can start by using your website. (Or you can of course develop a strategy using both your online and offline resources in parallel.)

Initially selling direct can be cost effective, because you can start by using your existing personnel and add resources as you need them. Some of your existing sales team can deal with your overseas customers and you can generate sales by telephone and e-mail, supported by occasional sales visits. You can see how things develop, without making major investments, and then decide what other strategies to adopt. You have full control of both the marketing and selling processes. As your export business develops, you can make changes to the way that you market your products and if you decide that some products would be even better suited for overseas markets with modification or further development, this can easily be carried out.

The pros and cons of selling direct:

- Pros:
  - You can start by using your existing personnel and add resources as you need them.
  - You can see how things develop and then decide what other strategies to adopt.
  - You have full control of both the marketing and selling processes.
- Cons:
  - You are a long way from the market.
  - You will be responsible for the logistics of shipping your goods.
  - You have to manage all the risks of exporting yourself, including the risks of possible non-payment of your invoices.
  - If the language of your target market is not your own, you will need to consider recruiting a qualified person who speaks that language or provide language training for your staff.

Setting up an overseas operation

Setting up your own operation in an overseas market is the most expensive and time-consuming option for market entry. It is not likely to be the option that you would choose if you are new to exporting and looking at one of your first target markets, but if you are an established exporter and you are prepared to make the investment, it is one of the best methods for a company to get established and achieve rapid growth in a new market. In certain countries you may find restrictions that mean you can only establish a joint venture with a local company or set up a company together with a local businessman.

There are four main ways of establishing your own overseas operation:

- Set up a local office. You can set up a local office staffed by your own employees. In its simplest form this could involve transferring one of your own staff or employing a local who would work from home. The advantage of employing a local is that you immediately get someone who speaks the local language and understands the local way of doing business.
- Set up a subsidiary company. You can establish your own locally registered subsidiary in your target market. The company would be subject to the local employment and tax regulations. The company could be run by one of your existing employees or by a local that you recruit. Additional local staff would be recruited as required.
- Purchase a local company. You can consider purchasing an existing local company. This could be a local competitor, a local distribution company or even your own existing distributor.
- Establish a joint venture. A joint venture is a partnership with a local business, where you set up a new business usually with 50 per cent owned by each party. Joint ventures are predominantly set up for manufacturing and it is not uncommon in major markets, such as China or India, for the local partner to have an existing factory, part of which can be sectioned off and used by the joint venture company.

The pros and cons of setting up your own operation:

- Pros:
  - Your local presence means that you are well placed to identify and exploit opportunities.
  - You have control of your operations.

- You keep all of the profits from your operations.
- You can plan for the long term.
- You can expand or contract your operations if the local situation changes.
- Your customers will see you as a local supplier.
- You can provide the level of after-sales service that your products require.
- If things go wrong, a locally established subsidiary company limits your liability.
- If you set up a joint venture, you share the profits, but on the other hand you also share the risks. You also get the benefit of your partner's local knowledge.
- Cons:
  - The financial cost of setting up a local enterprise is high.
  - You will need professional advice on the legal and financial ramifications and requirements.
  - A local operation will require greater resources to set up, manage and operate than alternative methods of market entry.
  - If you don't use a local partner, you take on all the risks yourself.
  - It can be costly and difficult to extract yourself if things do not work out. This is particularly the case with a joint venture.

Using a sales agent

A sales agent acts on behalf of your company by introducing you to customers and helping you to obtain orders from them. They are sometimes called commission agents, because they are paid a commission on any sales that they make. The level of commission varies and it is usually only paid once the order is complete, the goods have been shipped *and paid for*. A good sales agent gives you a high degree of local knowledge and because he is only paid his commission once you have been paid, he has a vested interest in making sure that you get paid. In choosing a sales agent, you need to satisfy yourself about their market knowledge and the level of contacts that they have in your target industries. Make sure that they have experience of selling your type of product, ask for references and examine their client list. In large markets such as Germany or the USA it is not uncommon for companies to appoint sales agents for either a specific region of the country or for specific industries. The level of commission would usually be set based on the type of business, the value of individual contracts or orders, annual turnover with particular customers and the amount of involvement (ie number of hours) that the agent will have to spend on that particular customer. Be fair about how you set up the commission schedule, because you cannot expect a sales agent to get involved with business that they will not be paid for. Make sure that you get good legal advice before setting up an agency contract. (You should also be aware that many Middle Eastern countries do not differentiate between an agent and a distributor.) The key thing about any agency arrangement is to get the relationship right at the start. Otherwise you may well end up with a relationship that doesn't work, but which may be difficult to extract yourself from.

The pros and cons of using a sale agent:

- Pros:
  - The right agent will be able to identify and exploit opportunities.
  - They should already have good relationships with the buyers at key potential customers.
  - This means they should be productive from the start, whereas setting up your own arrangements would take time.
  - You avoid the costs of using your own employees in the marketplace on a day-to-day basis, although you will still need to train the agent and support him with regular visits.
  - Using an agent gives you greater control over things like price and conditions than if you were using a distributor.
  - You can control your brand and how it is used much more than you could if you were operating through a distributor.
  - Based on their experience, an agent can give you advice on the creditworthiness of a particular customer.
- Cons:
  - You still have to manage shipments from your works to the end customer, including paperwork and customs clearance formalities.
  - You need to specify in the agent's contract what matters they will deal with on your behalf.

- If you want them to carry out proper credit checks on customers locally, you will need to include that in the contract and the commission structure will need to reflect the costs of this.
- Since the agent will be the main contact with your customers in the target market, you will certainly lose some control over marketing and your brand image.
- Most agents will not handle after-sales service as well as you would yourself, since they have already been paid their commission on the supply contract.
- You have to be prepared to allow access to your sales ledger as part of the process of paying commissions.

Using a distributor

The difference between a distributor and a sales agent is that a sales agent finds you customers, whereas a distributor is your customer. A distributor buys goods from you and resells them in the overseas market. Depending on your type of product, many distributors will also hold stock of your product (or at least of spare parts and consumables) at their premises to support your customers in the market. In this way an overseas distributor operates in much the same way as a distributor would in your home market.

As with sales agents, you should do your homework and make sure that the distributor has experience of selling your type of product and has existing customers for the type of product that you sell. It is also very important to make sure that they do not sell products that compete directly or indirectly with your own. Distribution law is complex and you should make sure that you get good legal advice before setting up a distributorship agreement. Distributors will normally expect to get a long period of exclusivity, but you need to make sure that the agreement is initially for a sensible time period and includes a 'get-out' clause if they fail to perform.

The pros and cons of using a distributor

- Pros:
  - A distributor takes on all of the logistics problems of getting your goods to the customer in your target overseas market.
  - A distributor takes over many of the trade-related risks, including supplying credit and getting paid locally.
  - An established distributor will already have a list of contacts that they can introduce your products to.
  - An established distributor can use their reputation to support the introduction of your (new) brand into the market.
  - A distributor will take over the marketing and sales promotion functions for your products in the overseas market including producing sales literature in their own language, carrying out advertising and taking part in exhibitions. They will probably expect some financial contribution from you to support some of these activities.
  - Most distributors keep stock of the products that they sell. Depending on your type of product the stock may be complete items or just spare parts.
- Cons:
  - A distributor will expect large discounts on the products they buy from you.
  - They will also expect more extended payment terms than you would offer in your home market.
  - The customers become *their* customers and not yours. Most distributors keep their customer lists to themselves.
  - Distributors add their own mark-up, so you lose any control over the selling price for your products in the target marketplace.
  - If the selling price they set is too high and inhibits sales growth they will probably ask for a larger discount rather than reducing their own margin.
  - A distributor may rebrand your product, sell it under their own name or change the brand image from the image that you have developed in your home market.
  - Distributors will usually demand a long period of exclusivity and you need to make sure that you have adequate safeguards in place to allow you to part company if they clearly do not perform.

Example

In Chapter 5 we looked at the UK company Precision Vacuum Products as they developed their export strategy and export plan. They decided to move into direct exporting and decided to use distributors in their target export markets and to sell directly to some key original equipment manufacturers (OEMs). We will look at the reasons that they chose to use distribution rather than a different approach.

As a small company with limited resources, they know that developing sales in their target export markets will be a gradual and slow process. They do not have the resources to set up their own sales units in individual markets, but also they can see that, even if they did, it would not make commercial sense with the level of sales they hope to achieve in the first three years of their plan. They decide not to use agents because of the high level of technical expertise required to sell their products and the level of after-sales support that is necessary.

Precision Vacuum Products can justify selling directly to key OEMs on the basis that their sales will be repeat sales of a standard unit and the level of sales to each OEM (probably several hundred thousand pounds annually) will justify individual sales and support visits. The balance of their sales will be developed using local distributors with good technical sales teams, a knowledge of the vacuum market and the ability to provide local stock and after-sales service.

Deciding which entry strategy to use

Exporting will generate additional sales for your company, but exporting does not just involve selling. You will need to handle paperwork, shipping, customs clearance, warehousing and after-sales service and you will have additional legal, financial and accounting requirements to those that you would have to deal with in your domestic market. Selling directly gives you overall control of your operations, but it also brings with it all of the costs. Although you have less control when you use an intermediary, they will handle the importation, paperwork, warehousing and shipping of your goods to the end customers.

In deciding which entry strategy is right for you, you should consider the following:

- Do you have the necessary skills, including the language ability, to make contacts and generate sales?
- Do you have the necessary time and does your company have the financial resources to set up and manage a local office or subsidiary?
- Are there local restrictions that would limit the way you can operate in your target market? In some countries only a national can own a company. In others you need a local partner or have to form a joint venture with a local company.
- What are the usual distribution channels for products like yours in your target market?
- Are your key competitors present in your target market, and if so, how do they operate?
- Are your products of a standard type that lends itself to warehousing and distribution or are they custom made depending on the technical requirements of the customer?
- Does your product require specialist after-sales support that would need to be provided by your own company? If so, direct sales, even if supported by a local agent, would be more appropriate than selling through a distributor.

You also need to decide whether it is more important for you to keep costs down to a minimum or to have control of the selling process. Remember that an intermediary will have their own priorities, which may or may not always be the same as yours.

Marketing channels

The things that you require from distribution in an export market are the same as those that you would require from distribution in your home market.

Distribution involves:

- marketing channels;
- physical distribution;
- customer service.

The main difference is that in export markets you expect your local presence, whether it is a distributor or your own entity, to have the local channels to market and you also expect them to handle the physical distribution of your goods to the customer and the customer service function.

The marketing channels that can be used for exporting are the same as those that can be used in your domestic market. The difference is that in your domestic market you will control how you use these channels, but in export markets some of these channels will be used by your distributor. Potential customers may still look at your website, but they will also look at your distributor's website and it will be the distributor that uses e-marketing and direct mail. Figure 6.2 shows the range of marketing channels that are available to you in most markets.

FIGURE 6.2 Marketing channels

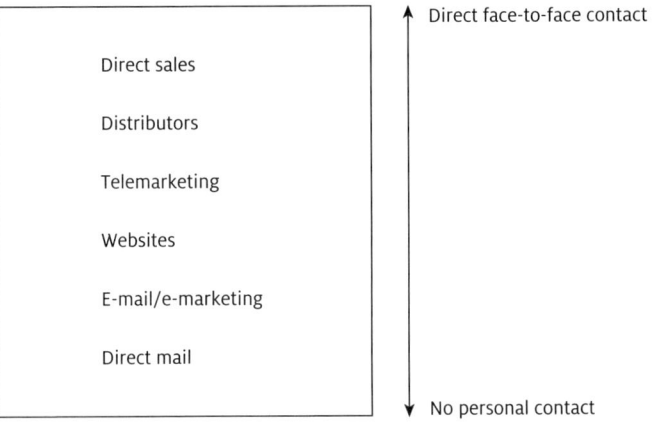

As with most things in exporting, there is no 'one size fits all'. If you decide to set up your own company in a particular export market, the available channels to market will be similar to those available in your own country. If you decide to use distribution, the available channels to market will usually be as shown in Figures 6.3 for indirect selling or 6.4 for direct selling.

FIGURE 6.3 Marketing channels – indirect selling

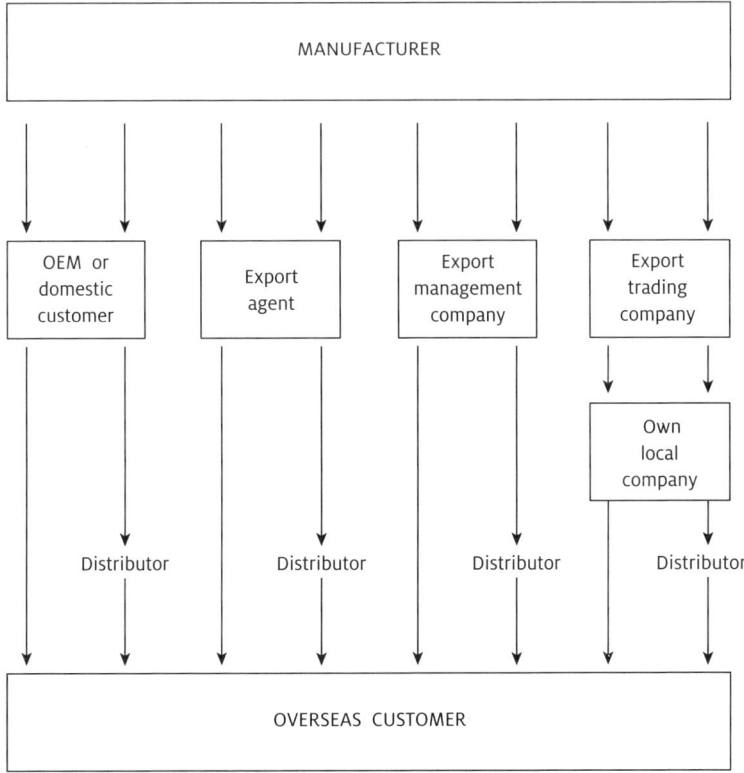

Exporting services is different from selling manufactured goods overseas, because normally there is no actual product on the shelf. There may be a standard product as in the case of items such as media products, software, etc, but hard copies of these products are likely to be produced locally in the overseas market by a local company, a franchise holder or a local distributor. Marketing channels for selling services overseas are shown in Figure 6.5.

FIGURE 6.4 Marketing channels – direct selling

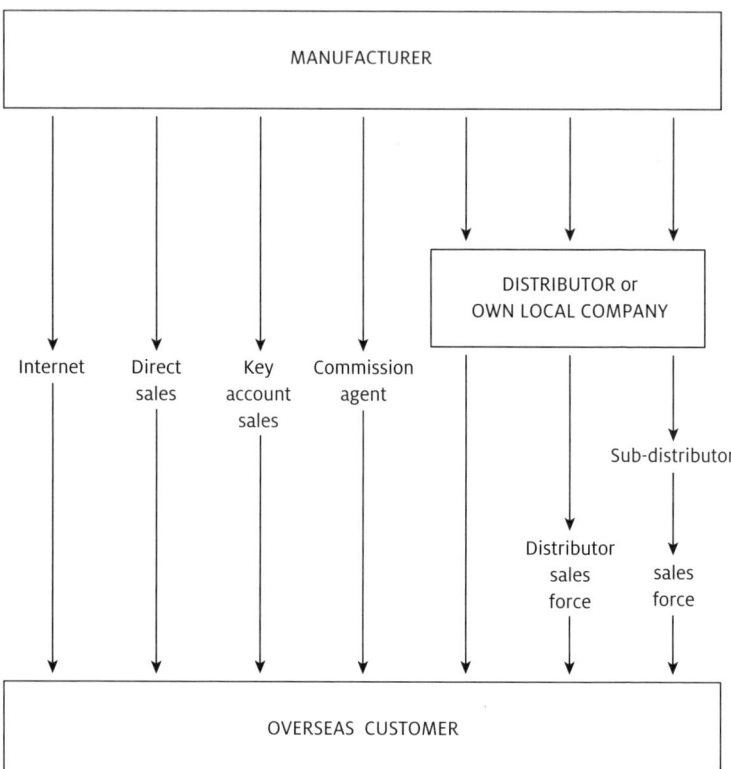

Summary

The most suitable market entry strategy for you will depend on your product and will be influenced by a number of factors, including the size of your business and your willingness to accept risk. The strategy that you adopt may be different for different markets, and depending on your product and the target market, you may need to adopt a combination of entry strategies.

The main forms of indirect exporting are through export agents, export management companies or export trading companies. It is quite common for a company to adopt a strategy by which they develop direct export business with markets that are easier to manage and use indirect methods for selling to other, more difficult markets.

FIGURE 6.5 Exporting services

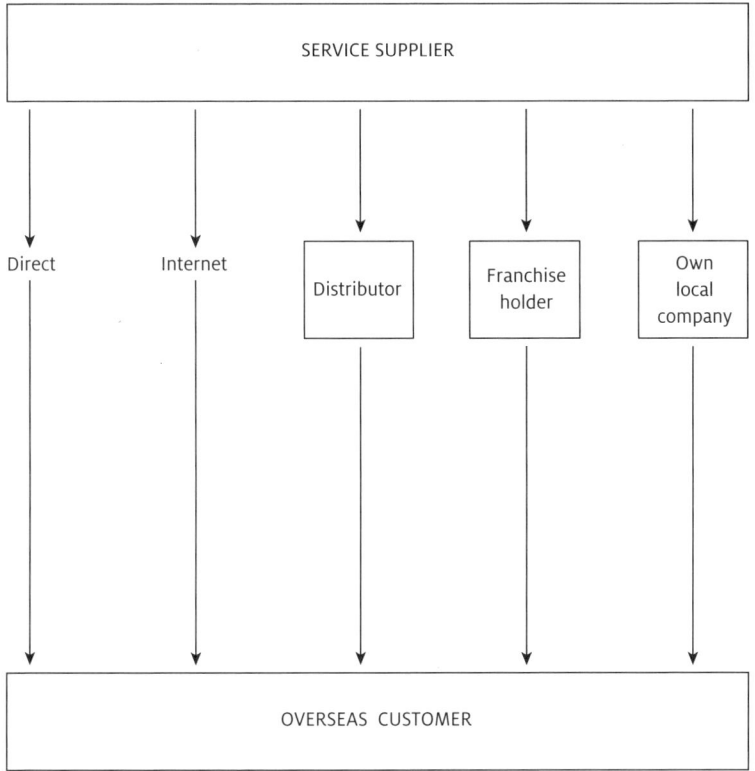

Direct exporting can involve selling direct from your home base, setting up an overseas operation or using a sales agent or distributor in your target market. Selling direct from your home base is an easy way to start. Setting up your own operation in an overseas market is expensive and time consuming and an alternative is to use the services of sales agents and distributors. The things that you require from distribution in an export market are the same as those that you would require from distribution in your domestic market. The main difference is that in export markets you expect your local presence to have the local channels to market and you also expect them to handle the physical distribution of your goods to the customer and the customer service function.

CHAPTER SEVEN

SETTING UP AND MANAGING OVERSEAS DISTRIBUTION

Because it is not easy to manage overseas business at a distance, most exporters decide to set up a local presence in some or all of their target markets. The most common approach is to use a local distributor or agent. Before we look at how you find and select agents and distributors we need to look at the differences between the two types of operation and how they compare. The most important thing to understand is that the main difference between a sales agent and a distributor is that a sales agent finds you customers, whereas a distributor is your customer.

The type of product that you are selling and the nature of your business will determine whether you should be looking for an agent or a distributor. A company bidding for infrequent, high-value contracts would probably use an agent. A company selling a product that needed a local supply of spare parts would probably decide to use a distributor.

TABLE 7.1 Agent and distributor compared

Agent	Distributor
An agent does not buy the goods from the supplier (principal) and never owns the goods.	A distributor purchases products from the supplier (principal) and owns the goods.
An agent finds customers for the principal and is paid a commission. The supplier invoices the end customer.	A distributor adds his profit and resells the goods.
The supplier determines the selling prices and the terms of sale.	A distributor determines the selling prices and the terms of sale.
The supplier knows the identity of the end customer.	The supplier does not usually know the identity of the end customer.

TABLE 7.2 Typical characteristics of business through agent and distributor

	Agent	Distributor
Order value	high	low
Order frequency	low	high
Local margin	low	high
Local stocking	no	yes
Control of pricing by principal	yes	no

Finding and selecting overseas agents and distributors

The key to success in selling through distributors or sales agents is to do your research properly. You need to make sure that you select a distributor or agent with a good market knowledge who is fully qualified to sell your type of product, who has a good existing customer base and who can show a strong track record of selling similar types of products. As a rule of thumb, where possible you need to find and research enough companies to be able to make a final shortlist of at least three. It is also very important to select a distributor or agent that you feel comfortable with and feel you can work closely with on a personal basis.

How to set about finding an agent or distributor

There are many organizations that can help you to find representation in your target market. In most major exporting countries, these include government organizations as well as commercial companies. You should consider any or all of the following:

- Your local contact at the government organization that provides support to exporters in your country.
- Word of mouth. Your existing business contacts can also help. If you already do business with one or two customers in your target market, ask them who they like to deal with locally. If you have contacts in other companies with similar or complementary (but not competing) products, who have been successful in your target market, ask them for recommendations. If you have a successful distributor in a neighbouring market, ask them what they think; eg if you have a successful distributor in Australia, they may be able to recommend some companies in New Zealand.
- Trade associations. You can find contact details of trade associations for your industry from the Trade Association Forum, **www.taforum.org**.
- The internet. Search for 'Export agents' and 'Export consultants'.
- Yellow Pages, **www.yell.com**, or the business-to-business search engine Kompass, **www.kompass.co.uk** (covering 60 countries worldwide).
- Your local Chamber of Commerce.
- An organization set up to encourage trade between your country and your target market. For Indian companies wanting to trade with

the UK or UK companies wanting to trade with India, this would be the UK India Business Council (UKIBC), **www.ukibc.com**.

● UK Exporters Ltd. This independent company that runs the British Exporter's website, **www.exportuk.co.uk**, offers a range of subscription services including an 'Agents wanted' service.

● A commercial organization that specializes in helping companies to find suitable representation in specific markets. eg Foreign Market Consulting, **www.fmcon.com**, for Turkey, and One Agenda, **www.one-agenda.com.uk**, for countries in central and eastern Europe.

● Major banks.

● By taking part in an exhibition in your target market.

● By taking part in a trade mission to your target market.

Overseas Market Introduction Service (OMIS)

Of particular interest to UK exporters is the Overseas Market Introduction Service (OMIS) offered by UKTI. For a competitive fee, you can commission research through UKTI into a particular market. This can include preparation of a list of potential distributors in the country and even help in setting up meetings with these potential distributors. OMIS uses the services of the UKTI trade teams located in the British embassies, high commissions and consulates across the world. Using their local staff means that you have access to their local language skills, market knowledge and commercial and political contacts.

Example

I used this service to find distribution in Austria. Providing the local trade adviser with a brief that included details of our company and our products, together with product literature and some material in the local language, I received a list of about 20 potential distributors. I narrowed this down to about six companies and the local trade adviser contacted them on my behalf. Four were interested and I set up a visit to the market to meet with them. The local trade adviser offered to set up the meetings, provide translation services and even allow use of the embassy facilities for meetings and presentations. The whole exercise took only about six months.

The key factors to consider when choosing an agent or distributor

The key factors to consider when selecting a distributor or agent to represent you in a particular overseas market are:

- Are they well established in your target market?
- Do they have a good reputation with key customers/potential customers?
- How to they compare with their main competitors?
- Are they located in the market's major business centre?
- Do they have good coverage of the rest of the market?
- What product lines do they have?
- Will your product fit in well with their existing product portfolio?
- Do they sell any competing lines?
- Do they have a good and experienced sales team?
- Do their salespeople have experience of selling your type of product?
- Do they have experience of selling to your target industries?
- Is their sales team well managed, with incentive schemes based on achievement?
- Are you confident that they can provide you with realistic sales forecasts to feed into your budgeting process?
- Do they employ people who can deal with you in your own language? (It is important that they have people who can manage your day-to-day business in your own language and not just the owner or managing director who speaks it.)
- Do they have the warehousing, servicing and other facilities that you require for your products?
- Do they have a good credit rating? You should use a company such as Dun & Bradstreet to carry out credit checks on the companies that you shortlist. The report you get will also tell you what sort of credit limit other suppliers give them and what their payment record is.

Agent/distributor questionnaire

A good way to make sure that you ask all the right questions and get them answered is to prepare an agent/distributor questionnaire and to get the prospective agents/distributors that you are evaluating to complete it for you. An example of such a questionnaire is shown below.

Agent/distributor questionnaire

Please answer all questions as fully as possible. Attach your company brochure, sample sales literature, financial statements and any other material that you think would be helpful to us in evaluating your company.

Full company name:

Address:

Tel no:

Contact e-mail address:

Date your company was established:

Name of chief executive:

Name and position of the person completing this form:

Number of employees:

Annual company turnover:

Please give a brief description of your company business:

Please list the main product lines that you sell:

Please indicate the main industries that you sell to:

Please detail the geographical area that you cover:

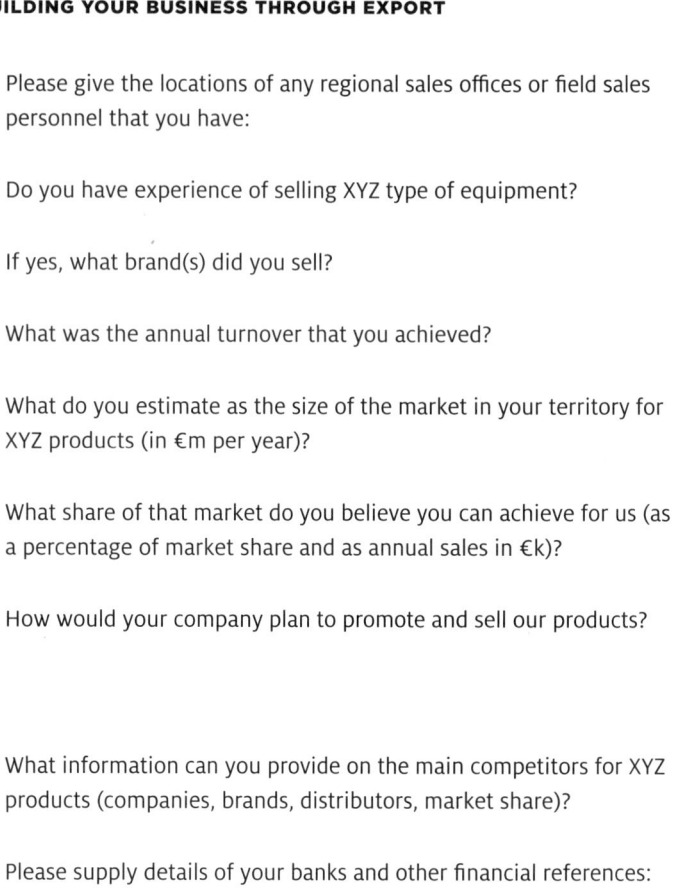

Please give the locations of any regional sales offices or field sales personnel that you have:

Do you have experience of selling XYZ type of equipment?

If yes, what brand(s) did you sell?

What was the annual turnover that you achieved?

What do you estimate as the size of the market in your territory for XYZ products (in €m per year)?

What share of that market do you believe you can achieve for us (as a percentage of market share and as annual sales in €k)?

How would your company plan to promote and sell our products?

What information can you provide on the main competitors for XYZ products (companies, brands, distributors, market share)?

Please supply details of your banks and other financial references:

Date:

Authorized signature:

Legal aspects of dealing with agents and distributors

The laws relating to setting up and dealing with agents and distributors are complex and difficult for a layman to understand. For that reason,

I would strongly recommend that before you start to work with overseas agents and/or distributors you consult a specialist lawyer to get some broad guidelines and then use the same company to help you to draft out standard agency and distribution agreements.

The key to dealing with any agent or distributor is to do your homework and make sure that you feel comfortable working with them. Working with an agent or distributor is like a marriage. It requires give and take on both sides and divorce can become both vitriolic and expensive. Some companies only start to look at the small print of their agreements when things go wrong, but by then it is too late.

In general terms agency law is more onerous than distribution law with regard to termination and compensation, but distribution is covered by detailed competition laws, whereas genuine agents are not. Add to this the fact that some countries, including many in the Middle East, do not differentiate between an agent and a distributor and you can see that these laws hold many pitfalls for the unwary.

Within the UK the key EU directives and applicable laws are:

- Agents: EU Directive 86/653 (18 December 1986);
- The Commercial Agents (Council Directive) Regulations 1993;
- Distributors: Articles 81–82 EC;
- The Competition Act (1998).

Although the EU directive on agency agreements covers all EU countries, the local legislation, often with local interpretations, varies from country to country. Although these laws only apply to EU countries many other countries around the world have similar legislation.

Some key factors relating to agency law are:

- The objective of agency law is to protect agents (not suppliers!).
- The law of the country in which the agent operates will apply.
- Verbal contracts are as binding as formal written contracts.
- Operating as an agent is sufficient in law to assume that a contract exists.
- Your failure to put limits on the territory and products covered will result in unlimited territory for all products.
- In some countries, once you have appointed an exclusive agent, they can block the import of your products to any other party, whether they perform or not.
- Agency termination usually requires a notice period and a termination payment.

- The requirements are different in different countries. In most European countries the compensation payment will be up to 12 months' commission, but in some countries it can be as high as 24 months'.

So if you decide to sell through agents you need to use a clear legal agreement to control territory, product range, pricing, targets, reporting requirements, negotiating limits and commission rates.

In many ways distribution law is less onerous than agency law, but it is just as important to have a clear written agreement. Many of the areas to be covered in a distributor agreement are similar to those in an agency agreement, but many are different, too.

Some key factors relating to distribution law are:

- In most countries distribution law tries to be reasonably fair to both parties. (There are some countries where the local law favours the distributor.)
- You can specify in the agreement which country's law applies to the application of the agreement.
- You can specify the place and method of arbitration of any disputes relating to the agreement.
- Exclusivity and pricing arrangements need to take into account EU and US competition and anti-price-fixing legislation. Distribution contracts should not include any attempt to set customer prices, anything designed to place restrictions on the market or anything that could distort the operation of a free market.
- Distribution agreements are not bound by agency legislation.
- Notice periods must be reasonable, but payment on termination is not legislated (except in a very few countries, including Belgium).

In most countries distribution law is more evenly balanced than agency law (which tends to favour the agent). If you decide to sell through distributors you should use your agreement to specify your prices and discounts to them, the products included, the area of exclusivity, the period of the appointment, termination arrangements, the obligations and reporting requirements of the distributor, the obligations of the principal (including details of any promotion contributions that you will make) and the situation with regard to sales by the principal. (You may want to specify that you will continue to supply the local unit of a multinational company directly and not through the distributor.)

As indicated above, the one area where distribution law is more complicated than agency law is in the area of complying with unfair competition legislation. Article 81(1) EC and member states national law equivalents prohibit agreements which affect trade between EU member states and that have an anti-competitive object or effect. In particular they prohibit agreements that fix prices or other trading conditions, limit production, or share markets. The distinction between agency and distribution is key in the application of EU competition laws. The rules don't apply where a principal uses a 'genuine agent'. Under EU law rules, to be considered a 'genuine agent' they must bear little or no financial or commercial risk in relation to the activities for which they have been appointed. This means that they must just be acting on the principal's behalf and must not be exposed to contractual risks with the customers or be required to purchase and hold stock from the principal for resale to the customers.

Competition law affects all trade within the EU and EEA and similar legislation affects the USA. If you are a supplier with less than 15 per cent market share you are unlikely to breach the act. If you have a significant market share you should take professional advice and use block exemptions in exclusive agreements.

If you are a supplier, you must not:

- dictate the prices charged by your distributors;
- impose unfair purchase conditions;
- apply different conditions or prices to similar transactions (with the same or with different distributors);
- restrict who your distributors can buy from;
- restrict who your distributors can supply to;
- act to limit competition in the market;
- limit production or markets to the consumer's detriment.

Distributors should not:

- collaborate with others to fix prices or limit competition;
- promote products outside the area covered by their agreement with the supplier.

On their website, the law firm Kemp Little, **www.kemplittle.com**, have a 'Distribution checklist' to determine the probable impact of EU competition laws on distribution arrangements.

Distribution checklist

Source: Kemp Little, 'European Distribution – a checklist for competition law compliance' (2005)

1 Is the 'distributor' actually an agent (ie do they take no commercial risk and not hold stock)?
2 If no, are the parties' market shares both less than 15 per cent? (Article 81 does not apply to parties who can prove that they do not hold more than a 15 per cent share of the relevant market.)
3 Does the distribution agreement contain any 'blacklisted' provisions (eg terms that fix resale prices or share markets or customers)?
4 If no, is the supplier's market share less than 30 per cent? (If market share is less than 30 per cent the agreement will be exempted under the Vertical Agreements Block Exemption Regulation if it contains no 'blacklisted' terms.)
5 Finally, are there any prohibited conditions (such as lengthy non-compete clauses)?

Agency and distributor contracts

Once you have decided on the agent or distributor that you want to work with in your target market, it is important to prepare and conclude an agreement with them. The agreement should be a clear and detailed written contract covering all of the key points that will be important to your working relationship.

I would strongly recommend that you get proper legal advice with regard to the preparation of both agency and distributorship agreements. This means not just using your existing company lawyer, but using a law company that specializes in international contract law. They may be expensive, but you will only need to use them to work with you to prepare a standardized contract. Once you have this you can use it for all of your future agency and distributorship agreements. The alternative can be very costly. You could find yourself in a relationship that is not working, but which you cannot get out of for a number of years. You could find that your contract is not legally binding in your target country. In some countries you could even find that you are legally obliged to pay a huge settlement to the agent or distributor for their loss of profits if you terminate your agreement in the wrong way.

You should have a standard distributorship and agency contract produced at the same time by the same lawyer. This will ensure that you have similar wording for similar sections of both agreements. The individual sections of the contract are usually called 'clauses', although some European lawyers call them 'articles'. If a clause is divided into sections, then each section should be individually numbered for clarity. So clause 8 could be divided into sections 8.1, 8.2 and 8.3 or into sections 8 (a), 8 (b) and 8 (c).

Requirements for a typical distributorship contract

A typical distribution contract would include a clause on at least each of the following:

- Type of agreement. It should state that it is a 'Distributorship contract'.
- The parties. The names and registered addresses of the principal and the distributor and confirmation of the appointment.
- Definitions. There should be a list of definitions that will be used throughout the agreement. This would define who 'the principal' is and who 'the distributor' is. It would also include such things as 'products' (a clear description of the goods) and 'territory' (the geographic sales area covered by the agreement), and depending on your type of product and how it is sold, it could also include 'industries' or 'applications' (if you are setting up separate distribution for separate major industries) and 'customers' (the type of customer covered by the agreement). This is particularly important if you want to exclude a key major customer or OEM (original equipment manufacturer).
- Products. This would either list the products included in the contract or refer to a separate enclosure at the end of the contract, if the list is too long or complicated to be included in the main text.
- Industries (or applications). This would list the industries covered by the contract.

- Territory. The geographical sales area covered by the agreement.
- Exclusivity. An agreement may be exclusive, open or selective. An exclusive agreement means that the distributor will handle all of the principal's business in the territory for all of the principal's products. An open or non-exclusive agreement means that the principal is able to sell directly into the territory and may also appoint other distributors. A selective agreement could mean that the principal only grants exclusivity to the distributor for the sale of certain products or for the sale of products into certain industries. This type of agreement is common in large markets like the USA where separate distributors may be appointed for sales into unrelated industries such as pulp and paper, waste water and the chemical industry. A selective distribution agreement can also be used where the principal wants to reserve the right to continue to sell directly to customers specifically listed in the contract.
- Period of appointment (and termination). The period of appointment that you initially offer would depend on the type of company and market. In developing markets it is quite normal to include a term of only one year. In established markets with established distribution companies, it is more likely that the term would be two years. The longer the period of initial appointment, the greater problem you have in extricating yourself from the agreement if it does not work out. Rather than having to renegotiate a new agreement every few years, you can use a rolling agreement where the agreement continues for the specified period, but then 'continues thereafter unless and until determined (terminated) by either party giving to the other notice in writing' (notice is normally six months). This is in effect the termination clause and the exact wording of this is important and should be drafted out by your lawyer.
- Obligations of the distributor. This states what we expect from the distributor in terms of promoting the products in the territory, quoting and following up enquiries and acting loyally to the principal.
- Sub-distributors or agents. Agreement for the distributor to appoint sub-distributors or agents if needed for specific purposes.
- Undertaking not to compete. This confirms that during the term of the contract the distributor will not represent or manufacture any products that directly compete with those included in the contract.

- Sales organization. This includes details of what is expected of the distributor in terms of a sales and after-sales organization.
- Advertising and exhibitions. This details what is expected in terms of sales promotion and who will pay for what. It can also include a requirement to discuss and agree annually on the advertising and sales promotion for the following year.
- Sales targets. This includes a provision for agreeing and setting annual sales targets. It would usually include details of minimum annual sales turnover that needs to be achieved with the option to the principal to cancel the contract if it is not.
- Principal to be kept informed. This lists what the distributor agrees to provide the principal in the way of information and regular reports on their activities, market conditions and competitor activity in the territory.
- Obligations of the principal. This usually covers what the principal is expected to supply in terms of products, training, samples, catalogues and support materials as well as advance notice of new products or the superseding of products.
- Supply of products. This covers such things as how individual orders will be handled, how prices will be calculated (based on price lists and discounts), the definition of delivery terms (Incoterms) and delivery times and the warranty offered. It could also include details of the standard payment terms offered by the principal, although this is often the subject of a separate clause.
- Stock of products. The distributor's obligations with regard to stocking the product and its spare parts. It usually also includes details of the principal's stock return or exchange policy.
- After-sales care. Details of the after-sales and service arrangements that the distributor is expected to provide.
- Trademarks. Describes how the distributor may and may not use the principal's trademarks, trade names and any other symbols.
- Confidentiality. Summary of what is considered confidential and should be treated as such. Usually includes the contract itself and can include such things as information, drawings, technical data, designs, etc.
- Limitation of liability. Establishes the extent of liability for both parties.
- Extraordinary termination. Reasons that the contract may be terminated immediately. This can include reasons such as fraud or

dishonesty, but usually also includes situations where the distributor becomes insolvent or bankrupt or where the ownership or management of the distributorship changes.

- Consequences of termination. Who gets what and how in the case of termination. What has to be returned to the principal such as documents, samples, confidential material; what happens to stock that the distributor has, etc.
- Sales by principal. What the principal is allowed to do in terms of selling product directly into the territory and whether, in such cases, any commission would be paid to the distributor.
- Rights of assignment. Whether either party can assign rights or duties arising out of the contract to any other party.
- Previous agreements. There is usually a clause stating that this contract supersedes any previous agreements between the two parties.
- Applicable law. States which country's laws govern the contract and the individual sales resulting from it.
- Arbitration. Details where and how arbitration will take place on any dispute arising from the contract. (Usually this would be under the Rules of Conciliation and Arbitration of the International Chamber of Commerce.)

In addition there could be a number of enclosures at the end forming part of the agreement. These could include such things as:

- a list of products covered;
- a list of end customers excluded from the agreement;
- a list of other products represented by the distributor;
- a list of discounts applying to individual products or product ranges;
- the principal's general conditions of sale;
- details of minimum stock requirements for the distributor by product.

Requirements for a typical agency contract

Many of the requirements for an agency contract are the same as or similar to those for a distributorship contract, but there are some important differences.

In an agency contract the clauses on the supply of products, stock of products and after-sales care would be removed and a number of new clauses would be added that are specific to agency contracts:

- Acceptance of orders by the principal. This would detail the limits of negotiation that the agent is allowed to use in negotiating orders with the customers, the conditions under which the principal would accept orders and the conditions under which they would be entitled to reject orders transmitted to them by the agent.
- Financial responsibility. The agent's responsibility to make sure that they only transmit orders to the principal from companies that they have checked to make sure that the companies are financially sound and solvent.
- Complaints by customers. The agent's responsibility to immediately inform the principal of any complaints received from customers.
- Agent's commission. Details of when and under what conditions the agent is entitled to a full rate of commission or a reduced rate and how these rates should be agreed. Actual commission rates are usually included in a separate enclosure at the end of the contract.
- Method of calculating commission and payment. Details of how commission would be calculated and paid. Normally based on the net value of invoices, payable in the currency of the sales contract and only after full payment has been received by the principal from the customer.

When you conclude an agreement with an agent or distributor, the most important thing is to make sure that both you and the agent/distributor end up with a signed copy of the contract. This might sound silly but I can assure you that it is amazing how many people finalize an agreement, sign two copies of the contract and send them to the agent or distributor to sign and return. In some cases busy people may get distracted by other things and forget that they haven't received a signed copy back – until some problem arises! Although it may seem over the top, I would strongly recommend that you send off two *unsigned* copies of the contract and ask the agent/distributor to sign and return both copies. You then also sign both copies and return one copy to the agent/ distributor. In this way you are sure that both copies of the contract have been signed by both parties and that you are both in possession of one copy. (Obviously you can avoid this problem if both parties are present together to sign the contract.) In addition to signing the contract on the last page, both parties should initial each individual page. (This avoids the possibility, however unlikely, that a devious agent/distributor could modify and insert a substitute page in their version of the contract.)

Managing distributors

Day-to-day management

A good distributor will have a number of key product ranges – often as many as six. Ideally, you want to be sure that your product range is one of their top product ranges, but you have to accept that the same sales people who sell your product range will be putting in time selling other companies' products. If you try to support the business from your office with just phone calls and e-mails, you should not be surprised to find that another company's products are getting more sales time. To manage a distributor properly you need to visit them regularly, both to review progress and to give support where needed. Ideally you should visit distributors in your own region three or four times a year. The length of visit may range from one day to several days depending on the requirement for you to give training to their personnel or make customer visits. If your product is technical in nature you may need to make joint visits to key potential customers.

Promotional and presentation material

If the language in your target market is not your own, there is little point in providing end customers with sales material and presentations in your own language. They will need to have these materials in their own language. If you are going to carry out training of your distributor's sales team, the material you will be using needs to be sent out to the distributor prior to the training so that it can be translated into the local language. It is also useful if you or your distributor can do some work ahead of the training to establish the size of the market in their area/ country and the key potential customers.

Overseas distributor meetings or conferences

An overseas distributor conference is similar to a sales conference, but involves a company's overseas distribution. It has much the same aims as a management conference, but with the emphasis on sales and growing them. The delegates would normally be the key sales and management personnel from a company's major overseas distributors.

The number of delegates would probably be between 20 and 50, depending on the number of distributors that you have.

Distributor conferences are often organized to take place in the spring or early summer – before the holiday season starts. The results and agreed targets resulting from the conference can then be fed into your company budgeting process in the autumn. Typically a distributor conference would last two to three days.

Summary

Because it is not easy to manage overseas business at a distance, most exporters decide to set up a local presence in some or all of their target markets. The most common approach is to use a local distributor or agent. The main difference between a sales agent and a distributor is that a sales agent finds you customers, whereas a distributor is your customer. You need to make sure that you select a distributor or agent with a good market knowledge who is fully qualified to sell your type of product, who has a good existing customer base and who can show a good track record of selling similar types of products.

There are many organizations that can help you to find representation in your target market. In most major exporting countries, these include government organizations as well as commercial companies. Taking part in an exhibition or trade mission to your target market is also a good way of finding representation.

The laws relating to setting up and dealing with agents and distributors are complex and you should consult a specialist lawyer for advice. In general terms agency law is more onerous than distribution law with regard to termination and compensation, but distribution is covered by detailed competition laws, whereas 'genuine agents' are not. With regard to the preparation of both agency and distributorship agreements you should get proper legal advice. To manage a distributor properly you need to visit them regularly, both to review progress and to give support where needed.

CHAPTER EIGHT

SALES PROMOTION

Sales promotion includes such things as websites, sales literature, presentations, advertising, exhibitions and trade visits. Sales promotion is an essential sales tool in any market and this is just as important for export markets as for your domestic market. When planning your sales promotional activities for overseas markets, it is important to bear in mind that each market is different. This means that some sales promotional activities are more suited to some markets than others and even the same activity may need to be modified or varied to suit the requirements of different markets or to take into account different languages and different cultures.

Understanding your target market

For each of your target markets you need to understand who your potential customers are, the factors that motivate them to buy and how you can get your products in front of them. You need to understand the methods of sales promotion that are used locally, since these may be different from those used in your domestic market or they may be used in a different way that reflects local cultural differences. You also need to find out how established competitors operate in the market and the methods of sales promotion that they use. To get information on all of these things, you need to carefully research the market and use the results from this research to help plan your approach to sales promotion.

As a minimum you need to find out the following for each of your target markets:

● What are the main methods of communication used? Press, TV, internet, e-mail, direct mail?

- What methods of sales promotion are used?
- What marketing tools are currently used?
- What cultural issues could affect marketing or sales promotion?
- Who are the potential customers?
- What motivates them to buy?
- What are the best ways to reach potential customers in this market?
- Who are the main competitors?
- How do these competitors operate?
- What media methods do they use?
- What is the level of their advertising and sales promotion?
- Do they have a local website in the local language?
- Can you obtain copies of the major competitors' brochures, data sheets, audiovisual material?

Refining your positioning, your product and image

Because every market is different you may need to modify your product, or modify the way that you position your product for a new target market. The way that you position your product will reflect the different requirements and preferences of your potential customers and the way that the market works. This will have a direct impact on the way that you promote your product in the marketplace.

You need to consider:

- the product price or pricing structure;
- how customers will buy it;
- why customers will buy it;
- how to handle sales;
- how to handle customer service.

In your domestic market you may use the image of your company as a reliable supplier with local support and service just round the corner to help you to sell your product. In an overseas market you would be reliant on your distributor to develop the same image. This may or may not be possible and you may decide to use a different image and promote your product in the target market as a robust and well-engineered product or a state-of-the-art ultramodern product.

Example

Quality, reliability and luxury are all ways that major products have been rebranded in overseas markets. An example is Stella Artois lager. The Belgian beer market is full of high-quality, specialist beers, many of which have a high alcohol content. In Belgium Stella Artois is sold as a run-of-the-mill medium-strength lager. It has a reasonable market share, but it is competing with the more expensive specialist beers. In the UK Stella Artois is marketed completely differently. It is advertised as a fantastic high-quality lager that people would die or cheat to get their hands on.

Your market positioning for your target market needs to take into account:

- Customer expectations. What do local customers expect from your type of product? You need to make sure that your product will appeal to local tastes and preferences.
- Market trends. Is your product in line with local market trends or may it even be ahead of them (or behind them)?
- Image. Should you rebrand your product or change the way that you portray your company for this market?
- Your product. Is it suitable for your target market as it is? Does it comply with local regulations and health and safety standards?
- Packaging. Do you need to modify your product's packaging? Do you need to include information in the local language on your packaging?
- Distribution. Is your type of product sold through different channels in your target market from those that you use in your domestic market?
- Competition. Are the main competitors the same as in your home market? Are there strong local competitors?

All of this is important in deciding how you will sell and promote your product in the target market and the level of pricing that you will adopt.

Reviewing your sales promotion for overseas markets

If you are already successful in your domestic market, you will already have a range of promotional materials at your disposal. Some of these may already be suitable for use in overseas markets, but most will need some modification or even a complete revamp. If you want to get the best out of your sales promotional materials for export markets I would recommend that you get them reviewed by an export communications consultant. Many overseas government organizations offer such support to their exporters. One of the best schemes available is the Export Communications Review (ECR) which is available to UK exporters.

The Export Communications Review (ECR)

The Export Communications Review (ECR) offers companies impartial and objective advice on language and cultural issues in order to help them develop an effective communications strategy for existing and future export markets. The scheme is offered by UK Trade & Investment and managed by the British Chambers of Commerce. The reviews are carried out by accredited export communications consultants, who have been trained in the discipline of export communications by the British Chambers of Commerce. All of the ECR consultants are multi-skilled, have experience in exporting and international marketing, are linguists and have lived and worked abroad. They discuss how a company tackles (or plans to tackle) the language and cultural issues that arise when trading overseas. They can identify communication strengths and weaknesses and offer unbiased objective advice.

The consultant can review all written and spoken communications with a specific overseas market or they can focus on a company's specific export activity, such as:

● press releases and promotional materials, technical documentation and manuals, catalogues and packaging for international audiences;
● preparation for and representation at an overseas trade show or exhibition;

- preparation for a presentation to an international audience;
- improving relationships with overseas agents and distributors;
- international sales and invoicing processes;
- systems for handling foreign phone calls and e-mails;
- training of overseas staff;
- language training needs in the UK;
- recruitment of export staff;
- international website strategy.

The consultant will provide the company with a customized written report including:

- a table of strengths and weaknesses of the company's current communications against international best practice, addressing written, telephone, face-to-face and electronic communications;
- practical recommendations, tailored to the company and summarized in an action plan;
- information about possible suppliers and costs to implement the recommendations;
- how-to guides, with more general advice on how to implement the recommendations.

UK exporting companies that have been trading for at least two years, employing less than 250 staff, can benefit from three UKTI-subsidized reviews. Each review costs only £500 and more than half of this cost can be recovered in government subsidies, so the actual cost is minimal. Companies can apply for the scheme online at **www.britishchambers. org.uk/ecr**. Robin Godfrey, who manages the scheme, says: 'This scheme helps hundreds of companies every year and has been so successful that other countries across the world, such as Hungary, Poland, Iceland and Ireland, have shown an interest in adopting the Review as a model for their own export companies.'

Websites

As well as providing companies with a major sales channel for all types of products, the internet has become the main channel for customers and potential customers to find out about companies and their products. This makes your company's website a key support tool for your export drive. Having said that, you should be aware that the development and use of the internet and access to high-speed broadband networks are still not uniform around the globe.

Language is also a great divider. If you work for a US company and you are looking for a particular product on the internet, your web search will bring up suppliers not only in the USA, but also in Canada, the UK, India, Australia, South Africa and many other countries. The same web search carried out in Russian by a non-English-speaking employee of a Russian company would be very much more restricted.

If you intend to expand your business into major countries where your own language is not commonly spoken, you need to consider developing your website so that it can be accessed and used in other languages. This is not easy and it is obviously also more expensive than developing and maintaining a website in just one language. In an interview with *Springboard* magazine in 2010, the internet guru Martha Lane Fox said: 'You can certainly build strong businesses through Europe, but it's not like in America where you're dealing with the same-sized market, but with everyone speaking the same language. Adapting your business, your website and your services to a multilingual market is tougher. Expanding in Europe, and elsewhere, is complicated by language and that raises costs as you have to adapt the front end of your website.'

The best way to decide what changes you need to make to your website is to have it reviewed by an export communications consultant. UK companies can arrange this as part of an Export Communication Review (ECR). A website review should involve a comprehensive analysis of your website covering:

- the technical aspects involved in setting up an international website;
- the optimum design, structure and navigation of the site for overseas visitors;
- inclusion of appropriate international content;
- translation and localization for target export markets;
- promotion of the site in overseas markets, including a 'localized' approach to search engine optimization;
- monitoring of the site's performance;
- managing the impact of a successful site.

Sales literature

For your domestic market you will have a range of sales literature available. Depending on your type of product, this will probably include a corporate brochure, sales brochures, leaflets and possibly also datasheets. These will all be available in your own language. So what should you do for overseas markets where the local language is different? What should you prepare and how should you go about it?

My suggestion is to look at the preparation of foreign-language material cautiously. If your target market is Brazil, but you haven't even made a first visit to the market, don't get all of your sales literature translated into Portuguese before you start. If you have already made several visits to the market and have just appointed a distributor there, then the situation is somewhat different.

For any target market where your own language is not spoken I would suggest that you adopt a two-stage approach to producing any of your literature in a foreign language.

Introductory leaflet

Stage one is material that you need in order to make your initial entry into your target market and to find effective distribution. It doesn't matter if you are a US company looking to start selling to Peru or a South African company wanting to sell in Angola – you cannot assume that the key decision makers at major customers or potential distributors will fully understand the information that you provide about your company and its products if it is not written in their own language.

I have found that for market entry what you really need is a high-quality two-sided single-page leaflet with one side printed in your own language and the other side giving exactly the same information in the language of your target market. The leaflet should include details of your company, your products and the applications that your products could be used for.

For all items of sales literature the foreign-language translation needs to be produced by a technically competent person who is translating into their mother tongue and it needs to be checked locally in the target market to make sure that it is technically accurate. Remember that it should also not just be a word-for-word translation and the text should be adapted stylistically and perhaps even tonally to make it appropriate for the individual market. If you contact your local trade adviser, you may be able to get the translation produced or at least checked by someone in the local embassy.

Another important point is that even with the same language there are differences in the words and grammar used in different countries. Not only is UK English different from US English, Australian English, Indian English and South African English, but there are significant differences between Spanish Spanish and Latin American Spanish and between French French and Canadian French. To be sure, you should get the translation done (or checked) by someone who is a native speaker to your target country. Also remember that European countries use literature in the A4 format, but the USA and a number of other countries use the quarto format. The wrong format will look strange in your target market and will also be difficult to photocopy or store.

Product and other literature

Once you have appointed a local distributor in your target market and their salespeople are starting to make customer visits, they need to have some support material printed in their own language. This does not need to be all of your sales leaflets and data sheets, but does need to cover key products that they want to discuss with end customers. You need to make the files containing these key sales leaflets and data sheets available to the distributor, so that they can use either their own qualified staff or a local agency to produce versions of these in their own language.

Presentations

Presentations make very effective sales tools. When selling overseas, your sales presentations can be easily modified by your local distributor for use by their own sales force. If the local language is different from yours they can translate the text of the presentations into their own language. Simplicity is important in presentations and you want to make sure that the main features and benefits of your products are clear to see.

Some tips when preparing and making a presentation:

- Use large font sizes for the text and an easy-to-read typeface such as Times New Roman or Arial.
- Don't try to get too many lines of text on a slide – about 10 is ideal.
- Use introductory slides with key headings and follow these up with separate slides expanding each of these headings.
- Bring bullet points in one by one to avoid the audience trying to read the whole slide rather than listening to your presentation.
- Consider using a background colour to enhance the impact of your presentation.
- Prepare a 'slide master' or 'background template' with your company name and logo on it.
- Include horizontal lines top and bottom to give your slides an 'active area'.
- Enhance your presentation by importing tables or graphs from Microsoft Excel (if applicable).
- Import suitable photos into your slides (if applicable).
- You can copy an open webpage onto a PowerPoint slide by pressing the 'Control' (Ctrl) and 'Print Screen' (PrtScr) buttons together and then using the paste function in PowerPoint.

Advertising

The level of advertising that you will use in your target market will depend on your type of product and the way that you are distributing it. If your product is a consumer product then levels of advertising would probably need to be similar to those in your domestic market. If you are selling industrial products, or capital goods, your advertising is likely to be more specific and targeted around things like product launches or major exhibitions.

When planning to advertise in overseas markets it is important to discuss your advertising campaign with your local agent or distributor. Local agents or distributors may be prepared to fund and manage advertising themselves, but more often than not they will expect you to fund part, if not all, of the cost. It is important to use their local knowledge to make sure that your advertising is tailored to the market, uses the appropriate messages and is in the local language. You may decide that it would be more effective to combine the advertising of your product with your distributor's own advertising programme.

Example

I recently worked for the European Division of a US company manufacturing industrial products. They brought out a new range of industrial vacuum pumps. They were very proud of the advert that they had prepared for the US market. It showed a boxer with cartoon strip-type bubbles for speech and the headline was something like 'Kerpow! Our XXX product gives you the old one-two.' They offered me the artwork to use the same advert in the technical press in Europe. I didn't use it. I could imagine the reaction of Dr Muller in Germany.

The advert had worked perfectly in the US market, but was just too brash to use for industrial advertising in Europe.

Exhibitions and trade shows

Exhibitions/trade shows are an important promotional tool and can be a good showcase for your products. With regard to overseas markets, taking part in an exhibition can be a good way of taking a first step into the market.

It gives you the opportunity:

- to meet customers face to face;
- to demonstrate your products;
- to find out what customers in your target market really want;
- to meet with potential distributors/agents;
- to see who the competition is and what products they are offering in this market.

One of the main advantages is that there will be a large number of potential customers all concentrated in one place. Also, if you exhibit as part of a country group you have the opportunity to network and to gain from the experience of other, more experienced exhibitors from your own country.

You need to select your exhibition carefully. Ideally you want to take part in an exhibition that is specific to your type of industry or product and not just a 'general' trade fair, where most of the visitors will be ordinary members of the public and not potential customers. As with any exhibition, you need to have a plan and decide what you want to achieve from it.

If it is your first time exhibiting in the country your goals may be:

- to meet with and evaluate the three distributors on our shortlist;
- to meet with potential customers and find out what they really want from our product;
- to assess the competition and their products;
- to see what new products or technologies are on offer;
- to network with other exhibitors from our country.

If you are already established in this market your goals could be:

- to get 30 new sales leads;
- to take orders on the stand to a value of at least £Xk;
- to discuss the ABC project with the customer;
- to meet with our top five local customers (listed) and develop our relationships;
- to assess the competition and their products.

Most major countries offer support to their exporters and this usually includes either financial or material support for taking part in overseas exhibitions and trade shows. Many international exhibitions have country 'pavilions', so at a trade fair such as the Hanover Fair in Germany, there would be a US Pavilion, an Indian Pavilion, a South African Pavilion and many more. At a major event such as the Shanghai International Trade Fair a country pavilion would probably be an individual structure, but at many events, it would be a grouping of stands in one section of an exhibition hall. The pavilion would include the stands of a large number of exhibitors from that country together with a support stand from the government support organization. US pavilions frequently host a US Commercial Service Business Information Office (BIO).

Tradeshow Access Programme

In the UK, UK Trade & Investment provides support for participants in overseas exhibitions and seminars through the Tradeshow Access

Programme. Participation is usually as part of a group, which is a big advantage for inexperienced businesses. The group is often on a UK stand, which is split into individual sub-stands for the participating companies. Grants are available to help SMEs with the cost of overseas exhibitions that are supported by the programme. Most events are sector specific, so the Association of British Mining Equipment is the Accredited Trade Organisation (ATO) for the International Mining and Machinery Exhibition in Kolkata, India, and the Engineering Industries Association is the ATO for METAL in Stuttgart, Germany, and METALEX in Bangkok, Thailand. Generally, the higher grant levels apply to selected shows outside Europe. Some major exhibitions such as the Hanover Fair or the IFAT exhibition (both in Germany) cover such a wide range of industries that they are not handled by one specific trade organization. Instead they are managed by the Birmingham Chamber of Commerce, which has a specific section that handles the support for a large number of exhibitions. These large exhibitions can have as many as 20 separate exhibition halls and often each hall is specific to a particular type of equipment. So although there is still a UK section/stand at these exhibitions, some companies decide that they need to be in a different sector-specific exhibition hall to attract visitors interested in their type of product. In such cases it is often possible for them to participate as solo companies and still qualify for grants.

Example

I have used the Tradeshow Access Programme on a number of occasions. When I participated in the Hanover Fair a few years ago everything was organized by the Birmingham Chamber of Commerce. Registering for the grant was easy, with the option of taking a part of the UK stand or booking our own stand. Because we needed to be in a different exhibition hall from the UK stand we booked and built our own. But we were still kept informed of all the joint publicity events organized for the UK contingent and were able to use their stand facilities such as phone lines and meeting rooms. Although the grant only covered a small part of the cost of participation, the fact that we were getting it made it much easier to get our budget for the exhibition approved by head office.

Sector-focused trade missions/visits

Trade missions are organized visits to target markets. They usually last between three and eight days and are often specific to a particular industry or event. They offer companies an excellent opportunity to research overseas markets. They can also be used to generate business opportunities, meet potential distributors or agents or to assess possible sales and promotion strategies. They are an ideal way to visit a market that you are unfamiliar with and you can gain from the experience of the mission leader and others on the mission as well as from the local contacts that you make.

To make the most of a trade visit you need to set clear objectives of what you want to achieve from it. The objectives could be:

● to help you to understand the market structure in the target market;
● to understand the level of acceptability of your product in the target market;
● to assess different market entry strategies;
● to visit an industry-specific exhibition and learn about local competitors and their products;
● to identify potential distributors or agents for your product;
● to meet with key potential customers;
● to generate specific business opportunities;
● to find partners for a joint venture.

If you take part in a trade mission, you should always take appropriate product literature with you, translated into the local language.

In the UK, small businesses taking part in these trade missions are eligible for travel grants to cover up to half the cost of the visit. The process works in a similar way to exhibition support and is often managed by a Chamber of Commerce on behalf of UKTI.

Example

In 2004 I was looking for distribution in Russia. At that time I had never visited Russia. There was an industry-specific exhibition taking place in October of that year in Moscow that looked to be an ideal place to meet possible distributors. When I contacted my International Trade Adviser she told me that there was a planned trade mission to Moscow that coincided with the exhibition. A colleague and I were able to book onto the mission and we had four months to plan our trip. As part of the trade mission there were several briefing meetings at the offices of the Chamber of Commerce that was managing the trade mission. This was in the East Midlands and the mission was led by Russian specialist Tim Jelley, a Senior International Trade Adviser who has been leading annual trade missions to Moscow for over a decade. At these briefings we were given a large amount of information about doing business in Russia and how to get the most out of our visit. We were also given a contact at the British Embassy in Moscow whom we could contact for information on anything relating to our visit. One thing that was made clear was that most people we would meet speak only Russian and that without some literature in Russian we would be wasting our time. At that time UK Trade & Investment had a service called the 'Subsidized promotional leaflet service'. For the amazing price of £320 I was able to get 1,000 copies of a high-quality two-sided leaflet with one side in English and the other side in Russian. The leaflet included details of our company, our products and the applications that our products could be used for. The Russian translation was produced by a contact at the British Embassy in Moscow who liaised with me to make sure that the translation was technically accurate. The embassy also provided us with a list of 30 potential distributors for the type of equipment that we wanted to sell in Russia. From this list we decided that there were eight companies who might be worth seeing. The embassy arranged meetings with these companies for when we would be in Moscow. Our hotel and flights had been booked through the mission organizers, but our contact at the embassy arranged everything else that we needed for our visit – safe transport from the airport, a car and driver to take us to our business meetings (and also to the exhibition) and an interpreter for the meetings. When we arrived in Moscow, the first day was spent at the embassy for detailed briefings on doing business in Russia and also on how to keep safe (important if it is your first visit). Subsequently all of those on the mission met up in the evenings, but during the day we all carried out our separate business meetings. The two-sided leaflet was of considerable help in giving our interpreter an understanding of our products so that she was able to make good accurate translations. Our visit was a success thanks to the huge amount of assistance that we received from UKTI in the East Midlands and the local embassy staff in Moscow.

Austrade organize a wide range of trade missions, many of which are related to the industry 'clusters' that Austrade support as part of their export strategy. Examples are the automotive industry, water industry (eg USA Water Industry Tour series) and the MedTech Australia Cluster. In June 2011 Austrade ran the MedTech Australia Global Opportunities Cluster US Mission. The main part of the mission was from 12 to 17 June to attend the conference of the Independent Medical Distributors Association (MDA) and the Military Healthcare Convention and Conference (MHCC) in San Antonio, Texas, with a side trip to Philadelphia to visit the DLA Troop Support (Medical) organization. The mission was designed to assist Australian companies to pursue opportunities in the US healthcare markets, both private and military, and to provide access to independent speciality distributors. Delegates were expected to pay their own travel and accommodation, but Austrade provided funding under their 'Global opportunities program' for exhibition and attendance costs at the conferences and arranged mission coordination, the production of mission marketing material and the setting up and running of networking meetings.

In the United States, the US Commercial Service organizes trade missions. Although many are industry related and often timed to coincide with industry-specific exhibitions, many cover a range of industries for one country. As an example, the 2011 Trade Mission to Italy, organized in conjunction with the Italian-American Chamber of Commerce, took place from 5 to 7 April 2011. The cost of the mission was $900 per delegate. The mission placed significant emphasis on private matchmaking meetings customized for individual companies and aimed to set up meetings with pre-screened potential business partners, distributors, agents and buyers as well as with US executives already successful in Italy, government officials and US embassy staff. Market intelligence and Commercial Service support were provided to participants both before and after the mission.

Summary

Websites, sales literature, presentations, advertising, exhibitions and trade visits are key sales promotional tools. For each of your target markets you will need to understand who your potential customers are, the factors that motivate them to buy and how you can get your products in front of them. You need to understand the methods of sales promotion that are used locally, since these may be different from those used in your domestic market or they may be used in a different way that reflects local cultural differences. The way that you position your product in your target market will also reflect the different requirements and preferences of your potential customers and the way that the local market works.

Most of your promotional materials will need some modification or even a complete revamp for use in overseas markets. If you want to get the best out of your sales promotional materials for export markets you should get them reviewed by an export communications consultant. Many overseas government organizations offer such support to their exporters.

Your website is a key support tool for your export drive, but it will be necessary to carry out a website review looking at optimizing the design, structure and navigation of the site for overseas visitors and to include appropriate international content. Adopt a cautious approach to the preparation of foreign-language sales materials. Your sales presentations can be easily modified by your local distributor for use by their own sales force and they can translate the text of the presentations into their own language. The level of advertising that you will use in your target market will depend on your type of product and the way that you are distributing it.

Exhibitions and trade shows can be a good showcase for your products. Taking part in an overseas exhibition gives you the opportunity to meet customers face to face, demonstrate your products and meet with potential distributors/agents. Trade missions are an ideal way to visit a market that you are unfamiliar with and they are a good way to make initial exploratory visits to countries that are particularly complex or difficult to deal with.

CHAPTER NINE

SELLING GOODS ONLINE

The internet offers significant advantages to all companies wanting to do business internationally. The scope and depth of a website are determined by the range and diversity of a company's products and not by the size of the company. Small companies can have a website that is as good and comprehensive as those of their larger competitors and can give the impression of being larger and more influential. Another advantage of using the internet to develop your international sales is that if a company is doing its selling, marketing and advertising online, it can avoid some of the costs that it would have to incur developing international sales by traditional methods.

Websites for international e-commerce

According to the International Telecommunications Union (ITU), about 10 per cent of the world's population used the internet in 2002 but this had grown to a quarter of the world's population by 2010. In the 2010 survey 'From surviving to thriving – doing business overseas', UKTI reported that 15 per cent of companies considered selling online to be an important sales method and 4 per cent of businesses said that they relied on the internet for most of their overseas sales.

Your company's website can be a key support tool for your export drive. But you need to understand that you cannot handle overseas business on your website in exactly the same way that you handle domestic sales. Even if the requirements for order handling and after-sales service for export business are similar whether you are dealing with them on- or offline, there are additional national and international regulations relating to e-commerce. You should also be aware that access to high-speed broadband networks is still not uniform around the globe. When you look at developing countries, even getting access to the internet is not as easy as in the USA, Europe and Australasia. Not every country currently has the broadband access and speeds that South Korea has, but clearly this will change in the coming years.

Types of site

Ordinary website or e-commerce site?

A website needs to be well constructed and easy to navigate so that customers will use it and will come back to it. Not all companies need to take orders on their website and not every company needs to have a true transactional e-commerce site. Many companies selling overseas just use their website to provide their potential customers with information about the company and their products and not to actually transact business on the site. Other companies need to be able to provide individual quotations for individual jobs or projects, so that although the details of the enquiry can be taken on the website through the 'Contact us' page, a separate quotation would then need to be prepared and e-mailed to the customer. But if your product is easy to store, pack and dispatch, it is likely to benefit if you have an e-commerce site.

Domain names

Your domain name is the title and address of your website. Most website owners try to buy a domain name that says something about their business or what their site does, or one that incorporates their main brand or company name.

A domain name is the first part of the web address after www. that is entered into a web browser to find a web page on the internet. (It is also the part after the @ sign in an e-mail address.) So in the web address **www.mycompany.com**, 'mycompany' is the domain name.

The second part of the address, '.com', is called the TLD (top-level domain). For international business it is best if you can get the TLD

'.com' or, failing that, '.co' or '.eu' (for European Union) for your main website. But it is also useful if you can purchase the local country codes '.co.uk', '.fr' or '.au' for individual local markets that you intend to trade in. A local country domain name can increase local brand awareness and brand loyalty. It can also help you to increase your search engine ranking on search engines that are popular in your target market. If you only intend to have one website, you can still own local domain names and arrange to redirect users to your main website.

In June 2010 the Internet Corporation for Assigned Names and Numbers (ICANN) met in Brussels to finalize the application process and timetable for the liberalization of domain names, with a whole raft of new TLDs being made available for use from 2012. With the liberalization of domain names, almost any TLD from '.airlines' to '.zulu' will be made available, but they will be sold to the highest bidder. Someone winning the bid for '.airlines' would be able to sell variants of the suffix, such as easyjet.airlines or japan.airlines, to the world's airlines.

In selecting a domain name exporters need to consider a number of things:

● The name needs to be short, simple and most importantly it needs to be memorable to potential customers in the target markets. But it needs to be memorable for the right reason. **www.mist.com** may sound good for a company selling humidifiers, but not if they plan to sell in Germany where the word 'mist' means 'muck'!

● Not all domain names will be available – you may have to compromise. So if **www.autos.de** is not available you may have to settle for **www.motors.de** and **www.motors.com**.

● Remember that there are no spaces in a domain name. A recent article in the *Sunday Times* mentioned that a company called Choose Spain which offers holiday villas on its website took the domain name **www.choosespain.com** and only realized their mistake when it was too late!

In the UK domain names are held with Nominet (**www.nominet.org.uk**), but registration is made via an agent, who would normally be your web hosting company. Your web hosting company may be able to register you for some overseas domain names, but you may need to do it yourself and registration requirements can vary from country to country. If you intend to do business in a country such as Russia or China, bear in mind that you can purchase domain names written in the Cyrillic rather than the roman alphabet or even using Chinese characters.

Make your website user friendly for foreign visitors

If you already have a website and want to use it for international trade, it makes sense to get an export communications consultant to carry out a review of your website. They can advise you of changes that you can make to your website to make it more user friendly to overseas customers. They can also help you to develop a website specifically for international trade. An international website needs to be designed and set up in such a way that the structure and navigation are simple for overseas visitors. You need to make sure that the language used in your website is clear and understandable to people whose mother tongue is not your own, and to avoid the use of unexplained jargon or unnecessarily complicated language. You must make sure that you include an appropriate amount of international content.

If you intend to expand your business into major countries where your own language is not commonly spoken, you need to consider developing a website in the local language. You need to use a specialist agency to do the website design and the translations. The design of the site needs to be in keeping with the local culture and the language used needs to be adapted stylistically. You don't just want a word-for-word translation. This type of work can only be done by a native speaker who is very familiar not only with the language but also with websites in the target market.

Web hosting

A web hosting service is a type of internet hosting service that allows individuals and companies to make their own website accessible via the World Wide Web. Web hosts are companies that provide space on a server they own or lease for use by their clients as well as providing internet connectivity, typically in a data centre. In recent years, companies large and small have turned to web hosting companies rather than using their own IT resources. The site hosting companies have large banks of computers which will store all of your information for a monthly fee. Also, they are able to handle large amounts of traffic, which significantly reduces the possibility of your website crashing (this is particularly important if you are using your website for international business, where different time zones mean that the pattern of people accessing your website will be different from that expected just from your domestic market). The companies offer better protection for your information as well as better protection from crashes and at the same time you can save money on equipment and staff. Most companies select a web host based in their own country, but in some circumstances there can be advantages in using a web host based in the target market itself.

E-commerce sites

Setting up a site

If you want to sell online rather than use your website just to provide information on your company and products to your international customers, you need to have an e-commerce site. As with an ordinary website, the options with an e-commerce site are to buy a package from a web hosting company or to have one built for you by a web design company. With the additional factors necessary to conduct overseas trade, most companies that want to use the site to export their product choose to have it built for them by experts.

Web analytics

Web analytics software allows companies to track which pages of their website are most popular, which promotions are clicked on most – basically which parts and which products seem to attract users and which parts don't. It allows you to monitor traffic to your website in real time. You can track where users enter and where they leave, where they come from (which search engines, etc) and where they go next, how long they stay on the site and how many pages they look at while they are there. You can log the number of daily visitors and where in the world they are all located. This allows you to make comparisons between domestic and overseas visitors to your site and to understand if your site is as easy to navigate and understand for an overseas visitor as for a domestic one.

Search engine rankings

The huge increase in the number of companies operating and selling on the internet has dramatically increased the competition between companies to get visitors to their websites rather than to those of their competitors. When carrying out a web search, most people will only look at the first page of search results and often only at the top two or three results. So making sure that your site gets high up in the results is important to the success of your website and search engine rankings are just as important for attracting overseas customers as for attracting domestic ones. Good rankings mean success and you can improve your search engine ranking by using search engine optimization (SEO). If you have decided to set up a website in your target market, or to use a local domain name, you may need to get specialist SEO advice from an export communications expert. This is because many local search engines filter the search results in such a way that they only display local country domains. You would also need to make sure that you are registered with search engines that are popular in your target market.

Getting paid

Fortunately most e-commerce website packages include facilities to make taking orders from overseas easier. As well as accepting credit card payment, most packages include the facility for you to take payment via PayPal or WorldPay or even by electronic funds transfer (EFT). With regard to postage and packing, most e-commerce packages allow you to set up special rates which users can select before they reach the checkout. These can include rates for shipment to Europe or the USA or a facility for the customer to receive a quotation for postage and packing by e-mail.

Online fraud

Online fraud is a potential risk with any online transaction, even when accepting established credit cards issued by major banks. Fraud rates on international online business can be as high as 2 or 3 per cent of business transactions and companies need to be vigilant and put systems in place to try to weed out transactions that are obviously fraudulent. You can reduce the risks by taking sensible precautions:

- Ask the customer to enter the card verification number (CVN). This is a three- or four-digit security code usually on the back of the card.
- Ask your credit card processing company to help you install an address verification system (AVS). This is a system used to verify the identity of the person claiming to own the credit card.
- Don't process orders without carrying out further checks if the billing address and delivery address are different or even in different countries.
- You can also set up your system so that it only accepts orders from certain countries. In this way you can exclude countries where the risk of credit card fraud is high. (But you need to list your exclusions on the website, so that potential customers from these countries are aware that they cannot purchase from you online.)

The effects of online fraud are not always immediate. According to Cybersource's 2010 annual online fraud report, 50 per cent of fraud claims were accounted for by 'chargebacks', where the card holder's issuing bank requests a reversal of charges on behalf of the cardholder, and 50 per cent were claims made by the card holder to the issuing bank, which then issued their own credit on the account. These charges can hit you weeks or even months after you have received payment and shipped the goods. So whatever you do, you have to accept that you will suffer from some level of fraud with your online business.

Shipping the goods

The process of shipping goods purchased online is the same as that for shipping goods purchased from you directly. This means that you will have the same types of costs and the same requirements with regard to export regulations, tariffs and taxes, and reporting requirements as with orders placed by other means.

Tax requirements

In addition to needing to understand and state in the terms and conditions on your website which taxes and tariffs are included in your price, you also need to make yourself aware of any international arrangements that would affect your online business with your target markets. For instance, European Union member states tax the sales of electronically supplied goods and services from non-EU companies to customers located in the EU. Non-EU online providers of goods and services are required to register with a tax authority in one of the EU member states and to collect and remit value added tax (VAT) at the VAT rate of the member state where the customer is located. It is likely that other countries will take a similar approach in the future.

E-commerce regulations

Companies that sell or market products or services online must comply with e-commerce regulations. E-commerce includes selling goods or services over the internet, by e-mail, on interactive digital television or by using mobile phone text messages. Many of the rules are similar to those that have been in existence for many years to regulate businesses that carry out 'distance selling' using methods such as mail order, catalogue selling and offering goods by phone or fax. All countries have rules and regulations that regulate e-commerce. But if you want to trade online internationally, you need to comply not only with your own national regulations, but also with international requirements.

The main international e-commerce regulations are aimed at protecting consumers and sensibly regulating commercial e-mails. The main e-commerce regulations derive from the European Commission (EC) Directive 2000/31/EC on Electronic Commerce, the EC Directive 2002/58/EC and the US CAN-SPAM Act of 2003 and their subsequent updates.

The EC Directive 2000/31/EC

As this is a European Directive, the regulations apply to all European Union member states and affect e-commerce taking place between and within member states. This means that companies in non-EU countries wanting to trade electronically with EU countries also need to take them into account. Information about the directive can be found on the Europa website, **www.europa.eu**, but it is easier to go to the website for the UK government's Department for Business Innovation & Skills, **www.bis.gov.uk**, click on 'Publications' and enter 'e-commerce regulations' in the search function. This brings up two publications, including the very useful 'Beginners guide to the e-commerce regulations 2002', which can be downloaded for free as a PDF file. This relates to the UK regulations brought in to comply with the EC directive, but the regulations relating to other EU states would be broadly similar.

The regulations relate to companies that:

- advertise goods or services online;
- sell goods or services to businesses or consumers online;
- transmit or store electronic content or provide access to a communication network.

They include provision for:

- the national law that will apply to online services;
- the information an online service provider must give a consumer, including discounts and offers in online advertising and how to conclude contracts online;
- limitations on service providers' liability for unlawful information they unwittingly carry or store.

The information requirements can be divided into three categories – information requirements, commercial requirements and electronic contracting.

Information requirements

These include companies providing their end users with:

- the full name of their business;
- the geographic location;
- contact details, including an e-mail address, to enable direct and rapid communication with their customers;
- details of any relevant trade organizations to which they belong;
- details of any authorization scheme relevant to their online business;

- their VAT number, if their online activities are subject to VAT;
- a clear indication of prices, if relevant, including any delivery or tax charges.

Commercial communications

Any form of electronic communication (such as e-mail advertising) that is designed to promote goods, services or image, must:

- be clearly identifiable as a commercial communication;
- clearly identify the person and/or organization on whose behalf it is sent;
- provide clear identification of any promotional offers being advertised, eg any discounts, gifts, competitions, games;
- provide a clear explanation of any qualifying conditions regarding such offers;
- provide a clear indication of any unsolicited communications being sent.

Electronic contracting

These requirements apply to anyone who enables end users to place orders online.

The company must provide end users with the following information in a 'clear, comprehensive and unambiguous manner' *prior* to an order being placed:

- the different technical steps to follow in order to conclude the contract so that end users are made aware of what the process will involve and the point at which they will commit themselves to the contract;
- whether the concluded contract will be filed or not and whether it will be accessible;
- the technical means of identifying and correcting input errors made by an end user prior to placing an order so that end users know how to correct any mistakes that they make;
- the languages offered for the conclusion of the contract;
- if the company subscribes to any codes of conduct they must supply the details and advise end users how they can access them;

- if you supply end users with terms and conditions applicable to their contract you must make these available in such a way that the end user can store and reproduce them, ie download them onto their computer and subsequently print them out;
- if an end user places an order online, the supplier must acknowledge receipt of the order without delay and by electronic means;
- the supplier must also make available appropriate, effective and accessible technical means which will allow the end user to identify and correct any input errors *prior* to the placing of the order.

Note: These requirements do not apply to transactions between two businesses (ie B2B transactions) if both parties agree to opt out of them.

A company is required to comply with these regulations not just for business within their own country, but even if they are providing their service in a different EU country. The EU also prohibits the transfer of personal data to non-EU countries that do not meet the EU requirement for privacy protection. This means that companies from countries outside the EU wishing to trade online with businesses or consumers within the EU need to be able to prove that they comply with the EU regulations. Some countries, such as the United States, have set up 'safe harbour' agreements with the EU under which their companies can self-certify the fact that they comply with the requirements.

Privacy and Electronic Communications (EC Directive) Regulations 2003

These regulations updated the Telecoms Data Protection Directive in the light of new technologies and in particular ensured that the privacy rules applicable to phone and fax services should also be applied to e-mail and to the use of the internet. There are four key provisions:

1 Anyone who uses cookies (whether they process personal data or not) and similar tracking devices must provide information and offer subscribers or users who are not content to accept them with the chance to refuse.

2 Allows for the provision of value-added services based on traffic or location data, either by network operators on their own or in conjunction with third parties. There is no restriction on the type

of services that may be provided as long as subscribers give their consent and are informed of the data processing implications.

3   Gives subscribers the right to decide whether or not they want to be listed in subscriber directories. Subscribers must be given clear information about the directories in question, including any reverse search-type functions, for which additional specific consent is required.

4   Requires that unsolicited commercial e-mail and SMS to individual subscribers is subject to a prior-consent requirement, so that it may only be sent if the recipient has agreed in advance. There is an exception to this rule in the context of an existing customer relationship, where companies may continue to market their own similar products or services on an 'opt-out' basis.

The US CAN-SPAM Act

Despite its name, the CAN-SPAM act doesn't just apply to bulk e-mail. It covers all commercial messages, including e-mail, that promote content on commercial websites. The original 2003 Act was amended in 2008 and the original four requirements were extended to seven. The main requirements are:

1   Don't use false or misleading header information.
2   Don't use deceptive subject lines.
3   Identify the message as an ad.
4   Tell recipients where you are located.
5   Tell recipients how to opt out of receiving future e-mail from you.
6   Honour opt-out requests promptly.
7   Monitor what others are doing on your behalf.

You can find out more information about the CAN-SPAM Act on the Federal Trade Commission website, **www.ftc.gov/spam**, including a useful explanatory document entitled 'The CAN-SPAM Act: A compliance guide for business', which can be downloaded as a PDF file.

The key difference between the CAN-SPAM Act and the EU directive is that the EU directive requires prior consent from the recipient before any direct-marketing e-mail messages can be sent ('opt-in'), whereas the CAN-SPAM Act allows direct marketing messages to be sent to anyone, without permission, until the recipient explicitly requests that they cease ('opt-out').

Summary

Most companies use their websites to provide information on their products and to publicize new products and sales successes. If you want to develop business internationally you need to make your website user friendly to overseas visitors and if you want to develop your business online you need a true e-commerce website.

When setting up an e-commerce site for international trade, you should include additional safeguards with regard to payment and additional options with regard to shipping methods and costs. Because the potential risk of online fraud is greater with international online business than with domestic online business you need to take sensible precautions and put additional security systems in place.

Companies that sell or market products online must comply with e-commerce regulations and all companies that wish to advertise or sell their products or services online internationally should acquaint themselves with e-commerce regulations applicable to their target countries. The European Union has e-commerce regulations that relate to companies that advertise goods and services online, sell goods or services to businesses or consumers online, or transmit or store electronic content. There are also EU and US regulations covering what can and cannot be included in commercial messages, including e-mails that promote content on commercial websites.

CHAPTER TEN

QUOTING FOR INTERNATIONAL BUSINESS

The general concept of quoting for overseas business is no different from quoting for business in your domestic market. The key difference is that in quoting in your domestic market you are familiar with everything from packaging requirements to your terms of payment for that particular customer. When quoting for overseas customers many things are different. The packaging requirements will depend on whether goods are being shipped by road, sea or air, documentation requirements will depend on the type of product and where you are shipping to, and there is a wide range of delivery terms (Incoterms) and payment methods available.

Pricing for export business

The most common methods that companies can use to determine their export pricing are cost-plus, top-down and marginal costing. But export pricing is not just determined by analysing your costs and it is important that you understand that cost is only a part of the equation. You also need to take into account the market demand and the competition in your target markets. GDP per head and the size of the middle-class population are also important factors in determining the demand for most consumer products. When selling these types of product local prices are likely to be lower in developing markets than in developed countries.

Special products and standard products

There are many different types of exporters with many different types of product, but from the point of view of export pricing I would suggest there are two main ways that a company can categorize its products. It can divide its products into 'special' products and 'standard' or semi-standard products (some companies will only have one of these two types):

- Special products. Special products may not be considered special by the company that makes them, but by their nature they need to be costed up individually or the price needs to be recalculated due to changes in costs of raw materials or components. So the price of this type of product needs to be calculated for each quotation.
- Standard or semi-standard products. This type of product covers everything from nuts and bolts to large machines and from jars of jam to laptop computers. Pricing for this type of product can be set on a regular basis (usually annually) and an export price list prepared.

In putting together a quotation for a 'special' product, you have to include the usual costs and margins that you would include for your domestic business. Typically, this would be the cost of raw materials, manufacturing and overheads with your profit margin added. For products that you are selling overseas there would be additional costs and it is quite normal to also add a margin to cover the additional risks and financial costs of international trade.

Companies that are already active in selling overseas have usually prepared their own standard charges that can be added to the quotation for such things as export packing and FOB (free on board) delivery. These sorts of additional charges are usually calculated as a rate per unit of weight or volume, with a minimum charge for items below a certain minimum size. The costs of more specialized types of packaging, additional documentation or certification and for different delivery terms would probably need to be calculated by an experienced person such as the shipping manager, who would need to get outside quotations for many of these.

Although all companies quoting for overseas business add their additional costs into their quotations, at the end of the day it is a competitive marketplace and on major projects you will find yourself competing with companies from around the world. This often means that you have to decide whether you can risk being uncompetitive or if you have to reduce your selling price from the price that you calculate taking into account all your additional costs and your full margin. If you feel that your price for a project will be on the high side, the most important things to bear in mind are:

● How much you want this business.
● Will it really lead to more business in the future? Bear in mind that once a market price has been established, it may prove difficult to increase it.
● Make sure that you add in sensible additional costs, but do not be overcautious.
● If you have some history of the price level with a particular customer, aim to have your price 'within negotiating range'. Do not give too much away and do not offer your lowest price so that you have no further room for negotiation.

If you have to make a price reduction, make sure that you really understand what you are doing. Don't just think in terms of taking the price reduction off your selling price; understand that you are taking it from your margin. If you have a 40 per cent margin and reduce your price by 10 per cent, this all comes from your margin. So you are reducing your margin by 25 per cent.

Standard products and export price lists

If your product is of the type that lends itself to having a price list, you will probably already have a price list for your domestic market. Price lists make it easier for your sales personnel to put together quotations and can also be used by your overseas distributors to calculate the cost of purchasing goods from you. You can prepare export price lists in your own currency and can also convert them to other major currencies, if much of your export business will be conducted in those currencies.

If you are just starting to export, then deciding on the price level of your export price list is a decision that will have a profound impact on your ability to develop your export business. Remember that your export price list includes two potential margins. It includes your distributor's margin and below that your company's margin, so you often have to be a little creative to ensure that you stay competitive. But remember also that some countries have anti-dumping laws and if your net selling price is too low, you may have to justify why this is, to prove that you are not using differential pricing to unfairly sell your product.

Price lists should always give your ex-works prices. This way you know exactly what your margin should be. Remember that if you sell through a distributor in your target market, their net price will also include freight costs, customs duties and tariffs and that once they have added their margin, they will also have to add local sales taxes to reach their selling price. It is not unusual for the end-customer selling price in some overseas markets to be 50 per cent higher or even double your normal domestic selling price. But this price level needs to be competitive, if you are to succeed in that market.

Pro forma invoices

Most companies will have a standard format for export quotations which will include details of the products being offered together with details of the packaging included, the terms of sale and the payment terms that are being offered. But there is a standard format that is used internationally that overseas customers can use in situations where they need to apply for an import licence, open a letter of credit or arrange finance for the purchase. This is the pro forma invoice. In most cases the customer will react to your quotation by asking you to send them a pro forma invoice. This usually means that they have decided to accept your offer and need this document to arrange the finance or letter of credit.

A pro forma invoice is a formal document. On the invoice it should clearly state that it is a 'pro forma invoice' and should include a statement saying that it is 'true and correct'. It should also clearly state the country of origin of the goods included in it. Some countries or banks insist that the pro forma invoice should be authenticated (officially certified as being true and correct) by your local Chamber of Commerce and some insist that it should also be accompanied by an authenticated certificate of origin. The information that you include on the pro forma invoice is important, not least because if it is being used to obtain a letter of credit, much of the detail will be included verbatim in the letter of credit itself. The invoice should include:

- the names and addresses of the buyer and the seller;
- the buyer's reference and the date of their enquiry;

- details of the products offered together with a description of each item;
- the price of each item and the currency (US$, euros, £ sterling, etc);
- the total gross and net shipping weights;
- the approximate total volume and dimensions of the consignment when packed for export;
- the delivery point and terms of sale (Incoterms);
- the estimated time for delivery;
- the terms of payment;
- the time that the quotation is valid for.

Keep the above information and particularly the description of the products offered simple. Complex language can result in errors in the wording on the letter of credit that is issued. Depending on your delivery point and terms of sale, you may also need to include the insurance and shipping costs. Since the main reason for issuing the pro forma invoice is to allow your customer to take out a letter of credit, it is wise to include confirmation of the total charges to be paid by the customer, because if you find when the letter of credit is issued that there are some costs that are not included, you will find it very difficult to get it modified. Bear in mind also that the estimated time that you give for delivery will be used to set the date of validity of the letter of credit. It is not unusual for a letter of credit to arrive several weeks after it was taken out, and if your terms of sale are FOB, you may find that ships to the customer's port of destination only leave once or twice a month. So if you would quote eight weeks for delivery to customers in your domestic market, it would be sensible to extend this to (say) 12 weeks on a pro forma invoice.

Export contracts

Having a proper written contract is important when trading internationally. Contracts should be clearly worded and should be in the form of a legal document so that there is no difficulty in interpretation and can be no misunderstanding. They should be prepared for you by a lawyer experienced in export contract law and who understands your business. For major contracts it is usual to have a standard format of contract into which the key information specific to that contract can be entered. Exporters selling a range of smaller or lower-value products may decide to have a standard quotation format and a separate standard set of terms and conditions that can be attached to every quotation. A written contract should include details of all of the key factors relating to the goods being supplied. This should include, as a minimum, a description of the goods, the price, packing details, trading terms (Incoterms), payment terms and the choice of law, which should make clear the jurisdiction under which arbitration or conciliation would be conducted. The description of the goods should be sufficiently detailed to avoid any dispute between the exporter and the customer and the detail should be such that the correct commodity classification code can be applied to the goods by customs on arrival.

Payment methods

A major variable in export quotations, particularly when quoting to customers in the developing world, is the method of payment. When you quote in your domestic market, even though you may have some customers on advance payment, most of your major customers will probably be on 'open account' with credit terms of 30 days. When selling overseas you have pressure, particularly from creditworthy major customers and distributors, to offer extended credit terms of 60 days or more on open account and you will have to balance this against the risks of non-payment and the sensible option, in many cases, of insisting on payment in advance or by letter of credit.

The methods of payment most commonly used in international trade are shown in Figure 10.1:

● Advance payment. This ensures that payment is cleared before the goods are shipped. The payment is usually made by a SWIFT inter-bank transfer, although for lower-value items it could also be made by credit card payment.

● Letters of credit. There are different types, but I would strongly recommend that you only accept irrevocable letters of credit that have been confirmed by a bank in your own country. Although a letter of credit is a relatively safe method of payment, you must make sure that all your staff are aware that in order to ensure payment, you must comply strictly with the documentary requirements of the credit. Letters of credit are governed by a set

FIGURE 10.1 Export payment methods

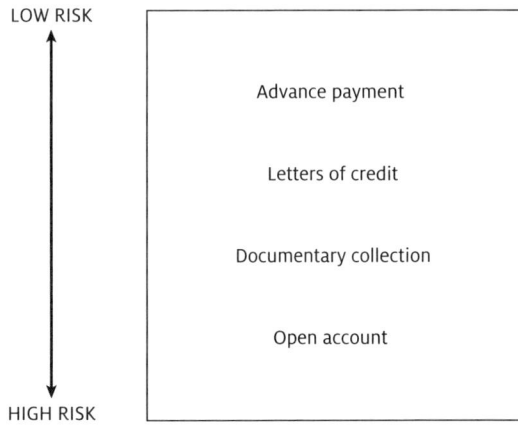

of rules from the International Chambers of Commerce (ICC). The latest version is called Uniform Customs and Practice, number 600 (UCP600) and over 90 per cent of the world's banks adhere to the rules in this document.

● Documentary collection (sometimes called 'cash against documents'). This is raised by the exporter and made out to the customer's bank. It is sent to the customer for acceptance and can be guaranteed by the bank for additional safety.

● Open account. The credit terms can be 30 days, 60 days or even longer and with 30 days the payment can be due from the date of invoice or from the end of the month of invoice, depending on what is specified. As with your domestic business, this type of payment method should only be used for creditworthy customers or distributors who have built up a reliable payment history. It is a method of payment that most companies will only consider from customers in developed countries, where there is a good system of debt recovery in place. Payments should always be made by bank transfer and not by cheque.

Clearly payment in advance is the best and most secure method of payment and if you are dealing with customers in developed countries it is usual to start working on the basis of advance payment and then to move towards an open account as you build up a trading history.

But when dealing with customers in developing countries, the foreign exchange regulations will often not allow money to be paid out overseas until it is clear that goods have actually been shipped. This is why the use of letters of credit is much more widespread with regard to the shipment of goods to developing countries. A letter of credit is an undertaking by a bank to make a payment to a named beneficiary within a specified time, against the presentation of documents which comply strictly with the terms of the letter of credit. A letter of credit provides security to both the exporter and the importer. When you ask for payment by letter of credit you are transferring the risk of non-payment to the issuing and the confirming banks and so you should understand that they are not going to pay you until they are certain that all the terms of the letter of credit have been met. So if you are going to conduct some of your export business using letters of credit you need to be sure that all personnel who will be involved – sales, finance and logistics personnel – understand the importance of checking the details on the letter of credit and making sure that they comply with them.

A letter of credit is a printed document and this means that spelling errors are possible as well as terms being included that you can immediately see are not possible to comply with. In such cases you need to request an amendment to the letter of credit or, if necessary, an extension to the validity. Examples are:

- Spelling mistakes in things like your name and address or the name or description of your product. These need to be corrected or your shipping documents will not comply with the letter of credit.
- A statement saying that all bank charges will be deducted from the final payment where you have stated in your pro forma invoice that all bank charges are to the client's account. This needs to be changed or you have to accept that you will pay the charges.
- The letter of credit will have a validity. If you cannot ship your goods and receive the shipping documents within this validity, you will not be paid. In such a case you need to request an extension to the validity of the letter of credit before you proceed with the order and not assume that you can extend the validity after shipment.

In their International Trade Guide entitled 'Letters of Credit – Best Practice', SITPRO, **www.sitpro.org.uk**, provides a useful list of essential checks to carry out when you receive a letter of credit. The complete guide can be downloaded from the SITPRO website.

SITPRO's letter of credit checklist

- Is the credit subject to UCP600?
- Are the names and addresses of the applicant and beneficiary complete and correct?
- Are there any terms or conditions of the credit that cannot be met? (If yes, immediate arrangements must be made with the applicant for the credit to be amended.)
- Do the terms cited in the credit match those in the sales contract? (Also check that the descriptions, names and addresses are consistent in both documents.)
- Are the prices correct?
- Are the description, price and quantity of the goods stated in accordance with the terms of the contract? (Underdrawing a credit may sometimes cause problems, although under certain circumstances, UCP600 allows a tolerance of plus or minus 5 per cent on quantity.)
- Can the goods be shipped within the stated period?
- Can the mode of transport specified be used?
- Can shipment be made from the port/airport specified?
- If part-shipments and transhipment of goods are prohibited, can the full quantity of the goods be exported on a vessel direct from the port of loading to the port of destination?
- Can the required documentation be obtained?
- Do any documents needs to be legalized?
- Are the insurance requirements of the credit acceptable?
- Are drawings under the credit negotiable?
- Are drawings under the credit payable in the UK rather than abroad?
- Can the goods be shipped within the period specified and documents presented to the bank within 21 days from the date of shipment (unless a shorter time is stipulated) but, in any case before the credit expires?

Note: The documents called for should fulfil the requirements stated in the sales contract.

So a letter of credit is not an easy option and I know many shipping managers who groan when they find out that a contract is being paid for by letter of credit. In some ways, until your staff get familiar with the process, handling a letter of credit can seem like running an obstacle course!

Note: in September 2010 the UK government closed SITPRO and announced that its activities would be merged into the Department for Business, Innovation and Skills (BIS). At the time of writing, SITPRO publications were still available to download as PDF files from a cached version of their website.

Terms of sale (Incoterms)

When quoting to an overseas customer there needs to be a common understanding of the delivery terms and it is important to use a delivery term that clearly defines where your responsibility for shipment of the goods ends and where the customer's responsibility begins. Incoterms (International Commercial Terms) are a set of rules for the interpretation of the trade terms that are most commonly used in international trade. They were first published by the International Chamber of Commerce (ICC), **www.iccwbo.org**, in 1936 and have been updated every 10 years or so since then. The terms in use at the time of writing are the 2010 revision, which came into force on 1 January 2011. The basic function of each Incoterm is to clarify how functions, costs and risks are split between the buyer and seller with regard to the delivery of goods as required by a sales contract. Each term clearly specifies the responsibilities of the seller and the buyer, and delivery, risks and costs are known at the critical points.

The choice of Incoterm is influenced by the mode of transport that you or your customer chooses to use. Some terms can be applied to any mode of transport, whereas others apply only to goods shipped by sea freight. The full rules for using Incoterms are available in the publication 'Incoterms® 2010', published by ICC Publishing SA.

Incoterms® 2010 was the first change to Incoterms® in 10 years and made some significant changes that reflect changes to the ways that goods are now being shipped. It is important that you use only Incoterms® 2010, because not only have four of the old rules (terms) from Incoterms® 2000 been deleted and two new rules (terms) been

TABLE 10.1 Group 1: Incoterms applicable to any mode of transport

Incoterm	Description	Transfer of responsibility
EXW	Ex Works	Named place
FCA	Free Carrier	Named place
CPT	Carriage Paid To	Named place of destination
CIP	Carriage and Insurance Paid To	Named place of destination
DAT	Delivered at Terminal	Named place of destination
DAP	Delivered at place	Named place of destination
DDP	Delivered Duty Paid	Named place of destination

added (reducing the total number of rules from 13 to 11), but there have also been some modifications with regard to obligations, risk transfer and cost sharing in the nine Incoterms that have been carried forward from Incoterms® 2000. In addition the main groupings have been reduced from four to two. Group 1 contains Incoterms applicable to any mode of transport and Group 2 contains terms that are applicable to sea and inland waterway transport only.

The rules in Table 10.1 can be used for any mode of transport. (This includes cases where a ship is used for part of the carriage.) The rules in Table 10.2 apply only to sea freight or inland waterway shipments, where the 'ship's rail' acts as the divider between one term and another. Containerized cargo (even if being shipped by sea) almost always uses the rules shown in Table 10.1, because a container is usually delivered to the carrier.

Incoterms® rules have traditionally been used in international sales contracts where goods pass across national borders. In various areas of the world, however, trade blocs, like the European Union, have made border formalities between different countries less significant. Consequently, the subtitle of the Incoterms® 2010 rules formally recognizes that they are available for application to both international and

TABLE 10.2 Group 2: Incoterms applicable to sea and inland waterway transport only

Incoterm	Description	Transfer of responsibility
FAS	Free Alongside Ship	Named port of shipment
FOB	Free on Board	Named port of shipment
CFR	Cost and Freight	Named port of shipment
CIF	Cost, Insurance and Freight	Named port of shipment

domestic sales contracts. As a result, the Incoterms® 2010 rules clearly state in a number of places that the obligation to comply with export/import formalities exists only where applicable. The ICC explains that two developments persuaded them to make this change. First, traders now commonly use Incoterms rules for purely domestic sales contracts. The second reason is the greater willingness in the United States to use Incoterms rules in domestic trade rather than the former Uniform Commercial Code shipment and delivery terms.

More detail on each of the Incoterm rules is shown below.

Group 1 – any mode of transport

- Ex works (EXW). The goods are made available to the buyer at the seller's premises. The buyer takes the goods and arranges and pays for onward transport, customs clearance and insurance. Selling goods 'ex works' minimizes the risks to the seller. Ex works tends to be used more for domestic sales or sales to customers within a trading bloc, where road transport can easily be arranged.
- Free Carrier (FCA) – where the main carriage is unpaid, but the seller must deliver the goods, cleared for export to the carrier appointed by the buyer. This is now the preferred rule for use where the goods are containerized. It is also the most appropriate rule for international sales with minimum obligations for the seller.

- Carriage Paid To (CPT) – where the main carriage is paid and the seller contracts for the carriage of the goods to the carrier nominated by the buyer and also pays the cost of carriage and other costs to bring the goods to the named destination. The risk passes to the buyer at the named place of delivery and the buyer takes all additional costs and any risks after the goods have been delivered to the nominated carrier.
- Carriage and Insurance Paid To (CIP) – same as CPT, but in addition the seller must take out insurance to cover the buyer's risk of loss of, or damage to the goods during shipment.
- Delivered at Terminal (DAT) – The seller must deliver the goods to the buyer at the named destination terminal, at the buyer's disposal, unloaded from the arriving vehicle, not cleared for import.
- Delivered at Place (DAP) – The seller must deliver the goods to the buyer at the named place of destination, at the buyer's disposal, ready for unloading, not cleared for import.
- Delivered Duty Paid (DDP) – The seller must deliver the goods to the buyer at the named port of destination, at the buyer's disposal, not unloaded, but cleared for import.

Note: All Incoterms beginning with 'D' mean that the seller covers all of the costs and all of the risks involved in bringing the goods to the named destination, which makes these the most onerous Incoterm rules.

In Incoterms® 2010 the new rules DAT and DAP were added and the old rules DAF, DES, DEQ and DDU were removed. Under both of these new rules, delivery occurs at a named destination: in DAT, at the buyer's disposal, unloaded from the arriving vehicle (as in the former DEQ rule); in DAP, likewise at the buyer's disposal, but ready for unloading (as under the former DAF, DES and DDU rules). The new rules make the Incoterms® 2000 rules DES and DEQ superfluous. The named terminal in DAT may well be in a port, and DAT can therefore safely be used in cases where the Incoterms® 2000 rule DEQ once was. Likewise, the arriving 'vehicle' under DAP may well be a ship and the named place of destination may well be a port: consequently, DAP can safely be used in cases where the Incoterms® 2000 rule DES once was. These new rules, like their predecessors, are 'delivered', with the seller bearing all the costs (other than those related to import clearance, where applicable) and risks involved in bringing the goods to the named place of destination.

Group 2 – applicable to sea and inland waterway transport only

- Free Alongside Ship (FAS) – where the main carriage is unpaid, but the seller must deliver the goods, cleared for export, alongside the vessel at the named port of shipment. Not now used where the goods are containerized.
- Free on Board (FOB) – where the main carriage is unpaid, but the seller must deliver the goods, cleared for export, loaded onto the ship at the named port of shipment. Under the terms of FOB shipment the seller is responsible for the goods until they pass the ship's rail, at which point the buyer assumes all risks and costs. Where the goods are handed over to the carrier at a point other than the ship's rail, the FCA rule should be used.
- Cost and Freight (CFR) – where the main carriage is paid and the seller contracts for the carriage of the goods. The seller must pay freight and other costs necessary to bring the goods to the named port of destination. The buyer takes all additional costs and any risks after the goods have been delivered over the ship's rail at the named port of destination.
- Cost, Insurance and Freight (CIF) – As with CFR, but in addition the seller must take out insurance to cover the buyer's risk of loss of or damage to the goods during shipment.

Note: Under the rules CFR and CIF the goods are handed over to the carrier at a point other than at the ship's rail.

Clearly the easiest and safest thing for an exporting company to do would be to try where possible to get the safest and most favourable terms of trade that they can. But exporting is a competitive business and it is also important to offer competitive terms to your customers. If you just stick with what is easiest for you, you may find that you lose out and hungrier competitors get the business.

Obviously the mode of transport that you use will limit the Incoterms that you can use. But normal practice also plays its part. In some countries certain terms are taken to be the norm and if you offer less favourable terms, again you could lose out. For shipments within the European Union it is standard practice for goods to be sold on a 'delivered' basis. Some countries even have regulations limiting the terms which may be used when shipping goods to their country. The purpose of these regulations is to let their local shipping and insurance markets benefit from importing rather than those in the exporting country.

In their International Trade Guide entitled 'Incoterms – an action plan and checklist', SITPRO provides a checklist, shown below, to use when deciding which Incoterm to use for shipping to a particular customer. The complete guide can be downloaded from the SITPRO website.

SITPRO's Incoterms checklist

- What method of transport is to be used?
- What are the terms currently used? Who chose these?
- Are there any company policies on which terms should be used and how much responsibility should be taken?
- Are there any restrictions on the term to be used by the country of importation?
- Are there any commercial norms in the country with which you are dealing?
- Discuss the terms to be used with your trading partner – it is important to take their point of view into account.
- Ensure that both parties understand and can carry out their obligations.
- Ensure that you are able to obtain enough information to give a quote for a certain Incoterm.
- Read Incoterms 2010. The introduction gives good advice and can clarify certain issues and the individual terms themselves are accurately described.
- Ensure all staff (especially those involved in sales and marketing) are properly trained in order to understand the basic principles of Incoterms and in particular the details of the individual Incoterms.
- Incorporate the terms decided into all relevant paperwork such as invoices, quotations, terms and conditions of sale.
- Review the terms periodically and change them if necessary.

Summary

The general concept of quoting for overseas business is no different from quoting for business in your domestic market. It's just a lot more complicated.

Pricing for export quotations can be determined using methods such as cost-plus, top-down and marginal costing. The main methods of payment used in international trade are advance payment, letters of credit, documentary collection and open account. The use of letters of credit is most widespread with the shipment of goods to developing countries. Using letters of credit is complex and not without its problems, but a letter of credit provides security to both the exporter and the importer and transfers the risk of non-payment from the exporter to the issuing and confirming banks.

Incoterms are a set of rules for the interpretation of the trade terms that are most commonly used in international trade. The basic function of each Incoterm is to clarify how functions, costs and risks are split between the buyer and seller with regard to the delivery of goods as required by a sales contract.

CHAPTER ELEVEN

MOVING YOUR GOODS

Exporting is not just about finding markets and taking orders. If you don't get your logistics right and goods are delivered late or arrive damaged, you will very quickly lose not only your existing customers, but also other potential customers, who will become aware of your reputation. As well as employing sales personnel who understand export markets, you also need to employ or train up logistics personnel. These personnel need to understand what they can organize themselves and for what and when they need to use the services of a freight forwarder. You will also need to train personnel in export documentation, the classification of goods and export reporting procedures.

Modes of transport

When shipping goods to a particular destination there will usually be a range of available routes and transport methods. Deciding on the mode of transport will be influenced by a number of factors, including the following:

- The destination. If the destination is on the same continent and not too far away, then road transport could be the logical choice. If you are shipping to the other side of the world the only choice would be by sea freight or airfreight.
- Availability. What are transport links like to the country of destination and what modes of transport are readily available?
- Speed. How quickly do you need to get your goods to their destination? Are they urgently required, eg emergency spare parts? Are the goods perishable?

- Cost. Obviously there is a difference in cost between different modes of transport.
- Type of goods. Are there any special requirements? Are the goods fragile? Perishable? Frozen goods, liquids, hazardous goods and delicate products such as computer equipment will need special packaging and may need special modes of transport.

Post

Small companies operating principally online and manufacturing or supplying small or relatively low-value items will frequently use the post as their main method of shipment for customers both in their domestic market and abroad.

Courier services

Courier services deliver goods door to door for a fixed price. The price for shipment to a particular destination will vary depending on things like whether you want same-day collection, whether you want delivery in 24 hours (in Europe) or several days, and whether you want delivery at the destination to take place at the weekend (if necessary). Prices are naturally higher than using postal services. Courier services are ideal for delivering things like emergency spare parts or small valuable items, but most companies would not use them for normal deliveries of their products, because of the cost. Courier services are operated by companies such as UPS, DHL and FedEx, who use their own vans to collect goods and either their own aircraft or scheduled services to transport the packages. Most couriers have a weight limit and packages normally cannot exceed 32 kilograms. The courier's charges include insurance and most have an online tracking service so that you can follow your package to its destination.

Road

Road transport is by far the most common method used for transporting goods – particularly to neighbouring countries or to countries that are linked by an adequate road transport network. Even where a short sea, tunnel or bridge crossing is required, road transport is still the method of choice. Using road transport it is possible to deliver goods door to door, either using the same vehicle or with the goods passing through a transport hub. More than 80 per cent of the UK's exports to Western Europe are by shipped by road. Although you can deal directly with a carrier to ship your goods in their vehicle, it is much more common to use a freight forwarder to organize the transport of your goods by road.

Rail

In some circumstances, rail transport can be cheaper than other modes of transport, particularly for transporting bulky goods over long distances. There is now also a significant market in intermodal containers carrying non-bulk goods, where the cargo is transferred between trains and other types of transport. Having said that, rail transport is not well suited to small consignments and generally exporters only use rail when other modes of transport are not suitable or are relatively expensive.

Airfreight

Airfreight is usually the fastest way of transporting goods – particularly between different continents – but it is often also the most expensive. It is the most cost-effective method of transporting high-value low-volume consignments, but is increasingly being used for shipping other goods, where the speed of delivery is critical, eg vegetables from Africa, seafood products from Asia, fruit from Chile. Much airfreight is now carried on scheduled passenger aircraft rather than on dedicated air cargo flights. Some 80 per cent of scheduled airfreight traffic is operated by members of the International Air Transport Association (IATA). IATA is the airfreight equivalent of shipping lines forming themselves into shipping conferences.

Sea freight

Transporting goods by sea may take longer than using other modes of transport, but it can be very cost effective, particularly if you are shipping large volumes. If you are shipping long distances, such as from Australia to China or from India to North America, it is the only method available apart from airfreight. There are many different types of ship that are used to carry different types of cargo or to transport that cargo in different ways. The main types are:

- Container ships. These carry their cargo in standard 6-metre (20-foot) or 12-metre (40-foot) containers, which are stacked both above and below deck.
- Roll-on/roll-off (ro-ro) ferries. These ships carry both lorries and cars.
- General cargo vessels. These carry all types of cargo packed in various different ways.
- Bulk carriers. These primarily carry large volumes of unpackaged goods, such as coal, ore, grain, etc.
- Tankers. These range from small specialized tankers to large supertankers and are used to transport liquids in bulk. They are primarily used for shipping crude oil, refined petroleum products and liquefied natural gas, but specialist tankers also ship liquified specialist gases (nitrogen, helium, etc) and bulk concentrated fruit juices.

Shipping routes reflect world trade flows. This means that sailings are more frequent and more numerous on routes where trade volumes are largest. The majority of exporters use conference lines for all of their sea freight consignments.

Groupage or consolidation

Freight forwarders often group together several consignments with the same destination. When shipping goods by road, this could mean them being able to book half a lorry or even a complete lorry. With container shipments groupage is quite normal to make sure that where possible only full containers are shipped. For airfreight shipments it is more common to talk about consolidation and the standard unit is referred to as a 'unit load device' (ULD). Using groupage or consolidation can significantly reduce shipping costs.

Dangerous goods

If you are shipping dangerous goods, then there are specific regulations relating to their shipment. Dangerous goods are classified using the United Nations classification system and should be marked with their name, description and UN number.

Using freight forwarders

The role of a freight forwarder is to help exporters (and importers) to transport their goods. All exporters use freight forwarders, but when you are starting to export, they can be particularly beneficial, because of their detailed knowledge about shipping to export destinations and the regulations that need to be complied with.

Freight forwarders can help you by:

- providing specialist advice;
- getting the best deal when booking transport on your behalf;
- grouping or consolidating smaller shipments to save time and money;
- having detailed knowledge of the paperwork and regulations that need to be complied with;
- arranging customs clearance for export consignments;
- acting as a go-between when transporting to a new territory.

If you have a consignment of goods to ship from one country to another, a forwarder will identify and book the best routes, best mode of transport and specific carriers for you depending on your requirements.

The main types of freight forwarder would fit into one of the following categories:

- local;
- regional;
- national with global partners;
- international brand (eg DHL).

In the UK you can find details of freight forwarders on the British International Freight Association (BIFA) website, **www.bifa.org**.

Using a freight forwarder makes shipping goods overseas relatively straightforward, but that does not mean that you should use a freight forwarder for absolutely everything. A UK company that has built up regular business with a distributor in Germany could easily arrange to send most shipments to them by using a road haulage carrier that they find to be reliable and cost effective. Equally, small, urgently required spare parts can easily be shipped by using a standard courier service.

Export packaging

The best way to make sure that your goods arrive in perfect condition is to make sure that you get your export packaging and labelling right. The packaging of goods for export shipment is more complicated than packing goods for delivery within your domestic market. What is adequate for domestic shipments will almost certainly not be adequate for shipping goods overseas. The correct marking and labelling of your goods is also important as these will help to make sure that the goods are properly handled while in transit to their final destination.

Export packaging is also sometimes referred to as transport packaging. It is one of the three main types of packaging that may be needed for exported goods:

- Export packaging is the outermost layer of packaging and is designed to protect your goods in transit. Typically, this would be wooden crates or boxes or plastic shrink-wrapping.
- Outer packaging is an intermediate layer of packaging which protects the final product packaging. For things like standard components or spare parts it could be a large box or carton protecting the smaller boxes that hold the components. For consumer goods, it could be a box containing multiple units that would eventually be opened out and used as a retail display unit.
- Sales packaging. This is the immediate layer of packaging around your goods, which remains in place when the goods reach their end user. Examples include the bottles or other containers for beverages and personal care products or boxes for items such as mobile phones or laptop computers.

Although we are primarily concerned with the outer layer export packaging, you should consider all of your packaging requirements together since they are interrelated.

When packing goods for export you should take the following into consideration:

- You should choose the most appropriate packing materials based on the mode of transport that you are using.
- You should find out whether the country of destination has any specific regulations with regard to the packaging of goods that you need to comply with.

- Where possible, consolidate smaller packages into one larger consignment to provide better protection and reduce shipping costs.
- Bear in mind that during shipment other consignments may be stacked on top of yours. Make sure your method of packaging will provide protection if this should happen.
- Secure and protect your goods within the packaging. Heavy goods may need to be bolted to the support. You should also consider using a filling material between the goods and the outer packaging.
- Make sure that you have adequate insurance in place while your goods are being packed. This is particularly important if you are using an outside company to carry out your export packaging for you.

Types of export packaging

The materials used in export packaging include wood, metal, plastic, paper and textiles. The main types of packaging in common use are:

- Cartons. These are the most widely used type of outer packing. Lightweight cartons may be suitable for short distances, but sturdier triwall cartons are more suitable for sea transportation. They are often stacked on pallets and shrink-wrapped for stability. They are particularly suitable for loading into containers, where less durability is required.
- Crates and cases. These are some of the most common options. Crates used to be made of wood, but this is less common now, because of the high cost of timber and the need to treat with pesticides and certify for certain markets. Crates normally have a strong outer skin and can be stacked without buckling. They can be handled by a forklift, a sling or a grab.
- Drums. Metal or plastic drums are commonly used to transport liquids and powders or goods that need to be kept dry.
- Sacks. These are available in a range of materials from paper to plastic. They are often used where containment is more important than protection.
- Pallets. These allow smaller packing units such as boxes or cartons to be grouped together. They are of standard designs so that they can be easily handled by forklift trucks, which simplifies the process of loading, unloading and warehousing. They are usually made of wood, although for airfreight, aluminium is used.

- Wrapping. Shrink-wrapping is often used with goods stacked on pallets to add stability and protect the goods.
- Unpacked. A wide range of bulk items are shipped 'unpacked'. These include materials like coal, grain and iron ore which are shipped in bulk carriers. But other large items such as heavy vehicles, cranes and large agricultural machines are commonly shipped loose or unpacked. With such types of equipment, making sure that they are stowed securely and cannot move in adverse sea conditions is more important than using protective packaging, which would be ineffectual in preventing damage.

Containers

There are a number of internationally recognized container types, including refrigerated units. There are two basic sizes – the 20-foot container with a volume of 33.2 cubic metres and the 40-foot container with a volume of 67.7 cubic metres. The goods inside will still need packaging, but the container offers protection and increased security from theft. The key advantages of packing goods into containers are:

- Very easy to use multi-modal transport.
- It gives you the opportunity to offer a door-to-door service.
- Loading and unloading are both quick and efficient.
- Your goods have a high level of security during transit.

Break bulk

The term 'break bulk' refers to goods carried as general cargo, rather than being carried in containers. They are usually packed in crates, rather than being just loose, but with this type of shipment there is a greater potential risk of damage during transit. To minimize the risk, it is usual to place a protective material around the goods to prevent damage from movement, moisture or other causes.

How to decide what type of export packaging to use

The main purpose of export packaging is to make sure that your goods reach their destination in perfect condition. The export packaging that you use needs to be able to protect your goods from damage caused by movement, handling and the elements. Most goods that are exported are loaded onto lorries or into containers, offloaded at ports or airports, loaded onto ships or planes and unloaded again at their destination. At each of the transfer points there is the possibility of mishandling or of the goods standing outside in adverse weather conditions for a period of time. There is also, of course, the risk of attempts being made to steal or tamper with goods whenever they are left unattended. According to the Transport Information Service from the German Insurance Association, **www.tis-gdv.de**, 5 per cent to 10 per cent of all insured losses on goods can be traced back to inadequate packaging.

The key factors that should help you to decide which type of packaging to use are the following:

- The type of goods being shipped. Factors such as whether the goods are bulky, very heavy, very light, fragile or valuable.
- Protection. The main purpose of export packaging is to avoid the risk of damage to your goods.
- Security. Goods that are being shipped will frequently be left unattended and you need to make sure that your packaging reduces the risk of your goods being stolen or tampered with. The use of containers helps with this and using container seals reduces the risk even further. Shrink-wrapping and the use of straps also make access more difficult for would-be thieves.
- Mode of transport. In general packaging for airfreight consignments will be lighter than packaging used for sea freight shipments.
- Cost. If you try to save money by using a level of packaging that is not up to the job, you will regret it. The very reason that standard options are standard is because they have proved to be reliable.
- Food and perishable goods. The same rules apply for food labelling and food safety throughout the European Union (EU). For countries outside the EU, standards and requirements vary. The rules are complicated and you should seek advice from your trade association.
- Dangerous goods. There are strict regulations for the packaging and transportation of dangerous goods. The rules vary depending on which mode of transport you are using.
- Wood packaging. There are international regulations and standards that apply to the use of wood packaging that have been introduced

to control the spread of insect pests and wood diseases. If you use wood packaging, you may need to provide a 'wood packaging certificate'. Some countries may also require you to apply for an import licence before shipping your goods. In such cases you may find it easier and more cost effective to consider using other packaging materials.

● Waste regulations. Many countries have waste regulations that favour packaging that can be easily recycled or disposed of. Some countries, such as Germany with its green dot system, go further and have stricter rules than the UK on packaging waste and collection. Even in the UK, if your business handles more than 50 tonnes of packaging a year and has a turnover of more than £2 million, you must register with your environmental regulator and make sure that you comply with the Producer Responsibility Obligations (Packaging Waste) Regulations.

Labelling

When shipping goods abroad every package in the consignment needs to be clearly labelled and identifiable. Regardless of the mode of transport that you are using, your consignment must have the correct shipping marks and numbers in accordance with the International Standards Organization standard ISO 780 and DIN 55 402.

The complete marking must comprise the following three parts:

● shipping mark;
● information mark;
● handling instructions.

The following details should be provided:

● Shipping mark:
  – identification mark, eg initial letters of receiver or shipper or of receiver's company name;
  – identification number, eg receiver's order number;
  – total number of items in the complete consignment;
  – the sequential number of the item in the consignment, eg 'Package 5 of 15';

- place and port of destination; not the full address, but check for places with the same name elsewhere in the world, eg Paris, France or Paris, Texas.
- Information mark:
  - The country of origin. Check regulations in the export country. Different countries can require the country of origin to be marked in different ways. For some products the country of origin may also need to be marked on the goods themselves or their individual sales packaging.
  - Details of the weight of the package (in kilograms).
  - Dimensions of the packages (in centimetres).
- Handling instructions. 'Handling marks' help to ensure that greater care is taken with cargo handling and storage. It must be possible to tell from the markings:
  - whether the package is sensitive to heat or moisture;
  - whether it is at risk of breakage;
  - where the top and bottom are;
  - where the centre of gravity is located;
  - where loading tackle may be safely slung.
- Special markings:
  - marking as per ISPM 15 for packaging containers made from solid wood;
  - hazardous goods must also be clearly marked.

ISO 780 and DIN 55 402 include details of the internationally recognized handling symbols, including a picture of a wine glass to show that the contents of the package are fragile and arrow symbols to show the correct upright position of the package.

Transport insurance

When shipping your goods abroad you will find that most companies in the supply chain that you use to move your goods operate under conditions that limit their liability in cases of loss, damage or delay. So if you want to have adequate insurance cover, to ensure that you can claim compensation if there is any resulting financial loss to your business, it is prudent to take out your own insurance. There is a range of different types of insurance cover available.

General cargo insurance

A typical cargo insurance policy covers goods in transit by road, rail, sea or air. It provides cover against accidental damage and other risks. The cost of the insurance and the circumstances in which you will receive compensation will depend on:

● the value of goods in transit;
● the expiry date of the insurance policy;
● whether the journey is domestic (eg to the docks or airport) or international.

Goods-in-transit insurance

The level of cover that you have will depend on the agreements that you have with your customers or suppliers. They are, however, likely to provide only basic cover and you should consider taking out additional insurance with a third-party broker or via your freight forwarder.

Basic shipping insurance cover (limited liability)

Under a variety of transport modal conventions, you automatically have basic insurance cover when shipping your goods by road, rail, sea or air. But this basic insurance offers you only the minimum of protection for your goods in the event of loss, damage or delay. It is therefore advisable to have additional insurance with a third-party broker or via your freight forwarder.

Most exporting companies operate in their domestic market as well as overseas and so will usually have a range of insurance policies covering the loading and unloading of goods at their factory or those of their customers and forwarders as well as taking out specific insurance for specific routes or individual shipments. Shipping insurance is a complex subject and if you are new to exporting it is wise to get advice from contacts that you have in your own industry or from your trade association or local Chamber of Commerce.

Export documentation

When shipping goods overseas they should be accompanied by the correct documentation. If you fail to ensure that all of the documents are correct you may not get paid on time and your customer may not be able to assume ownership of your goods or services.

Documentation such as bills of lading, airway bills and letters of credit have common formats that are pretty uniform throughout the world, but some export documentation still varies from country to country around the world. The European Union has made great efforts to ensure that standardized documentation is used throughout the EU, although some of the documentation will vary, depending on whether the goods are being shipped to another EU member state, within the EEA or outside Europe completely. Similarly US documentation has been simplified in recent years, particularly for shipment of goods within NAFTA. We can only give a short summary of key documentation here. This is a complex subject and even though most companies will use their freight forwarder to guide them in the preparation and completion of correct export documentation, any company involved in exporting needs to get professional training for their staff on this subject.

When transporting goods within the EU, it is not a legal requirement to carry invoices, and dispatch notes and packing lists are often used as accompanying documents. But many carriers still demand an invoice to make sure that they will avoid any possible delays at customs. All goods being exported outside the EU must be accompanied by an export declaration and another supporting document, which is usually the invoice.

Export documentation can be divided into four broad categories:

● transportation;
● commercial;
● insurance;
● payment.

Transportation documents

There are a number of documents that are commonly used for the movement of goods:

- Bill of lading. This is used as evidence of the contract between a company and the carrier it is using. It also acts as a certificate of title to the goods and is a fully negotiable document. Bills of lading apply only to maritime transport.
- Air waybill. This is issued by airlines to acknowledge receipt of goods to be transported by airfreight and serves the same purpose for air shipments that the bill of lading serves for sea shipments. Unlike the bill of lading, however, the air waybill is not a document of title to the goods and as such it is not required to be produced for delivery of the goods at their destination.
- The CMR Note (Convention des Marchandises par Route). This is, in effect, a 'road waybill' and is a standard contract of carriage which should accompany all consignments of goods that are being transported internationally by road. Again it is not a document of title to the goods.
- The CIM Note (Convention Internationale des Marchandises par Chemin de Fer). This is a 'rail waybill' and sets the conditions for the international movement of goods by rail. It is not a document of title to the goods.
- Standard Shipping Note (SSN). The SSN is used to accompany deliveries of non-hazardous goods in transit. By using an SSN you can complete the same standard document, regardless of which port, airport or clearance depot the goods are going to. An SSN tells the port how to handle the goods and using an SSN means that everyone with an interest in your consignment has adequate information at each stage until its final loading on board a ship or aircraft.
- Dangerous Goods Note (DGN). This is used to accompany hazardous goods in transit to the docks, to a forwarder or to an inland clearance depot.
- Export Cargo Shipping Instruction (ECSI). This is the instruction from the exporter to the freight forwarder or carrier. It gives everyone involved in the shipment complete, accurate and timely information about the consignment.

Commercial documents

The commercial invoice

A commercial invoice should be signed and dated and should contain at least the following information:

- a description of the goods;
- the weight of the goods (in kilograms);
- the value of the goods;
- the country of origin;
- details of the consignor and consignee.

It can also be useful to include the transport details.

Some countries have particular requirements with regard to the lay-out of invoices. You can get advice on this from your freight forwarder.

Other common commercial documentation:

- Certificates of origin. These specify where the goods were manufactured and are often required in countries that have preferential trade agreements in place. They are used to confirm that the goods originate in the exporting country so that the correct customs tariff can be applied to the goods. In North America, a NAFTA certificate of origin is required for goods traded among the NAFTA countries if the goods are NAFTA qualified and the importer is claiming zero-duty preference.
- Consular invoices. These are commercial invoices that need to be certified by a consular representative of the country to which the goods are being exported. This is a requirement for the exportation of goods to certain countries, particularly in the Middle East. In some cases the invoices may need to be 'legalized' by your local Chamber of Commerce first.
- ATA carnet. Certain types of goods that are temporarily exported can avoid all customs controls and charges by the use of an ATA carnet. The ATA carnet is issued by Chambers of Commerce and can cover three types of goods: exhibition goods, samples and professional equipment.

Insurance documents

For shipments to certain markets you may need to provide copies of insurance documents:

- Insurance policy. The most common situation is that exporters use a broker to approach insurance companies and agree an insurance policy to cover one shipment or in some cases multiple shipments with the same policy.
- Certificate of insurance. The insurance certificate provides documentary evidence that the cargo is insured and would be

included in a set of documents where this proof was required in order to get payment against a bill of exchange or letter of credit.

Finance and payment documents

- Bills of exchange are used for documentary collection. They are demands for payment that are presented to the importer through a financial intermediary, which is usually the importer's bank. Payment may be 'at sight', when the goods are delivered or 'at maturity', which could be after 30, 60 or 90 days. The safest option for the exporter is to only accept payment 'at sight'. With this method, the exporter retains control of the goods until payment is received. If the bill is not paid when the documents are presented, the goods will remain in storage until the bill is paid and could be resold or shipped back.

- Letters of credit. This is the most popular method of guaranteeing payment for international transactions, particularly when shipping to less creditworthy countries. It is, in effect, an advice issued by the importer's bank authorizing payment of a specific sum through an intermediary bank to a named beneficiary (the exporter) upon the delivery of certain documents. A letter of credit can be 'revocable' or 'irrevocable' and can be 'confirmed' or not. I would strongly recommend that you only accept irrevocable (ie the terms can only be modified by the bank after obtaining the approval of both the exporter and the importer) and confirmed (ie guaranteed by a local bank in your own country as well as by the importer's bank in their country) letters of credit. Letters of credit are governed by a set of rules from the International Chambers of Commerce (ICC). The latest version is called Uniform Customs and Practice, number 600 (UCP600).

Classifying your goods

If you trade internationally, it is essential that your goods are classified so that you can identify what duties and controls apply and ensure a correct customs declaration. Classifying your goods correctly will ensure that you pay the right duty and that you know whether an export licence is required. You have a legal responsibility to ensure that the correct classification is applied whether or not you have an agent who handles customs entries on your behalf. Incorrect classification can lead to delays in clearing goods, overpayment of duties and possible penalties. As well as being used in import and export declarations, the classification of commodities is used to collect data and trade statistics.

The Harmonized Commodity Description and Coding System (HS)

The Harmonized Commodity Description and Coding System, generally referred to as the 'Harmonized System' or simply 'HS', is a multipurpose international product nomenclature developed by the World Customs Organization (WCO), **www.wcoomd.org**. The HS, known generally as 'tariff numbers', is the coding system used for trade worldwide.

It comprises about 5,000 commodity groups; each identified by a six-digit code, arranged in a legal and logical structure and supported by well-defined rules to achieve uniform classification. The system is used by more than 200 countries and economies as a basis for their customs tariffs and for the collection of international trade statistics. Most of these countries set up their own national customs tariff, based on the HS system. Over 98 per cent of the merchandise in international trade is classified in terms of the HS.

According to the World Customs Organization, 'The HS contributes to the harmonization of customs and trade procedures, and the non-documentary trade data interchange in connection with such procedures, thus reducing the costs related to international trade. The HS is thus a universal economic language and code for goods, and an indispensable tool for international trade.'

The HS is also extensively used by governments, international organizations and the private sector for many other purposes such as:

● collecting internal taxes (such as value added tax);
● setting trade policies;
● the monitoring of controlled goods;
● rules of origin;
● freight tariffs;
● collecting transport statistics;
● price monitoring;

- quota controls;
- the compilation of national accounts;
- economic research and analysis.

The Harmonized System is governed by the International Convention on the Harmonized Commodity Description and Coding System. The official interpretation of the HS is given in the Explanatory Notes published by the WCO. The Explanatory Notes are also available online on the WCO website and on CD ROM, as part of a commodity database giving the HS classification of more than 200,000 commodities actually traded internationally.

The major complication with HS codes is that only the first six digits of the classification number are uniform among countries that use the HS. The first two digits are known as the HS chapter, the second two digits are known as the HS heading and the third two digits comprise the HS subheading. Most countries add a few further digits to classify the product in more detail, but these first six digits cannot be changed. To export your product you need to know the complete product classification code for your own country and also the complete classification code for the country that you are exporting to.

On the WCO website you can find a list of all of the countries and territories that apply the HS system. You can also purchase the Harmonized System Explanatory Notes. You can find details of your own country's version of HS coding from your own government support organization. There are examples below for the European Union and the United States. (It is unfortunate that every country or trading block seems to want to do their own thing.)

The European Union (EU)

EU countries classify goods for import or export according to the Tariff. This is a system of 'Commodity Codes' that are used across the EU based on the EU TARIC (Tariff Intégré Communautaire). Each community country has its own version and in the UK the classification is carried out using the Integrated Tariff of the United Kingdom ('the Tariff').

The EU commodity code is a 10-digit number, although an additional four or five digits may apply to certain products. For imports from outside the EU it is necessary to provide the full Tariff classification. For exports the first eight digits are sufficient.

The EU classification code is based on the European Union's Combined Nomenclature (CN). The first six digits of the code are based on the HS system and digits 7 and 8 are the CN subheading. (If there are additional digits, digits 9 and 10 are the TARIC subheading and digits 11 to 15 are additional TARIC codes.) So with these EU codes, only the first six digits would be the same as in other coding systems based on the HS system.

Using the Integrated Tariff of the United Kingdom, an example for a fully assembled bicycle would be:

HS Chapter	87	Vehicles, other than railway or tramway rolling stock and parts and accessories thereof
HS Heading	8712	bicycles and other cycles (including delivery tricycles), not motorized
HS Subheading	8712 00	other
CN Code	8712 00 30	bicycles
TARIC Subheading		in this example there is no TARIC addition so the CN code is extended by two zeros.

The full code for this item is: 8712 00 30 00.

Working out the code is complicated, but assistance is sometimes available. UK exporters can find the correct trade tariff for their products by using the free online tool 'UK Trade Tariff' on the Business Link website, **www.businesslink.gov.uk**.

The United States

The United States uses 10-digit codes to classify all products and commodities. As with other international classification systems, the first six digits are the HS number. The last four digits are unique to the United States and classify the product in greater detail. This complete 10-digit code is known as a Schedule B code. All Schedule B codes are contained in the booklet 'The Schedule B: Statistical Classification of

Domestic and Foreign Commodities Exported from the United States'. Schedule B codes are administered by the US Census Bureau and the booklet is available on their website, **www.census.gov**. The whole book can be viewed on the website or purchased through the Government Printing Office (GPO), **http://bookstore.gpo.gov**.

Using the Schedule B book, the example for a fully assembled bicycle would start in the same way for the first six digits:

HS	Chapter 87	Vehicles, other than railway or tramway rolling stock and parts and accessories thereof
HS	Heading 8712	bicycles and other cycles (including delivery tricycles), not motorized

But then under Schedule B there would be three alternatives, only one of which is shown in the EU coding:

Bicycles with both wheels not exceeding 25 inches diameter would be coded: 8712.00.1070

Bicycles with both wheels exceeding 25 inches diameter would be coded: 8712.00.2600

And bicycles 'other' would be coded 8712.00.6000 under the US coding rather than 8712.00.3000 under the EU coding system. (Similarly the EU coding system has codes for 'Bicycles without ball bearings' and for 'Unicycles', none of which exists in the US codings.)

On the US Census website under 'Schedule B Validation' you can type in your 10-digit number and it will check that it is valid and tell you the relevant product description. If you need further help you can consult a commodity specialist at the US Census Bureau Foreign Trade Division on (301) 763-3259 (durable goods), (301) 763-3484 (non-durable goods), or contact your local Export Assistance Center.

Handling product classification coding requirements

Determining product classification codes and the reporting requirements can seem complicated to inexperienced exporters, but there are
steps that you can take to simplify the process:

- Personnel. Classifying products requires specialized knowledge and
  becomes easier with experience. Arrange specialist training for at
  least two of your personnel who have a good knowledge of your
  products, including the components, materials or ingredients that
  make them up. (Training two people means that you have cover if
  one is absent or decides to leave the company.)
- Systems. Modify your computer system so that there is a field for
  the commodity code for each item, with a fail-safe mechanism
  that only allows items with a valid commodity code to be
  selected for overseas orders. If you are just starting to export,
  initially only complete this field for products that you expect to
  sell overseas.
- Suppliers. If you sell or resell products manufactured by other
  companies, try to get them to supply you with the commodity
  codes for these products. (Bear in mind that it is still your
  responsibility to use the correct codes, so you should still get
  your 'expert' to check them.)

Reporting procedures

Governments collect trade statistics and details of exports from and
imports into their country. The rules and regulations vary from country
to country, but in most countries exporters have a legal obligation to
provide details of their exports, including the tariff commodity codes
and values. This information is often collected by tax or customs
authorities on either export documentation or tax returns such as those
for value added tax in the European Union.

Reporting procedures for exporters from EU member states

The situation for EU member states is complicated by the fact that importers and exporters have to make separate declarations of transactions with other EU states and transactions with countries outside the EU.

The reporting procedures vary depending on the country that the goods are being shipped to:

- exports to other EU countries: Intrastat return;
- exports to EFTA countries: SAD;
- exports to the rest of the world: SAD.

The Single Administrative Document (SAD) was introduced in 1988 to replace over 150 customs documents in use at that time within both the EU and EFTA. In 1993 the EU itself moved over to Intrastat for reporting within the EU, but the SAD is still used for making export, transit and import declarations for shipments to EFTA countries and to all other countries outside the EU. In the UK the SAD is also referred to as Form C88.

Although in most cases UK exports are zero-rated for VAT, UK exporters are required by law to enter details of any exports that they make on their VAT return to HM Revenue & Customs. Companies that are VAT registered and have a high level of exports to EU states also have to submit more detailed declarations on an Intrastat return.

Intrastat is the system used to collect statistics on intra-EU trade. (The Intrastat system is only used to collect statistics on the trade of goods between member states and not the supply of services.) Rather than using the names 'exports' and 'imports', the movement of goods between EU member states are called 'Arrivals' (acquisitions, purchases or imports) and 'Dispatches' (removals, sales or exports). Intrastat thresholds are reviewed annually and the 2011 thresholds for needing to complete a return are £600,000 for Arrivals and £250,000 for Dispatches. The Intrastat return (Intrastat Supplementary Declaration or SD) has to be completed monthly and is only used for trade within the EU. For exports outside the EU, UK exporters have to report sales electronically to HM Revenue & Customs using the National Export System (NES) or by using the Single Administrative Document (SAD). New security laws mean that UK exporters have to declare goods leaving the EU. Exporters are covered if they supply normal export declarations such as the SAD for their goods. But if they are not declaring them in this way, they need to complete an Exit Summary Declaration. HM Revenue & Customs defines an export as goods sent from the UK to countries outside the EU. Countries outside the EU are known as 'third countries'.

Guidance on the reporting process and on submitting export declarations can be obtained from HM Revenue & Customs, either on their website, **www.hmrc.gov.uk**, or by phone. Support material is also available on the Business Link website, **www.businesslink.gov.uk**.

Reporting procedures for US exporters

US exporters have to complete a Shipper's Export Declaration (SED) where the value of the commodities being shipped, classified under any single Schedule B number, exceeds $2,500. The SED is used to control exports and is a source document for official US statistics. SEDs must be prepared and submitted for all shipments (regardless of value) that require an export licence or are destined for countries restricted by the Export Administration regulations. The US Census Bureau's Foreign Trade Division controls the SED. In 2008 the bureau made electronic filing of the SED mandatory using AESDirect. AESDirect is a web-based application that allows an SED to be filed electronically. Information is available on the website, **www.aesdirect.gov**.

So if your company is just starting to export you can see that the reporting procedures for your export sales are rather complicated. You need to train staff in the classification of your products by commodity code and you also need to train staff in the preparation and completion of the correct export documentation and in completing and making declarations of your export sales.

Summary

Exporting is not just about finding markets and taking orders. As well as employing sales personnel who understand export markets, you also need to employ or train logistics personnel. When shipping goods overseas, care needs to be taken when choosing the mode and route, because these factors can impact on transport costs. Freight forwarders can help exporters with their detailed knowledge about shipping to export destinations and the regulations that have to be complied with.

The packaging of goods for export shipment is more complicated than packing goods for your domestic market. The key factors in deciding which type of packaging to use are the type of product, the mode of transport being used, the cost and the degree of protection and security required. The correct marking and labelling of your goods are also important, as is supplying the correct documentation. If you fail to ensure that all of the documents are correct you may not get paid on time and your customer may not be able to assume ownership of your goods or services.

If you trade internationally, it is essential that your goods are classified so that you can identify what duties and controls apply and ensure a correct customs declaration. The Harmonized Commodity Description and Coding System (HS), known generally as 'tariff numbers' is the coding system used for trade worldwide. Over 98 per cent of the merchandise in international trade is classified in terms of the HS. As well as being used in import and export declarations, the classification of commodities is used to collect data and trade statistics.

CHAPTER TWELVE

MANAGING THE RISKS OF EXPORTING

The pattern of export trade that your company develops will be defined in large part by the type of business that you are and the type of product that you sell. When risk management companies are offering advice and insurance services to exporters, they will usually define the company's way of doing business as one of the following:

- occasional exporters;
- new exporters;
- companies supplying goods to overseas markets and to specific customers on a regular basis;
- companies supplying large 'one-off' sales contracts;
- companies supplying capital or semi-capital goods for major overseas projects;
- companies providing services.

Understanding the market

When dealing with overseas markets you need to understand the differences that exist in different cultures and different parts of the world. In most overseas markets, you will be dealing with a different language, a different business culture and probably also a different legal system. All of these can create potential problems. You can reduce the risks by researching the market thoroughly, getting advice where necessary and by either employing someone who speaks the local language or making sure that your distributor or agent has staff that you can deal with who speak your language.

Even where English is used, there are differences in the language and words used in different countries. This is particularly noticeable between the English that is used in the UK and that used in the United States, but there are also differences between the meaning and usage of certain words and phrases used in other English-speaking countries such as Australia and South Africa, and countries such as India, where English is used widely for business purposes. There are similar types of differences between the Spanish used in Spain and that used in South America and also between the French used in mainland France and that used in Canada.

You may find it surprising that even if your literature is suitable you will still probably need to get much of it reprinted for the US market. The United States uses the quarto format and literature and manuals printed on A4 will not photocopy properly and will look out of place in a pack of US quarto literature given out by your US distributor.

You also need to check that your trademarks and branding can be used in the countries where you are exporting to and that your products comply with local standards and have any necessary certification. This relates to all countries, but is particularly important when selling to major markets like the United States, EU, Japan, China and India.

Country risks

The country that you are dealing with may in itself present certain risks. It may be economically weak or politically unstable. The key potential risks that you need to consider are:

- Political:
  - changes in government which may affect trading policy or delay the transfer of payment for goods;
  - the imposition of import restrictions after your contract is signed, which prevent you from shipping the goods (which you may have already part-manufactured);
  - the imposition of embargoes, tariffs or other quotas;
  - internal or external threats to the country including war or civil unrest.

- Economic:
    - the willingness or ability of the government and government agencies to pay their debts;
    - the competence and stability of the banking system; collapses of the banking system are not uncommon in the developing world;
    - the availability of trade finance for exports to this particular country;
    - the ability of the private sector to pay for its imports;
    - lack of foreign exchange reserves;
    - the inconvertibility of local currencies;
    - the imposition of exchange controls which prevent the transfer of funds.
- Climate:
    - Climate is also a risk factor. Some regions of the world regularly experience natural disasters such as flooding, hurricanes, droughts or earthquakes. When these occur there may be major disruption to day-to-day business for the private sector and the government.

You can obtain information about country risks for specific countries by contacting your country's export support organization, your local Chamber of Commerce or one of the major banks.

In the UK, UK Trade & Investment's Overseas Security Information for Business (OSIB) provides UK companies with information on the security-related risks which companies face when doing business overseas. Through the UKTI website, **www.ukti.gov.uk**, you can access information about security-related issues for more than 90 different countries.

Customer risks

You should always check the creditworthiness of your customer. This type of information can be obtained by running a credit check though a reputable credit agency such as Dun & Bradstreet. Ideally you need to know the following:

- The identity of the customer. Do they have a legally established business in their country?

- Does the person you are dealing with have the legal authority to act for the company?
- The credit rating of the customer. Even in low-risk countries such as those in the EU or the United States customers can still pose a credit risk to you.
- Are they solvent? This does not just relate to payment for goods that you have shipped. If your customer were to become insolvent while you were still manufacturing the goods, you could be left with part-manufactured product which may be difficult to resell.
- What is the usual period of credit offered in your customer's country? (This will usually be longer than you would be used to when trading in your domestic market.)
- The trading history of your customer. Do they pay on time? Is their payment record consistent?
- Do your products fit with the business profile of your customer?
- Will your customer be able to pay their bill? (You can take out export credit insurance, even for low-risk countries.)

Creditworthiness

Once you have checked and confirmed that your customer or distributor is solvent, you need to decide how you want to trade. Do you want to offer credit or do you feel that you need to get paid for your goods before they are shipped? There is a range of options, including letters of credit to make sure that you receive payment for your goods, but most of these are more frequently used when dealing with developing countries or countries where there are generally perceived to be credit risks. When dealing with customers in the European Union, North America and parts of Australasia, it is normal to start by insisting on prepayment and then to gradually move to offering small and eventually larger amounts of credit as your relationship develops and the payment pattern proves that the customer is an acceptable risk.

When you start to offer credit to export customers, you need to decide how much credit you are prepared to advance. Before you do this you need to consider:

- How much credit you already have on your trading accounts, including credit outstanding in your domestic market.

- How much you know about your customer/distributor and his trading/payment record.
- What is the absolute maximum amount of credit that you do not wish to exceed with this customer?
- What would be the impact on your business if the customer delays payment or does not pay at all?
- Remember that payment terms for exporting are usually longer than in domestic markets – 30 days' payment terms for your domestic business often becomes 60 days or even more with export business.
- Can you finance the credit you will need to offer and if so, how will you finance it?

Financing credit and the risks involved constitute one of the most difficult problems facing would-be exporters. Steady growth in your export business is better than taking risks with credit to achieve rapid growth.

As a rule of thumb, your export business will cost you roughly twice as much to finance in credit terms as your domestic business.

In setting a credit limit for a regular customer or distributor, you need to take into account how much business you have on your books for that customer and not just how much debt is outstanding.

Example

A US company has a distributor in South Africa. The distributor sells a wide range of the company's products and places orders regularly every few weeks. The goods take about two months to manufacture and a further month to ship to South Africa by surface means. Payment terms are net 60 days (which partly reflect the fact that export shipments take longer to reach their markets than domestic shipments). If we take a point in time where the company has orders in house with a value of $100,000, goods being shipped with a value of $50,000 and invoices awaiting payment for a further $100,000, the company has an exposure to this one customer of $250,000 even though none of the payments may actually yet be due. To protect itself not just against possible non-payment for goods actually shipped but also the eventuality that the distributor could become insolvent and leave the company with partly manufactured product, the US company has a 'split' credit limit. It limits the value of goods shipped and not yet paid for to $200,000. It sets a total limit on the account of $350,000. The total limit includes orders in house but not yet shipped. Since the total exposure at present is $250,000, the company will only process a further $100,000 of new orders before receiving payment for outstanding accounts. Clearly it could reach a situation where if the distributor places a large new order, the company may require the distributor to pay some invoices that are not yet due, in order to keep within its credit limit.

The risks of currency and foreign exchange

If you develop a significant export business, foreign currencies and the fluctuations of the foreign exchange market are certain to impact on your business. If you sell goods in your own currency, you know what your margins are and how much profit you can make from a certain level of business. If you sell in a foreign currency, fluctuations in exchange rates can significantly impact your margins and profits. So you need to protect yourself against foreign exchange risk.

Buying and selling foreign currency

There are a number of ways to buy or sell foreign currency:

● Spot dealing. If you buy or sell currency on the 'spot' market, the exchange rate will be the rate at that point in time. Spot dealing is the simplest way for you to buy or sell foreign currency, but the risk is that you have no way of knowing what the rate will be until the transaction is carried out and the spot rate that you receive will be set by the market conditions at the time. This means that the rate that you get when you receive payment from your customer could be significantly different from the rate that you assumed when you originally quoted for the business.

- Forward contracts. Forward contracts are available for any period up to two years and if you take one out you know exactly how much you will get paid in your own currency, when your customer makes his payment to you. In return for the certainty of knowing how much you will be paid in your own currency, you forgo the possibility of making a foreign exchange gain if the exchange rate should move in your favour.
- Currency options. A currency option is similar to a forward contract, but as well as protecting you from adverse exchange rate movements it will also allow you to make gains if the market moves in your favour. Because of its flexibility, a currency option will cost more than a forward contract.
- Foreign currency bank account. Your company can also open a foreign currency bank account. This is particularly useful if you have both expenses and revenues in one particular currency, as you can use income in that currency to pay expenditure and minimize the need to actually exchange currencies.

There are three ways that you can deal with foreign exchange risks:

- Do nothing. This is a high-risk option. It means that as and when you need to convert foreign currency back into your own currency, you will be dealing with the spot market. If you do this, it will be impossible to properly plan and budget for your export business.
- Manage the effect of currency fluctuations yourself. This is a better option. If you do this, you will at least be able to calculate what your possible risks may be and take action accordingly.
- Take out foreign exchange contracts. This is the safest way to manage the risks. It allows you to fix the exchange rate so that you know exactly how much you will receive in your own currency when your invoice is paid.

Managing the effect of currency fluctuations yourself

If your company is based in the European Union, the United States or any other country with a stable and easily convertible currency, you can initially decide only to sell in your own currency. In doing so you are transferring the foreign exchange risk to your customers. Major customers may not be prepared to take this currency risk and may prefer to deal with your competitors if they are willing to sell in the local currency. So an alternative is to produce a price list in a currency that is the currency of your major customers. Apart from your own currency, it is really only sensible to consider having a price list in a major traded currency, such as the US dollar, the euro or the pound sterling.

Most-traded currencies (2011) – global foreign-exchange turnover as a percentage of the total:

1 US dollar 84.9%
2 Euro 39.1%
3 Japanese Yen 19.0%
4 Pound sterling 12.9%
5 Australian dollar 8.6%

Note: Total is equal to 200 per cent, because each transaction involves two currencies.

You may be surprised to see that the percentage of foreign exchange turnover involving the Australian dollar is now two-thirds of that of the pound sterling. Also, China has decided to handle more international transactions in its own currency, the renminbi. Several countries now buy renminbi rather than US dollars to pay for their imports from China and accept renminbi rather than dollars for the goods that they ship to China.

Once you are selling from a foreign currency price list you need to understand that currency fluctuations will impact on your business. Even if the amount of business that you are doing in foreign currencies is not a large percentage of your overall business, you need to understand its potential impact on margins and profits. If you are selling goods from a foreign currency price list a 10 per cent change in the exchange rate between that currency and your own will decrease or increase your selling price in your own currency by 10 per cent. But that will have a far greater impact on your margins. If you have a gross margin of 40 per cent on sales in the foreign currency, a 10 per cent reduction in the exchange rate will take away 25 per cent of that margin. Equally, an increase of 10 per cent in the value of the currency will increase your margin by 25 per cent.

A few years ago, I worked for the UK-based European subsidiary of a US company. Like many US companies, nearly 90 per cent of turnover was within the United States. In their domestic market, sales, purchases and profits were all in US dollars. Our situation in the UK was much more complicated. Our purchases from our parent company were all made in US dollars. We also purchased and manufactured ancillary equipment in the UK with costs in pounds sterling and purchased other equipment from Germany and Italy with costs in euros. Our sales were split about 50/50 into UK sales (in pounds sterling) and export sales, which were in either euros (to the eurozone) or US dollars (some major OEMs and sales to the Middle East). Our local sales budgets were set in pounds sterling (for the home market) and euros (for the eurozone), but as far as head office was concerned, all of our budgets were converted to US dollars. Exchange rate fluctuations could have a significant effect on our actual sales when converted back to US dollars and if the exchange rate was kind to us, we would be praised for increasing sales, even when the whole increase was due to the exchange rate. But the reverse was also true. To handle this complicated situation, we had bank accounts in pounds sterling, US dollars and euros. We tried, wherever possible, to use income in one currency to pay for purchases in that same currency. This worked well for most of our day-to-day business, but for individual large projects we used forward foreign exchange contracts.

Any company involved in exporting will set expected exchange rates for the key foreign currencies used for their overseas sales when they set their annual budget. If the value of your overseas sales in foreign currencies is significant, you need to manage the risks professionally.

Example

A company exports 20 per cent of its turnover to the United States. Sales are made in US dollars and the company calculates that it will make a gross margin of 30 per cent on these sales. In its budget for this year, it set the exchange rate at $1.5 : £1. It has taken no currency cover. The exchange rate moves to $1.75 : £1. The exchange rate has fallen by 15 per cent, but the margin on these sales has halved. Depending on the margin it is making on the other 80 per cent of its business, this loss of margin could easily reduce its overall margin by as much as 5 per cent, having a significant effect on its profits.

Taking out forward foreign exchange contracts

The safest way to deal with exchange rate risk is to use forward foreign exchange contracts. You can contract to buy or sell a fixed amount of one currency into another currency at a particular point in time at an exchange rate that is fixed when you take out the contract. An Australian company could take out a forward foreign exchange contract with their bank to convert 200,000 US dollars to Australian dollars at a fixed point in time and a South African company could take out a similar type of contract with their bank to convert 100,000 US dollars to South African rand. Both companies would know at the outset exactly how much they would be paid for their goods in their own currency.

Some countries in emerging markets have non-convertible currencies or have regulations in place that make it difficult or impossible to trade internationally in their currencies. In such cases you would need to consider dealing with them in a major 'hard' currency such as the US$ or the euro.

Example

When I was working for a UK company selling pumps, exports accounted for about two-thirds of our turnover. Our biggest customer was an OEM in the United States which accounted for over 20 per cent of our total annual turnover. They insisted on being invoiced in US$, which meant that we were taking on the full exchange rate risk for the business. The product we supplied was specific to that one customer and being OEM business, our margins were not exceptional, so we needed to protect them as much as possible. Shipments were made monthly, but the value shipped in any one month could vary between 50 per cent and 150 per cent of the monthly average. Based on historical sales we knew the approximate pattern of shipments throughout the year, although the actual level clearly depended on the level of business that the OEM was achieving in that particular year.

Our finance director set up a US$ account at our bank and an arrangement in which he purchased forward foreign exchange contracts for about 70 per cent of the expected monthly income that we would receive in US$. These contracts were for the sale of a particular amount of US$ on a particular date. The reason for setting up the contracts for only 70 per cent of the expected income was that these were fixed contracts. If one was for the sale of $100,000 on 5 August and we didn't have $100,000 in our US dollar bank account on that date, we would have to buy some US dollars so that we could fulfil the contract. Setting the value at 70 per cent made sure that we always had some excess dollars to cover fluctuations in the monthly level of orders. At any one time we had forward contracts going out about 18 months ahead. This protected our margins for at least the existing budget year and part of the following budget year.

At one point the US dollar fell rapidly by about 20 per cent against the pound over a period of a few months. This meant that if we had not had the forward contracts, we could have made 20 per cent of our turnover with this customer as excess profit – that would have been well over half a million pounds! But our finance director pointed out that we were businessmen and not currency speculators. If the exchange rate had gone in the opposite direction, we could have been in a situation where half a million pounds of our company's profits were lost. With the exchange contracts in place we knew exactly where we stood.

There is another important point that comes out of the above example. This is that forward exchange rate contracts can only protect your business for a limited period of time. They can be used to protect your business from risks during the period from when you take an order to when you are paid for it. They cannot protect your margins from long-term currency fluctuations. If you consider the US$:£ exchange rate over the last 20 years, it has varied from between very nearly $1:£1 to as much as $2.4:£1, but for most of the time it has probably been in the range of $1.4:£1 to $1.8:£1. Major fluctuations have also occurred between the US$ and the euro and the Japanese yen. Short term you can protect your margin by taking out forward foreign exchange contracts, but long term you have to decide if your company can accept the reduced margin, while you try to cut costs and also hope that the exchange rate will eventually move the other way.

Delivery delays and frustrated exports

When accepting large individual export orders or contracts, it is wise to try to get payment terms that include a significant down payment with the order. If you are supplying capital or semi-capital goods for major projects, it is not uncommon to find that the customer's time-scale has changed and that they would prefer to take the goods later. This can cause you significant financial costs if you have already commenced manufacture and are going to be unable to ship the goods when scheduled. Even worse is what is called a 'frustrated export'. This is when the customer refuses the goods or attempts to cancel the order at an advanced point in the manufacturing schedule. Your export strategy should include a plan to either resell the goods to another market, modify the goods for resale, reuse components or parts in other contracts or realize a salvage value for the goods. You should also have procedures in place for collection of the value of the invoice or for taking legal action against your client.

Intellectual property rights in international trade

Your intellectual property (IP) is the sum of the unique ideas, products and information which adds commercial value to your business. It can be a brand, the name of your business, an invention, a design or some type of artistic or written material that you create. Intellectual property includes copyrights, patents, trademarks and logos, but also extends to plants and seeds with national or variety rights and goods that infringe designations of origin or geographical indications. Intellectual property rights (IPR) give legal protection to your intellectual property, preventing others from profiting from it commercially. If you are not sure what you have in the way of intellectual property that could or should be protected, you can find out about intellectual property on the Intellectual Property Office website, **www.ipo.gov.uk**.

There are four main types of IPR which can be used to protect inventions or creations. These are:

● Patents. Patents protect what makes things work.
● Trademarks. Trademarks are signs (like words and logos) that distinguish goods and services in the marketplace.
● Designs. Designs protect the appearance of a product/logo.
● Copyright. Copyright is an automatic right which applies when the work is fixed, written or recorded in some way.

In protecting your IPR you need to make sure that you protect them both in your domestic market and overseas. Once you start exporting your products you need to consider how you can protect your IP from being copied or stolen in countries where IP protection is less comprehensive than in the major economies. But you also need to make sure that you have cover in place in all of the markets that you are in or may want to export to in the future. Although copyright is an automatic right that applies worldwide, other intellectual property rights are not so comprehensive and may be non-existent unless you apply for and receive cover.

Patents

A patent is an exclusive right to make use of an invention commercially in return for disclosing it and as long as you pay the fees. A patent is valid for up to 20 years, subject to annual renewal. Applying for a patent is a long process and if you want cover for all major markets, it can be quite costly, so you should also consider whether there may be other ways to protect your invention such as using registered design, registered trademarks, copyright or through private agreements. You are unlikely to be granted a patent unless your process or product is new or inventive or if anything already exists that can be deemed to cover part of what your invention does, or the way that it does it. So before you even think of registering a patent, get expert advice. You can get advice by contacting a patent attorney or your local Chamber of Commerce. Bear in mind that you must not have publicly revealed your invention before you apply for the patent and that it can take up to four years to get your patent granted. Patents are territorial rights, so if your patent is granted in the UK, you will have the rights for the UK only. If you want protection in other countries as well, you have to apply for a patent in that country, through the European Patent Convention or through the Patent Co-operation Treaty. In the UK for example, applying for a patent currently costs £280. But if you ultimately want patent protection in all major economies, you will find the cost to be several thousands of pounds, with annual renewal fees for each country as well. This perhaps explains why most small and medium-sized companies only take out a patent if they are sure that it will result in a major revenue stream. But if you already have a patent and are moving into exporting your products, you need to make sure that your patent has been extended and is currently valid in the major markets where you intend to do business.

Trademarks

A trademark is a sign which is used to distinguish your goods and services from those of other traders. It can be a name or brand identity and usually includes words, logos or pictures or a combination of any of these. If you register a trademark, the rights can last forever (with renewals every 10 years). You can use a trademark as a marketing tool, which customers of your products will recognize. Goods and services are divided into classes and trademark applications and registrations must specify the classes that cover the goods and services that the trademark is going to be used on. In the UK a trademark application costs £200 for a single class and £50 for each additional class. As well as individual country applications, which can be made at your country's patent office, you can apply for an EU Community Trademark, valid for all countries in the European Union at the Office for Harmonization in the Internal Market (OHIM), **www.oami.europa.eu**.

Registered design rights

Design relates to the physical appearance of an item or part of it. This IP is not concerned with how the item works, but concentrates on the appearance resulting from the features of the product or the way that it looks. Features contributing to a product's appearance can include:

● lines;
● contours;
● colours;
● shape;
● texture;
● material.

Registered design protection lasts initially for five years and can be renewed every five years for up to 25 years. Again, you can apply for it at your country's patent office or for a registered community design (RCD), covering all EU countries via the OHIM. For example, in the UK, design registration costs £60 for the first design and £40 each for additional designs within the same application.

Copyright

Copyright lasts for the lifetime of the creator plus 70 years. (Broadcasting and sound recording copyright lasts for 50 years.) Copyright gives you protection against your work being copied or reproduced throughout much of the world. Copyright protects literary works, music, art and film.

Example

Some time ago, the group that I worked for decided to buy a German company with manufacturing facilities in Germany and India. I took over the sales and marketing management for the new company. Its distribution network covered Germany, Austria, Switzerland, France, Italy, Benelux and Scandinavia. We decided to expand the distribution network and were particularly interested in developing outlets in Spain, the United States and parts of Asia.

The company was very much a niche player, supplying specialist equipment to the food, pharmaceutical and chemical industries. There were a number of major competitors supplying similar products and our big selling point was our well-known and well-respected brand name. We set up distribution in Spain and printed product literature in Spanish. We also started advertising in the local technical press. Then we received a formal letter from a Spanish law firm saying that our brand name conflicted with a trademark owned by their client. I immediately asked our legal department to look into the matter and was horrified to find that the company had only registered the brand name as a trademark in their domestic market. We hurriedly arranged to get trademark protection in other major countries, where we were already selling the products and also in major countries that we intended to expand into. We did some research on the Spanish company that owned the trademark for Spain. They were a large company, but only traded domestically in Spain. Although there was some overlap with our products, they did not directly compete. Nevertheless, they decided that they would not allow us to use our own brand name in Spain. This meant that to sell the product in Spain we had to use another brand name that we owned and prepare new literature using this new brand name (which we registered as a trademark). The new brand name had no track record and no reputation. For us, Spain changed overnight from a top target market to a market with virtually no potential. After that, whenever we set about acquiring a new company, I made sure that we did checks on their patent and trademark coverage!

Avoiding litigation

When selling to a number of countries, including the United States, you also need to check your product literature to reduce product liability risks. Customers in the United States are much more likely to take legal action if your literature fails to warn of potential harm that could result from the misuse of your product.

Personal and company risk

There are unfortunately still many countries in the world where the risks of exporting are not just limited to financial risks. Crime, both organized and localized, terrorism, bribery and corruption can all be very real risks to companies and also to company personnel involved in exporting.

You should not underestimate the personal risks that you run if you ignore sensible security advice. On a trade mission to Moscow, a significant part of the briefing at the British Embassy concentrated on making sure that we were aware of the risks of travelling on the metro after dark, hailing down cabs in the street or of having drinks drugged in nightclubs and waking up in the street minus wallet, credit cards and passport.

Bribery and corruption are also major risks in some countries. You may be sure in your own mind that you would never get involved in bribery, but remember that bribery works in two directions and you may find that you are offered bribes and put under significant pressure (or threat) when you turn them down.

Example

This is a rather extreme example and I quote it just to make you aware of the ultimate personal risk. In the 1980s I was travelling back to the UK from the Far East and I picked up a newspaper on the plane. There was a short news story on one of the inside pages. It stated that a British engineer had been sentenced to life imprisonment in Iraq for bribery. I looked at the name again and realized that I knew the person involved. He worked for a company I had worked for several years earlier and although he was not a personal friend, I did know him. When I got back to the UK, I spoke to several colleagues at my old company and it appears that he was the resident engineer on an infrastructure project in Iraq. Although it is not completely clear what happened, it seems that there was a dispute over paperwork and before he knew what was happening, he was arrested, given a summary trial and sentenced, with no leave to appeal. He spent seven or eight years in an Iraqi jail and was only freed at the end of the first Gulf War.

Risk management and insurance services

So should you manage all of the risks of exporting yourself or should you use the services of a credit management and insurance provider? In many ways this would depend on the type and range of your export business, the expertise that you have in house and the attitude of top management.

There are two extremes: if you have a limited amount of export business that you are developing and most of your sales are through distributors whom you have been working with for some time, then you can probably handle all of the risk management yourself. If you supply items of capital equipment for major long-term projects that take several years to complete and your customers are mainly in developing countries, then you probably need to take out credit insurance such as ECGD (Export Credits Guarantee Department) cover for every contract.

In my experience, if you have a competent credit management team in house and managing the risks is company policy agreed by top management, then you can handle most of the risks of day-to-day business yourself, but should still take out export insurance for large one-off orders or contracts. But if your top management does not want to take any risks as you develop your export business and your margins are sufficient to cover the additional costs of a credit insurance policy, you should take one out. (Even if you do this, you still need to be sensible in assessing the risks that you take.)

If you decide to manage the risks yourself you need to have a team that will usually consist of senior personnel from your sales, finance and logistics departments. These personnel need to have the expertise and resources to:

- research the country and associated risks;
- gather credit and background information about existing and potential customers and distributors;
- decide when and where you need to rely on credit insurance;
- select the most appropriate and cost-effective policy;
- manage the credit insurance policy to get the best out of it.

Insurance products and services

The insurance product that you select will depend on your type of business, but the following are the main products that are available:

- An arrangement with a credit insurer to analyse your existing business, consider your future plans and cover the risks on your exports. The service can be set up to cover all of your export sales or just large or key accounts. It can also be limited to specific products or individual geographic areas.
- A one-off policy for a particular contract. This type of policy would take into account specific factors relating to this one contract. This type of policy is ideal for contracts that are much larger or of longer duration than your normal day-to-day business and is particularly well suited to the sale of capital or semi-capital goods, which are often sold on extended credit with staged payment terms. Policies of this type can be set up with your credit insurance company, but in the UK the main provider of this sort of policy is the Export Credits Guarantee service (ECGD).

● A Managed Credit Insurance scheme. This type of arrangement is particularly suited to small exporters or companies new to exporting.

The Association of British Insurers, **www.abi.org.uk**, can provide a list of credit insurance companies and details of specialist advisers can be obtained from the British Insurance Brokers Association (BIBA), **www.biba.org.uk**.

The major credit insurance companies have a long experience and understanding of the risks involved in international trade. They provide a professional approach to export risk management. By covering your commercial debts and making sure that you get paid even if your customer fails to pay, they help to provide your export sales team with the confidence that they need to maximize your export sales growth.

Summary

When dealing with overseas markets you will be dealing with different languages, different cultures, different business cultures and different legal systems. You can reduce the risks by researching your target markets thoroughly and by getting advice where necessary.

The country that you are dealing with may in itself present certain risks, as may the creditworthiness of your customers, which should be checked by running credit checks through international credit agencies such as Dun & Bradstreet. Financing credit and the risks involved is one of the most difficult problems facing would-be exporters. Steady growth in your export business is better than taking risks with credit to achieve rapid growth.

If you develop a significant export business, foreign currencies and the fluctuations of the foreign exchange market are certain to impact on your business. So you need to protect yourself against foreign exchange risks. If you decide to sell from a foreign currency price list, you need to understand that currency fluctuations will impact on your business. Forward exchange contracts can only protect your business for a limited period of time. They cannot protect your margins from long-term currency fluctuations.

Intellectual property rights (IPR) give legal protection to a person or company's intellectual property, preventing others from profiting from it commercially. The four main types of IPR that can be used to protect inventions or creations are patents, trademarks, designs and copyright.

In protecting your IPR you need to make sure that you protect them both in your home market and overseas.

There are still many countries in the world where the risks of exporting are not just limited to financial risks. Crime, both organized and localized, terrorism, bribery and corruption can be very real risks to companies and also to company personnel involved in exporting. You should not underestimate the personal risks that you run if you ignore sensible security advice.

The major credit risk insurance companies have a long experience and understanding of the risks involved in international trade and they provide companies with a professional approach to export risk management.

CHAPTER THIRTEEN

INDIVIDUAL EXPORT MARKETS

If you want detailed information on individual export markets, you can download country reports from government websites. At the time of writing, the basic country reports can be printed or downloaded as PDF files without the need to register on most sites. This means that anyone can take advantage of them.

The individual country guides available online from UK Trade & Investment (**www.ukti.gov.uk**), the US Commercial Service (**www.export.gov**) and Austrade (**www.austrade.gov.au**) are ideal for learning all of the basic information that you need to know when you start looking at an individual export market. But it is useful to have some key summary information for some of the world's major export markets readily available. The key characteristics of some major export markets and an indication of local business etiquette are given below.

Europe

Germany

- The largest economy in Europe, Germany has a population of over 81 million.
- The UK's largest European export market and the UK's number-two export market worldwide (after the United States).
- Its trading practices are open and there is therefore competition from all over the world.
- It has a very wide industrial base, so it is extremely unlikely that any product will not have any local competition.

- Key industries for exporters include vehicles and automotive components, aerospace, oil and gas, healthcare, IT, biotech and environmental engineering.
- Although there are many large German companies, the typical German company is small or medium sized – 99 per cent of all German companies are SMEs.
- Typical distribution would be based in Hamburg, Düsseldorf, Frankfurt, Stuttgart, Munich and Berlin.
- There is also potential to sell components to German companies that are exporting equipment or plant.

The Germans have a well-deserved reputation for efficiency and quality. To get into the German market you must be good at what you do and to stay there you must be able to stay ahead technically. You must be prepared to meet buyers' requirements in design, price, delivery and standards and your literature must be available in German.

In business the Germans tend to be formal (particularly in the south of the country) and people who have been working together for 20 years will still refer to each other as 'Herr Schmidt' or 'Doktor Schmidt'. You should do the same. The American style of using first names at first meetings is not acceptable in Germany.

France

- France is the largest country in Western Europe with a population of about 64 million.
- The French and British economies are fairly similar in size.
- French industrial development has tended to favour the consumer goods industries and vehicle production. France also has well-developed defence and nuclear industries.
- France has nearly 30 per cent of the EU's usable farmland, and agriculture is a major industry.
- France is also the world's top tourist destination, with about 80 million visitors a year.
- Twenty per cent of the population live in Paris, which has assumed an economic and commercial importance greater than that of any other city in France.
- Paris is the centre of industry, banking, insurance and foreign trade, but if you want your product to be sold all over France your

distributor needs to have branch offices in cities such as Lyon, Marseille, Bordeaux and Nantes.

- Since 2004 France has been developing what it calls 'pôles de compétitivité' (competitiveness clusters). These include aerospace in Bordeaux and Toulouse, electronics and telecoms in Rennes, and nanotechnology in Grenoble.
- France suffers (in the same way as the UK) from a narrow industrial base. This means that although in many industries there is stiff local competition, there are many gaps that offer potential for companies with the right type and quality of product.

A knowledge of the French language is essential if you want to do business in France. This knowledge can come from a French-speaking member of your company or from the staff of your distributor in France.

There are regional differences between Paris, the west and the south of the country, and business tends to be conducted in a more formal manner in Paris than in the provinces. In business the French tend to be distant rather than formal. They may not be punctual themselves, but they will expect you to be punctual. If you are late for an appointment you will be received coolly – if at all. It is true that you will be expected to shake hands at the start and end of meetings, but this is just a habit. It takes a long time to build up personal relationships when conducting business in France.

The United Kingdom

- The UK is the world's sixth-largest economy and is the third-largest in the EU after Germany and France.
- It has a population of about 63 million.
- It is the largest market in Europe for exports from the United States and India and is South Africa's fourth-largest export market worldwide.
- Because of its liberal business climate, it is often seen as the essential entry market to the EU.
- Key industry sectors for exporters include aerospace, automotive components, food and drink, IT products, medical equipment, security products, environmental technology, renewable energy, travel and tourism.
- London is a major international financial centre and transport hub.

- Although there is some heavy industry around London, light industry predominates, with much high-tech industry located along the M4 corridor. Heavy industry is mainly located in the West Midlands (Birmingham), the North West (Manchester) and around the Glasgow area.
- Ideally you should have a distributor with offices in both the north and the south of England. You cannot assume that a distributor based in England will be able to cover the whole of the UK. Because of both distance and cultural differences, you should consider having separate distribution in Scotland, Wales and Northern Ireland.

Although there are many similarities in how business is conducted in the UK and in the United States and Australia, the business culture in the UK is more conservative. The pace of business tends to be slower, except perhaps in London. British executives prefer a more formal approach and tend to communicate more by e-mail or letter than by phone. They expect prompt acknowledgement of correspondence and a longer lead time to appointment schedules. Cold calling is likely to meet with a frosty response. If you are setting up a first meeting, make contact several weeks before and follow up with information by post or e-mail. Most business people will wear suits, although 'smart casual' is becoming more widespread in some industries, particularly in IT and the creative industries. If in doubt, always wear a suit.

The UK is a base for many international and multinational companies from around the world. The modern UK business culture rewards enterprise. Many UK companies are entrepreneurial and interested in new ideas.

Italy

- The GDP of Italy is about the same as that of the UK.
- It has a population of about 60 million.
- It has a good infrastructure and is a highly sophisticated market.
- Per capita incomes in the north of the country are among the highest in Europe.
- Due to the absence of raw materials, the Italian economy is reliant on manufacturing and the processing of goods.
- Key products are machinery, food products, vehicles, electrical appliances, packaging, textiles and clothing, building materials and ceramics.

- Italian industry is well known at home and abroad for the design and style of their products.
- Industry is concentrated in the large cities of the north, and the south of the country is predominantly agricultural.
- A distributor or local company should be set up in the north where most industry is situated.
- Italy is home to a high number of trade exhibitions with global appeal. In 2015 Milan will host World Expo. This is an event on a world scale and will include many large infrastructure projects.
- The importance of Italy as an export market should not be underestimated.

The Italians are less formal than the Germans and less distant than the French. They are very conscious of their level and status within their company and titles are very important. They can be volatile in temperament, but are always charming – even when saying no. They are well known for their lack of punctuality and it is wise to check by telephone beforehand that your arranged meeting is still scheduled to take place. The Italians love to haggle – especially over price – and they are not well known for prompt payment. Nevertheless there are plenty of business opportunities in Italy and perseverance pays dividends in the long run.

Other European countries

None of the other European countries can compare with the UK, Germany, France, Italy and Russia in population and industrial size. The most common way of selling into the smaller countries is therefore through a local distributor. There is much French influence in Belgium. Holland and the Scandinavian countries have their own individual styles with which the British and the Germans are familiar. The Scandinavians in particular buy and sell high-quality state-of-the-art products. The cost of doing business in these countries reflects the high cost of living and standard of living that their citizens enjoy.

Of the old eastern European countries, Poland, Hungary and the Czech Republic have now developed into market economies. There are also good possibilities in neighbouring countries such as Romania and Bulgaria, where the infrastructure is not so well developed and this may deter your competitors and give you opportunities if you are prepared to persevere.

Other top export destinations

The United States

- The United States is the world's largest economy and the GDP of just one state – California – would rank among the top five nations of the world if it was a separate country.
- Current population is in excess of 310 million.
- The US economy encompasses every major industry and since the US market is so large in itself, many American companies can make a perfectly good living without ever getting involved in exporting.
- Many American companies are only active in one state or one area of the United States.
- In the United States very few products are sold directly to the end user. They are usually sold through wholesalers, distributors or agents.
- You cannot deal with a company in New Jersey and assume that this company will be able to sell your product throughout the United States.
- If you choose to sell in the United States through a local company, you will probably find that this restricts your business to the geographical areas where this company is strong.
- Distributors in the United States tend to be successful in specific industries such as aerospace, chemicals, pulp and paper, water treatment. If your product is sold into two completely different industries you would probably have to run two completely separate sets of distributors for these industries.
- You will probably need to get much of your product literature reprinted for the US market, because the US uses the quarto format and not A4. Written content should be checked locally to make sure that it will be readily understood (British English and American English are not the same!).
- You need to check your literature to reduce product liability risks.
- You need to check that your trademarks and branding can be used in the United States and that your products comply with US standards and have any necessary US certification.

The sheer size of the United States and the cultural differences from region to region mean that it should really be treated as a series of regional markets with differing characteristics. Regional immigration patterns affect different areas. The fast-growing Hispanic population is becoming increasingly important in all US markets, particularly in the south and in California.

Networking is very important in the US market. Passive business styles do not work well. To grow your business you need to be proactive and establish relationships, attend events and build your brand.

The business culture is faster and less formal than in the UK. Even if your host may be dressed smart casual, it is still wise to wear a suit or at least a jacket and tie to business meetings.

Japan

- Japan's economy is the third-largest in the world after the United States and China.
- It is the UK's largest export market after Europe and the United States.
- It has a population of 127 million. Japan's consumers are highly educated, demand the highest standards and are early adopters.
- Contrary to popular belief, Japan is an open economy and there are no barriers to exporting to Japan if you have good-quality products that have something to offer.
- Japanese industry includes not only large, well-known companies with cutting-edge technology supported by a large level of R&D spending but also much greater numbers of smaller companies.
- Prospects are good for companies manufacturing quality goods and components at reasonable prices.
- Japan is the world's largest manufacturer of motor vehicles and is a major force in semiconductors, electronic goods, computer software and games, machine tools and industrial robots.
- Tokyo is the commercial and financial centre of Japan.
- The bulk of Japanese industry and population is situated in the coastal plain from Tokyo to Osaka.
- The pace of doing business in Japan is much slower than in the United States or Europe. Much stock is placed on personal relationships and doing things in the proper manner.
- If you want to do business with Japan you need to understand Japanese business etiquette.

- The biggest barrier to trade in Japan is the complex distribution system and this is a problem for new Japanese companies as well as for exporters to Japan.
- To do anything in Japan you need a local presence – whether this is a distributor or a local company.
- The Japan External Trade Organization (Jetro), **www.jetro.go.jp**, has offices in most major industrialized countries to help promote imports to Japan.

If you want to do business with Japan you need to understand Japanese business etiquette. There are many books dealing with this complex subject and you would be wise to read one before starting to deal with the Japanese. In Japan, 'face' is all important. The Japanese language is very complicated and it takes at least a year of full-time study to achieve a reasonable conversational ability. The Japanese will be extremely pleased if a foreigner makes an attempt to learn a few simple words, but attempts to use a limited knowledge of the language for business conversation will normally be counterproductive. Interpreters should be used in all business dealings. It follows that you cannot just get onto a plane and set off to do business in Japan. The UKTI through its website and also through its Japan Desk can provide a wealth of information and support materials to UK exporters entering the Japanese market. Their 'Doing business in Japan' guide includes a section on Japanese business etiquette and culture with a very useful 'Ten top tips' for meetings and presentations.

Brazil, Russia, India, China (the BRICs)

Brazil

- Fifth-largest country in the world – larger than the USA, Australia or the whole of Western Europe.
- A population of 185 million.
- Rapidly expanding middle class.
- Brazil accounts for more than 50 per cent of the GDP of the whole of South America.
- GDP per head is higher than in either China or India.

- Key industries include oil and gas, advanced engineering, agriculture, environment, healthcare/biotech, pharmaceuticals, science, sports and leisure infrastructure.
- Ten-year energy plan with planned investments of over £150 billion in the first five years.
- Main business centre is São Paulo, but there are over a dozen other cities with populations of over a million.
- Brazil is a complex market and is for experienced exporters.

Brazilian business culture is largely European with considerable influence from Africa and Asia. Establishing personal relationships is essential to conducting business throughout the country. Rio de Janeiro and the north of the country have a more laid-back feel than São Paulo and the south. For business meetings in the big cities, always wear a suit and tie. Smart casual dress is not acceptable. Brazilians are not always punctual for meetings and you should not interpret lateness as a sign of rudeness or lack of interest. When arranging a meeting always provide details of the subject of the meeting in advance.

At business meetings in Brazil first names are normally used. Even so, titles are important and if someone is 'Doctor' you should address them as such. When meeting business contacts expect a firm handshake, combined with strong eye contact. Although large Brazilian companies with an international outlook may have English speakers on their staff, do not assume that everyone speaks English. It is advisable to take an interpreter to your initial meeting with a potential business partner. Do not assume that Spanish will be welcome. If you decide to try to use Spanish, start by apologizing for not speaking Portuguese, otherwise your host may think that you do not know that Brazilians speak Portuguese and not Spanish!

Russia

- The largest country in the world.
- A population of 142 million.
- Its GDP is about half that of the UK and it is the fourth-largest market in Europe.
- Russia possesses a wide range of mineral and energy resources.
- Key industries include oil and gas, aerospace, the automotive industry, engineering and pharmaceuticals.

- In the long term Russia is a market of great potential to exporters, but it is not an easy market to get into.
- Russia is a market for experienced exporters.

Other European and Asian companies provide tough competition due to their proximity to the Russian market and their long-standing relationships with much of Russian industry. A complicated and slow-moving bureaucracy, the poorly established rule of law, complicated product standards and certification requirements, and a very different business culture and etiquette constitute major barriers to entry. The UKTI guide 'Doing business in Russia' is 104 pages long, compared with about 16 pages for their standard country guides. This gives some indication of the complexities of doing business in Russia. In the guide itself they say 'This guide is aimed at companies experienced in overseas trade that are new to doing business with Russia.' Among the questions it asks potential exporters to consider is: 'Do you need to be involved in Russia at all?' I would suggest that you ask yourself that question. If you are new to exporting, try the more straightforward markets of the EU and United States before you consider looking at the potential for your products in a very difficult market like Russia.

India

- A population of 1.21 billion people makes India the second most populous country in the world after China.
- More importantly, it has a middle class population of about 300 million people.
- The Indian economy is now the second-fastest growing economy after China.
- It is projected that by 2030 the Indian economy will have overtaken all European countries, putting it fourth in size to the United States, China and Japan.
- The second-largest market for mobile phones after China, predicted to be in the top five vehicle producers by 2014, ranked third in the Asia-Pacific region based on the number of biotech companies in the country.
- Since the early 1990s India has removed most trade barriers. By 2009–10 the peak tariff rate was down from 72 per cent to just 10 per cent.

- Quantitative restrictions on imports ended in 2001.
- India is a collection of linked markets rather than simply one large market. There are a number of distinct regions with linguistic and cultural differences, varying customer preferences and expectations, and varying distribution requirements.
- Business opportunities exist in the traditional economic heartlands of Mumbai, Dehli and Bangalore but also in emerging cities such as Pune, Jaipur, Nagpur and Ahmedabad.
- English is widely spoken in business circles.
- India should not be ignored by experienced exporters.

The distances separating major cities are often large and this is compounded by the lack of an adequate transport infrastructure. Although this is gradually improving, the difficulties that this poses for effective supply and distribution should not be underestimated.

In large cities, business meetings are conducted as in Western countries. The most common greeting is 'Namaste' with the hands folded as in prayer. It is normal practice to exchange business cards. Etiquette requires the use of the right hand when giving or receiving. Business contacts are usually addressed as Mr/Mrs/Ms and the surname. The use of first names is not common. Superiors are often spoken to as 'Sir' or 'Madam' and business superiors and those more senior in age are almost always addressed formally. It is not customary for business associates to be entertained at home.

The UK India Business Council (UKIBC), **www.ukibc.com**, is the leading organization helping UK companies grow and develop their business in India.

China

- China's economy is now second only to the US economy in size.
- China is almost the same size as Europe, but with twice the population (1.35 billion people).
- A recent report by Goldman Sachs projects that China's GDP will overtake that of the United States by 2041.
- China is the largest global producer of cameras, computers, textiles, toys and many other products.
- It is the world's largest consumer of iron, steel, coal and cement.
- It is not a single national market. It is made up of over 30 different provinces and municipalities.

- In addition to the well-known business centres of Beijing, Shanghai, Guangzhou and Shenzhen there are 270 cities with populations of over a million.
- Seventy per cent of the Chinese population live in the eastern part of China.
- Rapid and continuous industrialization and urbanization have created a vast and fast-growing consumer market.
- China offers huge export opportunities to large and small companies, but the complexity of the market and the speed that it is changing mean that it is certainly a market for experienced exporters.

The Chinese set great store on building personal relationships. Their philosophy is that you should first build a relationship and if it is successful, commercial transactions will follow. This means that you may have to accept that it can take several visits just to get to know several possible candidates for business partnerships. Introductions via a trusted intermediary can play a valuable role in opening doors, but there are no short cuts to relationship building.

You need to carry out reliable research before even thinking of trying to enter the Chinese market. On the UKTI website, **www.ukti.gov.uk**, you can find a guide to doing business in China that has been prepared by the UKTI's China Markets Unit in collaboration with the British Embassies and Consulates in China and the China–Britain Business Council. Read this first! The UKTI website also has much more information and reports on China.

The China–Britain Business Council (CBBC), **www.cbbc.org**, is the leading organization helping UK companies grow and develop their business in China. They work closely with UKTI and have a network of nine offices in the UK and a presence in 11 Chinese cities. UKTI and CBBC organize a large number of business events, seminars and workshops in the UK and China. Details of these events can be found on the UKTI website or on the CBBC website at **www.cbbc.org/events/**. UKTI and CBBC organize regular trade missions to China and the UKTI OMIS service can be used to support visits. This is almost certainly the best way to arrange your first visit to China.

Summary

If you want detailed information on export markets, you can download individual country reports from government websites. Basic country reports can be printed or downloaded without the need to register on most sites, which means that anyone can take advantage of them. Both UK Trade & Investment and the US Commercial Service have individual country guides. These are called 'Doing business in...' guides and are produced for more than 100 individual countries. These 'Doing business in...' guides are ideal for learning all of the basic information that you need to know when you start looking at an individual export market, including important information on the local business culture and etiquette.

GOVERNMENT SUPPORT ORGANIZATIONS

Almost all governments provide support for their exporters. This is just a small cross-section of the organizations in some major exporting countries.

UK

UK Trade & Investment (UKTI), **www.ukti.gov.uk**, was established by the UK government to assist UK exporters. UKTI has developed a national export strategy that for the first time consolidates all government support for exporters under one organization, integrating the activities of the Department of Trade and Industry, the Foreign and Commonwealth Office, overseas embassies and regional and local providers of export services in the UK. (According to information on their website, UKTI has a staff of over 2,400 people in 96 countries with a network of International Trade Advisers (ITAs) in the UK regions.)

In May 2011, UKTI launched its new five-year strategy 'Britain open for business', which sets out its plans to provide practical support to exporters and inward investors over the next five years. The key parts of the export strategy involve:

- targeting services at innovative and high-growth SMEs to encourage more companies to export, and help existing exporters reach more high-growth and emerging markets;
- winning high-value opportunities in overseas markets for UK businesses of all sizes.

As well as continuing to provide support to exporters selling to established export markets, UKTI has identified 19 priority high-growth and emerging markets where they will shift their resources to help UK exporting companies to seize opportunities. They are also introducing programmes of sector-based support across a range of innovative and technology-rich sectors, including advanced manufacturing, defence and security, infrastructure, healthcare and life sciences, and services.

In 2010 UKTI was named as the best trade promotion organization from a developed country by the International Trade Centre's Trade Promotion Organization (TPO) at the TPO awards in Mexico City. The award cited the excellence of UKTI's 'Gateway to global growth' programme. In 2009 UKTI supported 25,000 UK companies and created an additional £35 billion of exports which created £5 billion of additional profits for these companies.

United States

The US Department of Commerce and International Trade provides government support to US exporters. The US Commercial Service is the trade promotion arm of the US Department of Commerce's International Trade Administration. It uses the US government's export portal, **www.export.gov**, as its main online resource for US exporters for market research, trade events, trade leads and information on how to export. The US Commercial Service has a network of international trade specialists based in Export Assistance Centers in more than 100 cities throughout the United States. Services offered include market intelligence, trade counselling, business matchmaking and trade advocacy.

Australia

The Australia Trade Commission (Austrade), **www.austrade.gov.au**, provides support to Australian exporters. TradeStart is an Australian government initiative that delivers services through local public sector and industry organizations throughout Australia. Austrade/TradeStart programmes include 'Getting into export', which is designed to help potential exporters to develop the skills and knowledge that they need to start exporting, and the 'Global opportunities' (GO) programme, which provides export and investment facilitation services and funding support over a three-year period to eight industry clusters to help them expand their international business. Financial support is also available through the Export Market Development Grant scheme (EMDG).

Canada

The Trade Facilitation Office Canada (TFO Canada), **www.tfocanada.ca**, provides exporter training not just for Canadian companies but also to help exporters in developing countries to export to Canada. Services provided include exporter training, trade information portals, technical regulations, packaging, product adaptation and government-led export promotion.

China

The China Council for the promotion of International Trade (CCPIT), **http://english.ccpit.org**, is the largest and most important institution for the promotion of foreign trade in China. Its aims are to operate and promote foreign trade and foreign investment. It also operates under the name of the China Chamber of International Commerce.

India

The India Trade Promotion Organization (ITPO), **www.indiatradefair.com**, is the key government agency for promoting the country's external trade. It has been operating for nearly 30 years in the form of the Trade Fair Authority of India and the Trade Development Authority. Its promotional tools include organizing fairs and exhibitions in India and abroad, contact promotion programmes, product promotion programmes, buyer–seller meets, overseas department stores, market surveys and information dissemination.

South Africa

The main government organization supporting South African exporters is the Department of Trade and Industry (DTI), **www.thedti.gov.za**. The DTI markets South African exports internationally with teams operating from regional offices around the world providing market intelligence and identifying opportunities for South African companies. Their specialists concentrate on specific industrial sectors such as automotive, chemicals and mining, and offer advice on export processes and procedures. The DTI also provides incentives to exporters – with a special focus on small, medium and micro enterprises (SMMEs) and black economic empowerment (BEE) exporters – through the Export Marketing and Investment Assistance (EMIA) scheme.

New Zealand

New Zealand is a country of mainly small businesses. Only 4 per cent of companies employ more than 20 staff and a total of only 625 businesses are responsible for 91 per cent of merchandise exports. The New Zealand government established New Zealand Trade and Enterprise (NZTE), **www.nzte.govt.nz**, in 2003. NZTE's model takes an integrated approach to economic development that includes a focus on investment, trade, export and domestic capability to overcome the challenges of lack of scale and distance. Programmes include 'Path to market' which helps companies assess and realize their export potential, 'Beachheads', which is designed to help companies expand their presence in international markets and accelerate their market share, and 'Better by design', which helps to boost economic growth by the better use of design.

Some other major exporters

- Germany – Trade and Invest, **www.gtai.de**;
- France – Ministry for Foreign trade, **www.exporter.gouv.fr**;
- Italy – Istituto Nazionale per il Commercio Estero, **www.ice.gov.it**;
- Japan – Jetro, **www.jetro.go.jp**.

USEFUL WEBSITES

Government support for exporters – UK

www.ukti.gov.uk – government organization providing support for exporters, including market reports, country reports and support for exhibitions, trade missions, etc

www.businesslink.gov.uk – the government's online resource for businesses; the site includes support material for exporters

www.export.org.uk – Institute of Export

www.bis.gov.uk – Department for Business Innovation & Skills (BIS)

www.britishchambers.org.uk/zones/export – British Chambers of Commerce export information

www.sitpro.org.uk – Archived website of SITPRO, the UK trade facilitation agency

Government support for exporters – other countries

www.export.gov – US Department of Commerce

www.buyusa.gov – US Commercial Service overseas websites

www.austrade.gov.au – Australia Trade Commission

www.tfocanada.ca – Trade Facilitation Office of Canada

http://english.ccpit.org – China Council for the Promotion of International Trade

www.cbbc.org – China–Britain Business Council

www.indiatradefair.com – India Trade Promotion Agency (ITPO)

www.ukibc.com – UK India Business Council

www.thedti.gov.za – Department of Trade and Industry, South Africa

www.nzte.govt.nz – New Zealand Trade and Enterprise

www.jetro.go.jp – Japan External Trade Organization

www.gtai.de – Trade and Invest, Germany

www.exporter.gouv.fr – French Ministry for Foreign Trade
www.ice.gov.it – Istituto Nazionale per il Commercio Estero (Italy)

Other useful sites for exporters

www.wto.org – World Trade Organization
www.worldchambers.com – World Chambers Network, official global portal of Chambers of Commerce
www.iccwbo.org – International Chambers of Commerce
www.wcoomd.org – World Customs Organization
www.iccbookshop.com – ICC United Kingdom Bookshop (supplier of information on Incoterms)
www.europa.eu – European Union website
www.census.gov – US Census Bureau (administers Schedule B codes)
www.bifa.org – British International Freight Association
www.abi.org.uk – Association of British Insurers
www.biba.org.uk – British Insurance Brokers Association (BIBA)
www.tis-gdv.de – Transport Information service of the German Insurance Association
www.exportuk.co.uk – UK Exporters Ltd (publishers of British Exporters CD; offer international press release service, agent finder service and membership of British Exporters Club)

Government statistics

www.ons.gov.uk – Office for National Statistics (government statistics, including economy, regional trends, consumer trends and product sales reports (Prodcom information))
http://epp.eurostat.ec.europa.eu – Eurostat, provider of European statistics
www.thestationeryoffice.com – Largest supplier of official publications, both online and with various branches around the UK

Financial data

www.dnb.co.uk – Dunn & Bradstreet, financial information on
   companies

Market and sector reports

www.ukti.gov.uk
www.export.gov
www.euromonitor.com
www.frost.com – Frost & Sullivan
www.keynote.co.uk
www.eiu.com – Economist Intelligence Unit, country reports

Market research organizations

www.marketresearch.org.uk – Market Research Society
www.esomar.org – European Society for Opinion and Market Research
www.britishchambers.org.uk/emrs – UK government's export
   marketing research scheme

Trade associations

www.taforum.org – Trade Association Forum (find trade associations
   in your industry)

Trade and specialized directories

www.kompass.co.uk
www.kellysearch.com
www.yell.com – Yellow Pages
www.nridigital.com – information on industries and projects

Internet

www.nominet.org.uk – holder of UK domain names
www.hostingreview.com – reviews of web hosting companies

Distribution law

www.kemplittle.com – law firm specializing in distribution and
agency law

Intellectual property

www.ipo.gov.uk – Intellectual Property Office: patents, trademarks,
copyright
www.uspto.gov – US Patent and Trademark Office

Other general sources

www.oecd.org – Organisation for Economic Co-operation and
Development: GDP data and a wide range of statistics for OECD
members
www.eiu.com – Economist Intelligence Unit
www.kompass.com – 'the business-to-business search engine'
www.worldatlas.com – worldwide country information
www.wikipedia.org – free online encyclopedia
www.cia.gov – CIA website. Publishes *World Factbook*

APPENDIX 1

Types of government support services available

To show how extensive and helpful the tools and services offered by these government organizations can be, this section provides an outline of the services available to UK exporters from UKTI. Similar and equivalent support services are available to exporters in many countries from their local government support agencies, so this is a really essential avenue to investigate.

Example: government support available to exporters in the UK

The UKTI website, **www.ukti.gov.uk**, and the Business Link website, **www.businesslink.gov.uk**, provide the online interface for UK companies seeking export support. Although both sites cover a lot of the same subjects, the material and guides that you can download from the UKTI site is more related to export markets, market sectors, help in entering specific markets, making overseas visits, taking part in overseas exhibitions, trade missions, and so on. Typical guides include 'Doing business in France' and 'Making the most of your exhibition'. Although some of these subjects are covered on the Business Link site (and there are crosslinks between the sites), in addition Business Link has much more information on the 'nuts and bolts' of shipping your goods abroad. They have a wealth of information on things like export documentation requirements, customs regulations, VAT requirements, export insurance, etc and typical guides that you can download include 'International paperwork: the basics', 'International transport and distribution' and 'Getting paid when selling overseas'.

UKTI have a number of interactive assessment tools on their website. These include a questionnaire that will help you recognize your strengths and isolate your weaknesses as you get ready to break into export markets. There is also a tool to allow you to identify export opportunities in any chosen market.

How to start using the service

If you enter your postcode on the UKTI website it will bring up the name and contact information for your nearest International Trade Adviser. You can then call or e-mail this adviser for specific information and guidance. (But before you contact an adviser, it is worthwhile downloading some basic information to read through and even perhaps making an initial assessment yourself.)

UKTI's International Trade Advisers can provide professional advice on their range of services, including financial subsidies, export documentation, contacts in overseas markets, overseas visits, e-commerce, export training and market research. Virtually all of the UKTI programmes are personalized and specifically adapted to the requirements of individual businesses. Your adviser will identify if your company is new to exporting (in which case they will offer a set of services including 'Passport to export') or if your company is an experienced exporter (in which case they will offer services including 'Gateway to global growth').

Support is available for companies of all sizes and with all levels of export experience, but schemes that offer financial support or grants are normally restricted to what UKTI defines as small and medium-sized enterprises (SMEs). These are independent companies with less than 250 employees, with an annual turnover not exceeding 50 million euros or an annual balance sheet total not exceeding 43 million euros.

Individual services offered by UKTI

I will cover the main services below, but I would mention that programmes on offer may vary and may be changed from time to time and the financial support offered may be increased or cut, depending on changes in government spending. Also, new web pages will be added and some will be withdrawn. Nevertheless, having used the services for many years, I can assure you that the general trend has been to continually improve the service available and if financial support is withdrawn from one area, it is usually soon reintroduced in another.

Passport to export

Passport to export is a skills-based programme that provides new and inexperienced exporters with the training, planning and ongoing support that they need to succeed overseas. It offers a business health check, mentoring from one of their local export professionals, an individual export plan and a range of developmental training from which to choose.

Export Marketing Research Scheme (EMRS)

This is a subsidized service that the British Chambers of Commerce administer on behalf of UKTI. It helps companies carry out export marketing research on all major aspects of any export venture. This can include:

- market size and segmentation;
- regulations and legislation;
- customer needs, usage and attitudes;
- distribution channels;
- trends;
- competitor activity, strategy and performance.

Companies with fewer than 250 employees may be eligible for grants of up to 50 per cent of the agreed costs of export market research projects.

Overseas Market Introduction Service (OMIS)

OMIS is a service by which, for a competitive fee, you can commission research into a particular market. This can include preparation of a list of potential distributors in the country and even help in setting up meetings with these potential distributors. OMIS uses the services of the UKTI trade teams located in the British embassies, high commissions and consulates across the world. Using their local staff means that you have access to their local language skills, market knowledge and commercial and political contacts.

Tradeshow Access Programme

The Tradeshow Access Programme provides support for participants in overseas exhibitions and seminars. Participation is usually as part of a group, which is a big advantage for inexperienced businesses. The group is often on a UK stand, which is split into individual sub-stands for the participating companies. Grants are available to help SMEs with the cost of overseas exhibitions that are supported by the programme.

Sector-focused missions

Sector-focused trade missions last between three and eight days. Small businesses taking part in these trade missions are eligible for travel grants to cover up to half the cost of the visit. The missions are often specific to a particular industry or event. The process works in a similar way to exhibition support and is often managed by a Chamber of Commerce. They are an ideal way to visit a market that you are unfamiliar with and you can gain from the experience of the UKTI mission leader and others on the mission as well as from the local contacts that you make.

Other services for experienced exporters

Some of the services mentioned above, such as the OMIS and the EMRS, are used by experienced exporters as much as by newcomers. But there are some additional services that are specifically aimed at helping experienced exporters to grow their business.

Gateway to global growth

This is UKTI's flagship package for experienced exporters. It is a free service which offers companies a strategic review, planning and support to help them grow their business overseas. The solutions suggested could be complex and in some cases they may require services offered by other public and private sector companies as well as specific services offered by UKTI. They may require the acquisition of specialist information and skills or guidance on how to achieve specific objectives.

Overseas Market Introduction Service (OMIS)

This service will be extended with two new services for experienced exporters that will be piloted in 2012 – Global OMIS to provide longer-term support for larger companies who want to use UKTI services around the world to secure multiple orders and a bespoke service (linked to a success fee for UKTI) to help companies to win major trade contracts using dedicated UKTI and external specialist resources.

Export Communications Review (ECR)

This service is offered by the British Chambers of Commerce to provide companies with impartial and objective advice on language and cultural issues to help them to develop an effective communications strategy to improve their competitiveness in their existing and future export markets. It offers companies an on-site review of the way that they currently communicate with their export markets. Typically, this would include a review of the company's website and written materials and could also include meetings with the company's customers and agents/distributors. The reviews are carried out by accredited export communications consultants, who have been trained in export communications by the British Chambers of Commerce.

The Business Opportunities Service

The Business Opportunities Service is a free service providing sales leads that come via UKTI's global contacts network. Over 400 business opportunities are published each month. These may come from any industry sector in over 100 overseas markets. The leads range from market pointers to private sector opportunities, multilateral aid agency tenders to public sector leads. Any UK company can register for this service on the UKTI website. When you receive a lead that is of interest, you can contact the UKTI staff member who posted the opportunity to request more specific information if you need it or the contact details for the company.

High-Value Opportunities programme

Very large-scale, high-value international projects and contracts offer enormous opportunities for businesses of all sizes. This programme offers intensive 'high-level' support for larger companies seeking overseas contracts ranging in value from £250 million to £1 billion, with supply chain opportunities for SMEs.

Partnership with ECGD

UKTI and ECGD will work together to promote the Export Enterprise Finance Guarantee (ExEFG) to SMEs to guarantee lenders who facilitate the provision of short-term export finance lines of up to £1 million to exporting SMEs. Other new products include a bond support scheme to help exporters to raise tender and contract bonds, an export working capital scheme to facilitate access to working capital for specific export contracts and a foreign exchange credit support scheme to help exporters manage their exposure to foreign exchange rate movements.

Other services

Online peer self-help: UKTI is developing an online network of UK companies, so that they can support each other and share knowledge in order to internationalize their business. The online content will include financial, sector and market data, as well as information based on the practical experience and wisdom of users. This service will be rolled out during the course of 2012.

Social media: The UKTI website, **www.ukti.gov.uk**, was revamped in 2010 and is now state of the art with improved functionality and navigation. There are integrated social media feeds to the UKTI blog, Twitter, Flickr, YouTube and LinkedIn.

Springboard magazine: UK Trade & Investment publishes a magazine, *Springboard*, six times a year. This is free and you subscribe at **http://springboard.managemyaccount.co.uk**. Springboard includes news and updates on UKTI initiatives, features on export success stories, interviews with successful exporters and entrepreneurs, country focus articles and a directory of events.

APPENDIX 2
Example of a complete export plan

Precision Vacuum Products is a company based in the south of England. The company was founded 10 years ago and manufactures specialist components such as valves and measuring equipment used in vacuum systems. The company has rapidly expanded and now has a turnover of over £5 million. It has decided that further growth prospects in its domestic market are limited and has decided to look at exporting as a way to grow its business further. It has developed an export strategy and prepared the export plan that is shown below.

Export plan – Precision Vacuum Products

Contents

Executive summary
Introduction
1 Export Policy Commitment Statement
2 Situation/background analysis
 – Products
 – Operations
 – Personnel and export organization
 – Resources
 – Industry structure, competition and demand
3 Marketing
 – Identifying, evaluating and selecting target markets
 – Product selection and pricing
 – Distribution methods

   - Terms and conditions
   - Internal organization and procedures
   - Sales goals: profit and loss forecasts
4 Tactics: action steps
   - Primary target countries
   - Secondary target countries
   - Indirect marketing efforts
5 Export Budget
   - Pro forma financial statements
6 Implementation schedule
   - Follow-up
   - Periodic and management review (measuring results against plan)

   Addenda
   - Background data on target countries and market
   - Basic market statistics: historical and projected
   - Background facts
   - Competitive environment

Executive summary

After the rapid growth of recent years, we now feel that we are reaching the limit of expansion in our domestic market. Moving into export will allow us to widen our customer base and reduce our reliance on our domestic customers. The increased turnover will allow us to increase our production levels and improve the viability of our combined pressure switch/controllers.

Germany, Austria and Italy appear to offer the best prospects and we will initially target these markets. We intend to take part in the METALTECH 20X4 Exhibition in Düsseldorf in June of next year using government support and to set up distribution in Germany and Austria before the end of 20X4. To support this effort we will prepare German-language sales literature and appoint a German-speaking export sales manager. We will also use government support to find and appoint distribution in Italy before the end of 20X5.

We intend to develop export sales of at least £1.25 million annually by 20X6, both through distribution and by targeting key OEM customers. We see Germany as the market with most potential and aim to achieve sales in Germany of at least £800,000 by 20X6. By this time we expect to be generating annual sales to export OEMs of at least

£700,000. This expansion will help us to increase sales of combined pressure switch/controllers to 800 units a year, with half of these sales coming from our export business.

Introduction

The company was founded 10 years ago and since we introduced our range of controllers five years ago, our turnover has rapidly increased. Nearly 80 per cent of our turnover comes from our five main customers. Not only does this leave us vulnerable to changes in the marketplace, but also we see limited scope for significant growth in our domestic market. For this reason, we have decided to look at exporting to continue to grow our business.

Export policy commitment statement

We have decided to grow our business by exporting our electronic pressure switches and controllers. We have expanded rapidly in the last five years, but further growth in our domestic market is difficult, because we are already supplying most of the large users and exporting offers us much better opportunities. We intend to concentrate on developing sales in Germany, Austria and Italy. We will set up distribution in these countries and also target key OEMs.

Situation/background analysis

Products: Although we will offer our full range of equipment, including our vacuum valves, we believe that the main potential for us in our target markets is in pressure switches and controllers. In particular we see great potential for our combined pressure switch/controller. We also see potential for developing complimentary products such as a combined pressure switch/controller with an attached vacuum valve.

Operations: We have adequate capacity to expand production to meet the expected additional demand from export sales. If we achieve our target of doubling sales of combined pressure switch/controllers, this will help to increase the utilization of the Xonor machine from 45 per cent to 90 per cent.

Personnel and export organization: We have adequate internal sales resources to handle the export business initially, although we may need to recruit an additional internal sales person in the second or third year of the plan. We will appoint an experienced export sales manager to develop and manage the export business. Our sales director will concentrate on UK sales and overall marketing and will initially provide support to the export sales manager in dealing with key OEM customers.

Resources: We will have to fund ATEX testing and certification for the combined pressure switch/controller with an attached valve in order to sell it into the chemical industry. Apart from that the main additional costs of this plan will be sales and marketing costs.

Industry structure, competition and demand: All of the countries that we are targeting have major domestic vacuum pump manufacturers and major OEMs. This means that the demand for vacuum components and equipment is high. The market is much bigger than just the local markets, because at least 50 per cent of vacuum systems manufactured in the target countries are exported to countries such as China, Russia, India and Brazil. Our research tells us that our potential customers prefer to buy combined units to reduce the amount of in-house engineering that they have to do. The vacuum-coating systems market in particular is a quality 'high-price' market.

Marketing

Selecting target markets: We carried out a full evaluation of a number of potential target markets. We ruled out Poland and Russia, because of local competition and the lower price level of the markets. We decided to delay attempts to enter the US market until we have modified our products and obtained technical approvals. Our evaluation showed Germany offering the most potential, followed by Austria and Italy.

Products/pricing: We have used marginal costing to set the export prices for our pressure switch/controllers. As sales increase and utilization of the Xonor machine improves, actual margins will also improve.

Distribution methods: We will set up distribution for all markets using distributors with a good technical knowledge of the vacuum industry and vacuum systems. We will sell directly to key major OEMs.

Internal organization: Jenny Philby will take over internal sales for the new export business. She will continue to handle Vacuum Industries Ltd in the UK because of her good contacts within the company. John Markley will take over her other UK business. The new export sales manager will handle outside sales for the new markets with support from our sales director for key OEM customers. There will be no changes in finance or logistics.

Objectives:

- to increase export sales from zero in 20X3 to £1.25 million in 20X6;
- to increase sales to Germany to £800,000 by 20X6;
- to increase sales to Austria to £200,000 by 20X6;
- to increase sales to Italy to £250,000 by 20X6;
- to gain annual sales to export OEMs of £700,000 by 20X6;
- to increase export sales of combined pressure switch/controllers to 400 units a year within three years.

Sales goals:

				Forecast		
Year (all values in £k)	20X1	20X2	20X3	20X4	20X5	20X6
Germany				150	300	800
Austria				50	100	200
Italy					100	250
Total				250	500	1250

Tactics: action steps

Primary target countries

Our primary target countries are Germany, Austria and Italy. These countries are all part of the EU, which means that shipping and paperwork arrangements will be straightforward. Germany is by far the largest of the target markets for our products, being nearly twice as large as the Italian market. There are more potential customers in Germany than in either of the other two markets. German and Italian competitors are active in all of the markets, but we have a specific advantage with our combined pressure switch/controllers, which none of our competitors possesses. We feel that there are more barriers to entry into the Italian market, because there are fewer potentially qualified distributors and because the market in Italy is led more by price than quality (when compared to the German and Austrian markets).

Secondary target countries

The United States is also of interest, but we have decided to make it a secondary target because we need to modify the products which are all fully metric and we also need to have their products tested at the Vacuum Institute in Atlanta in order to get the technical approvals required for the US market. We will develop a suitable product and aim to get approvals within two years, so that we can then consider entering this market.

Strategies

Products

● Apply for ATEX certification for combined pressure switch/ controller with attached vacuum valve.

Pricing

● Determine sensible list price level for target markets.
● Produce euro price list and enter pricing into system.

Promotion

● Produce German version of main sales brochure and data sheets for pressure switches and controllers.
● Take part in METALTECH 20X4 exhibition in Düsseldorf in June 20X4 as part of the UK stand.

Place

● Use the Overseas Market Introduction Service to find and evaluate potential distributors.
● Use participation in METALTECH 20X4 to further evaluate potential distributors.

People

● Recruit export sales manager (ideally German speaking).
● Organize export training for key internal staff in sales, shipping and finance.

Processes

- Enter HS codes into the system for all standard items and modify order-handling system to make sure that orders can only be entered onto the system for items with a valid HS code.

Export budget

Partial profit and loss account (excluding fixed cost allocation):

	20X4 £k	20X5 £k	20X6 £k
Invoiced sales	250.0	500.0	1250.0
Cost of sales	100.0	200.0	500.0
Gross profit	250.0	300.0	750.0
Sales and marketing costs:			
Salaries	45.0	62.0	65.0
Recruitment	10.0		
Travel costs	10.0	15.0	20.0
Mobile phone	5.0	6.0	7.0
Literature	8.0	14.0	10.0
Exhibitions	30.0	35.0	40.0
Advertising	15.0	20.0	20.0
Sundry items	10.0	10.0	10.0
Total sales and marketing costs	130.0	162.0	172.0
Distribution costs	7.5	15.0	37.5
Total operating expenses (relating to plan)	137.5	177.0	209.5
Operating profit (relating to plan)	112.5	123.0	540.5

Implementation schedule:

Master schedule Year: 20X6			
Month	1 2 3 4 5 6 7 8 9 10 11 12		
Action plan		Dept	Person
German literature	⟶	Marketing	AJT
METALTECH 20X4	⟶	Sales/Marketing	MBN
OMIS Germany/ Austria	⟶	Sales/Marketing	MBN
Italian literature	⟶	Marketing	AJT
OMIS Italy	⟶	Sales/Marketing	MBN

This plan will be reviewed every 12 months or more frequently if conditions require.

Addenda:

Background data on target countries and market
Basic market statistics: historical and projected
Background facts
Competitive environment

APPENDIX 3

Example of an export marketing plan

The Pure Fruit Jam Company is a UK manufacturer of specialist jams and marmalades. They have been exporting for a number of years and each year they prepare a marketing plan for their domestic market and a separate marketing plan for their export business. These plans feed into their budgeting process towards the end of each year. When they decide to develop sales in a new export market, they prepare a marketing plan specifically for that market. As part of the expansion of their export sales they are targeting Japan and the United States. They have prepared individual marketing plans for both of these markets. Their sub-plan for the Japanese market is shown below.

Marketing plan for Japan

Contents

1 Introduction
2 Executive summary
3 Situation analysis
  – Assumptions:
  – Sales (history/budget)
  – Key products
  – Strategic markets
  – Key sales areas
4 Marketing objectives
5 Marketing strategies

6 Schedules
7 Sales promotion
8 Budgets/P&L accounts
9 Controls and update procedures

Appendices

1. Introduction

The Pure Fruit Jam Company is a manufacturer of specialist jams and conserves. The company uses only fresh fruits and ingredients and we have had considerable success with the trend towards organic and non-synthetic products. We intend to build on our success. We only started in the export market five years ago and have made considerable progress, so that export sales now represent 20 per cent of our total sales.

2. Executive summary

We have been working at the Japanese market for three years and have made some progress with sales of our gift packs and mini gift packs through the Seikokku Group. Seikokku are an upmarket department store with in-house food markets. We have also had success with the Golden Apricot hotel chain with our mini pots.

We will be repackaging gift packs and adding a mandarin orange marmalade and a sake-flavoured marmalade range. These products will be packaged with local-style packaging and may be sold as own label products through prestige stores such as Seikokku.

We are using government grants to produce Japanese sales literature and also to support taking part in the Nippon Food Show in Osaka as part of the British Pavilion.

Our contracts with Golden Apricot and Seikokku have given us good experience of how business is carried out in Japan. The Japanese like UK quality food products, which are considered to be very chic. With the prestige of British quality products we are confident of major expansion here. We consider there to be considerable potential for our products and plan to increase sales from £50k to £300k within the next three years.

3. Situation analysis

3.1 Assumptions

- Japanese GDP will continue to grow at a rate of 2 per cent per year over the next three years.
- The pound sterling will not strengthen against the yen during the timescale of the plan.

3.2 Sales (history/budget)

Sales area: Japan: total sales

				Forecast		
Year (all values in £k)	**20X3**	**20X4**	**20X5**	**20X6**	**20X7**	**20X8**
Marmalades (340 g)				15	40	60
Mini pots			20	60	105	150
Gift packs			30	45	80	90
Total	0	0	50	120	225	300

3.3 Key products

Gift packs

Gift packs consist of either two specialist standard-size jars of jam or marmalade or six mini pots of different flavours. This business has really taken off with Seikokku and we hope to secure other major contracts shortly.

Mini pots

We sell mini pots mainly to hotels and airlines. The Golden Apricot Hotel Group have started taking significant amounts of this product and we are near to securing a contract with the No Vacancies Group. We are also optimistic about securing contracts with major airlines. Our discussions with Japan Airlines are well advanced.

Marmalades

We have had no success with our full size jars of our standard marmalades, but Seikokku have expressed an interest in our whisky-flavoured marmalades and we have also agreed to manufacture mandarin orange marmalade and sake-flavoured marmalades for them.

3.4 Strategic markets

Our strategic markets are supermarkets/department stores and hotel chains. We are also optimistic about selling to Japan Airlines and All Nippon Airlines for their first-class cabins. Sales in these markets for 20X5 and forecasts for 20X6 to 20X8 are given below:

Sales in Japan by strategic market

Year (all values in £k)	20X3	20X4	20X5	Forecast 20X6	Forecast 20X7	Forecast 20X8
Quality shops/ supermarkets			30	60	120	150
Hotels			20	40	70	100
Airlines				20	35	50
Total	0	0	50	120	225	300

Supermarkets/department stores

This is a major market for us in the UK and in Japan it was our first success with the Seikokku chain taking our gift packs and mini gift packs. We are optimistic that we can sign up other chains that operate more in the west of Japan.

Hotel chains

Golden Apricot Hotel Group have started taking significant amounts of our mini pots and we are near to securing a contract with the No Vacancies Group.

Airlines

We have no business at present with Japanese airlines, but we are optimistic about selling to Japan Airlines and All Nippon Airlines for their first-class cabins.

3.5 Key sales areas

Year (all values in £k)	20X3	20X4	20X5	Forecast 20X6	Forecast 20X7	Forecast 20X8
East Japan			35	80	150	200
West Japan			15	35	65	180
Hokkaido				5	10	20
Total			50	120	225	300

East Japan

This area encompasses greater Tokyo and most of the eastern side of Japan. Our main contacts are in Tokyo and we have had major success with Seikokku, whose head office is there. We want to find other business through companies with their head offices and central purchasing in the Tokyo area. We are hoping to conclude a deal with the No Vacancies Group based in Shinagawa.

West Japan

This area is based on Osaka and covers the area also to the west. We have had success here with the Golden Apricot Hotel Group.

Hokkaido

We have been contacted by a chain of hot springs resorts on the northern island of Hokkaido. We have sent samples and are waiting to see the results.

4. Marketing Objectives

- to grow sales in Japan from £50,000 to £300,000 within three years;
- to increase our sales of mini pots to hotels from £20k to £100k within three years;
- to gain £50k a year of sales of mini pots to airlines within three years;
- to increase sales to quality shops/supermarkets to £150k within three years;
- to grow sales of gift packs from £30k to £90k within three years;
- to sell £60k a year of specialist marmalades in Japan within three years.

5. Marketing strategies

Product

- Repackage gift packs for the Japanese market – information in Japanese, but retain British quality feel.
- Add sake-flavoured marmalade to range.

Pricing

- Premium price alcohol-flavoured marmalades – particularly whisky and brandy.

Promotion

- Use government grant to produce Japanese sales literature.
- Take part in Nippon Food Show in Osaka as part of the British Pavilion, using government grant support.

Distribution

- Use British Embassy commercial section to help find representative in Osaka (for west of Japan) using the Overseas Market Introduction Service (OMIS).

6. Schedules

Master schedule Year: 20X6			
Month	1 2 3 4 5 6 7 8 9 10 11 12		
Action plan		Dept	Person
Japanese literature	———→	Marketing	LFR
Nippon Food Show	——→	Sales/Marketing	JNM
OMIS Japan	——————→	Sales/Marketing	JNM
Marmalade launch	—————→	Marketing	LFR
Press advertising	———————————→	Marketing	LFR

7. Sales promotion

We will not require any additional staff for our Japanese expansion project. We will be repackaging gift packs and adding a sake-flavoured marmalade range for the Japanese market. We are using government grants to produce Japanese sales literature and also to support taking part in the Nippon Food Show in Osaka as part of the British Pavilion. We will use the Nippon Food Show to relaunch our premium whisky- and brandy-flavoured marmalades. We will also be using the Overseas Market Introduction Service (OMIS) to help find a representative in Osaka to cover the west of Japan.

The costs of advertising expenditure are given in the next section and our action plans are included in the appendix to this plan.

Details of exhibition expenditure follow.

Nippon Food Show, International Exhibition Centre, Osaka

Dates: 12–14 May 20X6; stand size: 32 m² (4 m × 8 m); stand contractor: Brit-Ex Contracting.

Costs:	(£k)
Stand space rental:	6
Design, supply and build:	10
Artwork, photographic panels:	6
Rental of carpets, furniture, lights, phone, etc:	3
Hotel bills/expenditure for stand staff:	3
Air fares:	3
Total gross cost:	31
Less government grants:	3
Total net cost:	28

8. Budgets and profit and loss account

Operating expenses will increase significantly to fund the additional sales costs of the plan. The operating expenses budget for the export sales department for the first year of the plan follows.

Operating expenses budget for 20x6

Department: Export Sales – Japan Project; costs (£k):

Salaries:	10
Travel/entertaining:	30
Advertising:	50
Exhibitions:	28
Literature:	15
Sundry items:	5
Total:	138

Partial salaries have been included and the travel costs are those for the sales manager and sales director to support the Nippon Food Show in Osaka, Japan and to make additional visits to meet with potential distributors for the west of Japan. Advertising is mainly tied in with the exhibitions and we have assumed that local distributors will take over this expense after 20X6. The literature costs include the provision of a Japanese brochure and again we assume that local distribution will use our artwork to produce their own materials as sales develop.

A partial profit and loss account for the additional sales included in this plan follows.

Effect on P&L of export sales to Japan (excluding fixed cost allocation)

	20X6 £k	20X7 £k	20X8 £k
Invoiced sales	120	225	300
Less cost of sales	72	135	180
Gross profit	48	90	120
Sales and marketing costs			
Salaries	10	11	12
Travel/entertaining	30	25	28
Advertising	50	10	10
Exhibitions	28		
Literature	15	5	5
Sundry items	5	5	5
Total – sales costs	138	56	60
Distribution costs	4	6	8
Total operating expenses (excl fixed cost allocation)	142	62	68
Operating profit	(94)	28	52

9. Controls and update procedures

This plan is to be revised every 12 months.

Appendices

In the appendices we include details of sales by product, key market and key sales area, with forecasts for these for the next three years.

INDEX

(italics indicate a figure or table in the text)

accredited trade organization (ATO) 147
action plans 90–91
Africa 7, 42
agent *see* export agent
airway bill 193, 194
anti-dumping laws 169
Apple 45
Asia 37, 42
Asia-Pacific Economic Cooperation forum
     (APEC) 35
Association of British Insurers 224
Association of South-Eat Asian Nations
     (ASEAN) 33, 35
ATA carnet 195
Austrade (Australia Trade Commission)
     43, 67, 226, 240
   Export Market Development Grant
      (EDMG) 240
   Global Opportunities programme 43
   trade missions 150
   website 57
Australia 7, 29, 42, 43

Belgium 5
bill of lading 193, 194
bills of exchange 196
Brazil 28, 36, 37, 42, 142, 233–34
BRICs. the 36, 37, 233–37
British Chambers of Commerce 2, 5, 15,
     26, 59, 64, 67, 120, 148, 168,
     195, 207, 218
   Export Communications Review
      139–40, 251
   Export Marketing Research Scheme
      (EMRS) 15, 27, 68, 249
   website 140
British Insurance Brokers Association
     (BIBA) 224
British International Freight Association
     (BIFA) 185
British Pump Manufacturers
     Association 55

Business Link 21, 203
   UK Trade Tariff online tool 199
   website 26, 199, 247
Business Opportunities Service 251
Business Victoria 20
   export readiness checklist 20–21

Canada 42, 241
'cash against documents' 171
certificates of origin 195
China 3, 36, 37, 42, 241
China Council for the promotion of
     International Trade
     (CCPIT) 241
CIM Note (Convention Internationale
     des Marchandises par Chemin
     de Fer) 194
CMR Note (Convention des Marchandises
     par Route) 194
commercial invoice 194–95
Common Market of Eastern and
     Southern Africa
     (COMESA) 35–36
competition law 127
Complete Export Plan 96,
   format 97–98
   see also export plan
consular invoice 195
credit agencies 224
credit check 207–08, 224
credit management 223
creditworthiness 208–10
currency options 211

Dangerous Goods Note (DGN) 194
data protection 162–63
direct exporting 26, 105–11
   selling direct 105–06
   setting up an overseas operation
      107–08
   using a sales agent 108–10
   using a distributor 110–12

direct selling 105–06
distribution 113–16, 118–35, 138
  law 124–28, 246
distributors 110–12
  characteristics of business *119*
  choosing 122
  comparison with agent *119*, 135
  contracts 128–35
  finding and selecting 120–22
  legal issues 124–28
  managing 134–35
  questionnaire 122–24
distributorship agreement/contract 110, 129–32
Dun & Bradstreet 207, 224
Dusky Moon 46

e-commerce 15, 25, 102–03, 152–64
  contracting 161–62
  EU requirements 160–62
  international websites 152–53, 155
  online fraud 158
  payment methods 157
  regulations 159–64
  'safe harbour' agreements 162
  search engine rankings 157
  shipping the goods 158
  taxes/tariffs 159
  types of website 153–55
  web hosting service 155–56
EC Directive 2000/31/EC 159–60
ECGD (Export Credits Guarantee Department) 222
Economist, the 54–55
entry strategies 100–17, *101*
  deciding which to use 112–13
  direct 105–12
  indirect 103–05
  online 102–03
  passive/'domestic' exporting 101–02
E7, the 37
Europa 160
European Economic Area (EEA) 34
European Free Trade Association (EFTA) 34
Eurostat 61
  NAC Rev 2 coding system 62, 63
Euromonitor 55, 58
European Patent Convention 218
European Union (EU) 33, 41, 193
  classification of goods 198–99

Classification of Products by Activity (CPA) 63
Community Trademark 219
directives on agents/distributors 125
directives on e-commerce 159–60
Office for Harmonization in the Internal Market (OHIM) 219
Privacy and Electronic Communications Regulations 2003 162–63
reporting procedures for exporters 202–03
TARIC (Tariff Intégré) Communautaire 198, 199
exchange rate 11–12
export agents 118–35
  agency contract 132–33
  characteristics of business *119*
  choosing 122
  comparison with distributor *119*, 135
  contracts 128–35
  finding and selecting 120–22
  legal issues 124–28
  questionnaire 122–24
export audit 9, 16–17, 21–24, 25, 30
  example 23–24
  sales history 22
Export Cargo Shipping Instruction (ECSI) 194
Export Credits Guarantee Service (ECGD) 223
Export Communications Review 139–40, 141, 251
export contracts 169–70
export documentation 193–96, 204
  commercial 194–95
  finance and payment 196
  transportation 193–94
Export Entreprise Finance Guarantee (ExEFG) 252
export marketing plan 96, 98–99
  see also export plan
Export Marketing Research Scheme 15, 27, 68, 240
  Example 68
export markets 31–46, 226–38
  country selection chart *40, 41*
  factors to consider 38–46
    competition 39
    distance to the market 39
    economic climate 50
    import duties/tariffs 39, *40*

language 39, 41
local standards *40*
personal risks 221–22
political stability 39, *40*, 50, 221
size 50
industry sectors/clusters 43–44
overseas markets 49–52
pricing for 81–84
product considerations 44
rating charts 39–42
segmentation 38–39
selecting 37–38
targeting 42–43, 46, 75, 80
world market 31–33
see also overseas markets
export packaging 186–90, 204
break bulk 188
considerations 186–87
containers 188
deciding on type to use 188–90
handling instructions 191
information mark 191
insurance 187, 191–92
labelling/marking 190–91
layers 186
shipping mark 190–91
special markings 191
types 187–88
export plan 9, 73–74, 84–89, 96–99
assumptions 84
costs and budgets 91–95
example 253–60
format 96
see also marketing planning process
export readiness checklist 20–21, 27
export strategy 9, 70–73, 84–89
exporters
adaptives 15
passives 15
reactives 15
strategists 15
types 14–15
exporting
benefits of 7–8
choices 25–26
costs of 10–11
direct 26
domestic 25
getting started 14–30
indirect 25
online 15–16, 25

readiness 8–12
reasons for 6–7, 17–19
risks 9–10
top management support 12
exporting services 117

Food and Agriculture Organization
(FAO) 61
foreign currency bank account 211
foreign exchange risks 210–16, 224
Foreign Market Consulting 121
forward foreign exchange contracts 11,
211, 214–16
Fox, Martha Lane 141
France 5, 227–28
Free Trade Agreements (FTAs) 33
freight forwarders 184, 185
Frost and Sullivan 58
'frustrated export' 216

'genuine agent' 127
German Insurance Association 189–90
Transport Information Service 189
Germany 3, 5–6, 42, 56, 226–27
global purchasing network 102
Godfrey, Robin 15, 140
Goldman Sachs 36
government support organizations *see*
support services
gross domestic product (GDP) 31
comparison of EU and USA *33*
Gym Equipment Company 27–28

Harmonized Commodity Description and
Coding System (HS) 61, 204
codes 198
uses of 197–98
HM Revenue & Customs 202–03
National Export System (NES) 202
website 203

Incoterms (International Commercial
Terms) 2, 165, 174–79
applicable to any mode of
transport 175, 176–77
applicable to sea and inland waterway
transport only *176*, 178–79
checklist 179
India 36, 37, 42, 235–36, 241
UK India Business Council (UKIBC)
59, 121, 236

India Trade Promotion Organization   241
indirect exporting   25, 103–05
   example   105
   export agents   104
   export management companies   104
   export trading companies   104
Indonesia   37, 44
Institute of Directors   16
insurance   187, 191–92, 223–24
   credit   222, 223, 224
   documents   195
intellectual property rights (IPR),
      protecting   217–20, 224–25
   copyright   217, 219
   designs   217, 219
   patents   217, 218, 220
   trademarks   217, 218–19, 220
   websites   246
International Chambers of Commerce
      (ICC)   171, 174, 176, 196
   Uniform Customs and Practice 600
      (UCP600)   171, 196
International Monetary Fund (IMF)   6, 31
International Telecommunications Union
      (ITU)   152–53
internet, the   1, 16, 120, 141, 152, 246
   see also websites
Internet Corporation for Assigned Names
      and Numbers (ICANN)   154
Intrastat system   202
Ireland   42
Italy   5, 229–30

Japan   232–33

Kelly's Directories   60
Kemp Little   127–28
   distribution checklist   128
   website   246
Keynote   58
Kompass Directories   60, 120

language   141, 143, 206
letters of credit   2, 169, 172–73, 193, 196,
      208
   irrevocable   196
   revocable   196
logistics   11

Managed Credit Insurance Scheme   224
market research   47

Market.Research.com   58
Market Research Society
   Code of Practice   66
   website   66
marketing   20
marketing channels   113–16, *114*
   direct selling   *116*
   indirect selling   *115*
marketing objectives   85–87
marketing planning process   73–74
   assumptions   84
   costs/budgets   74
   evaluating/selecting target
      markets   80
   implementation schedule   74
   objectives/strategies   73–74, 85–97
   pricing for export markets   81–84
   research analysis   73, 74
   situation analysis   73, 75–80
   SWOT analysis   75–76, *76*
   written plan   74, 96–99
marketing research   47–49, 205–06
   aims   74–75
   carrying out yourself   52–54
   checklist   53
   collecting/analysing data   49
   company information   60
   country (market) reports   55–58
   defining objectives   48
   desk research   54–55
   field research   63–64
   government support   67–68
   industry (sector) reports   55–58
   information requirements   48
   market structure/segmentation
      53–54
   obtaining information   48–49
   overseas markets   49–52
   product/statistical information   61–63
   trade associations   58–59
   trade missions   64
   tradeshows/exhibitions   64
marketing research agency   64–68
   brief   65
   choosing   65–66
   proposal   66
   report   66–67
Mexico   37
Mintel   58
mobile phones   44
moving your goods   181–204

airfreight 183
classifying 196–201
courier services 182
dangerous goods 184
export documentation 193–96
freight forwarders 184, 185
groupage or consolidation 184
modes of transport 181–84
packaging 186–90
post 182
rail 183
reporting procedures 201–03
road 182–83
sea freight 183–84
Multilateral Trading System (MTS) 33

Net Resources International (NRI) 60
Netherlands, the 5
New Zealand 242
New Zealand Trade and Enterprise
      (NZTE) 242
Nominet 155, 246
North American Free Trade Agreement
      (NAFTA) 33, 35, 193
Norway 43

O'Neill, Jim 36
Office for National Statistics 42, 62, 63
One Agenda 121
online selling see e-commerce
Organization for Economic Co-operation
      (OECD) 36, 246
Overseas Market Introduction Service
      (OMIS) 27, 121, 249
overseas markets 49–52, 226–38
   competition 52
   country type 50
   customers 51
   distribution channels 52
   entry strategies 100–17
   industry structure 51
   infrastructure 50
   legal/regulatory issues 50–51
   product suitability 52
   size 51
overseas operation 107–08

packaging 138, 186–90, 204
Panasonic 44
Patent Co-operation Treaty 218
patents 218–19

payment methods 170–74, 171, 208
   advance payment 170
   creditworthiness of customers 208–10
   documentary collection 171
   Incoterms (International Commercial
         Terms) 2, 165, 174–79
   letters of credit 172–73
   open account 171
   terms 209
people/staff 88
place 87
Precision Vaccum Products (PVP)
   action plan 91
   distributors and 112
   export plan 253–60
   export plan assumptions 84
   export plan objectives 86
   export strategy 71–72
   competitor SWOT analysis 79
   market segment SWOT analysis 79
   operating expenses budget 92
   organization SWOT analysis 77
   pricing strategy 90
   product SWOT analysis 78
   profit and loss accounts 92, 95
   sales and marketing costs 94, 95
   sales forecast 86, 87
   target market evaluation 80
   target market objectives 88–89
   target market SWOT analysis 78
price fixing 127
PricewaterhouseCoopers (PwC) 37
pricing 81–84, 87, 165–69
   break-even analysis 83
   cost-plus 81–82
   fixed costs 83
   legislation 126
   marginal 82–84
   special products 166–67
   standard/semi-standard
         products 166–67, 167–68
   top-down 82
   variable 83
processes 88
Prodcom 63
product 87
   design features 219
promotion 87

quoting for international business 165–80
   export contracts 169–70

payment methods   170–74
price lists   167, 168
pricing   165–69
pro-forma invoices   168–69
special products   166–67
standard products   166–67, 167–69
see also Incoterms, pricing

rail waybill   194
Regional Trade Agreements (RTAs)   33, 42
registered community design (RCD)   219
risk management   222–24
risks of exporting   9–10, 205–25
    avoiding litigation   221
    climate   207
    country risks   206–07
    currency   210–11
    customer   207–08
    delivery delays/frustrated
        exports   216
    economic   207
    foreign exchange   211–14
    intellectual property rights (IPR)
        217–20
    personal   221
    political   206
    understanding the market   205–06
road transport   182–83
road waybill   194
Russia   36, 37, 42, 148–49, 230, 234–35

'safe harbour' agreements   162
sales agent 108–10
sales promotion   136–51
    advertising   144–45
    company image   137, 138
    exhibitions/trade shows   145–47
    introductory leaflet   142–43
    language   141, 143, 206
    literature   142–43, 206
    overseas markets   139–40
    positioning your product   137–38
    presentations   143–44
    sector-focused trade missions
        148–50
    Stella Artois example   138
    understanding target market   136–38
    websites   140–41
sea freight   183–84
Shipper's Export Declaration (SED)   203
shipping see moving your goods   181–84

SIC coding system   61–62
SITPRO   172–74
    Incoterms checklist   179
    'Letters of Credit – Best
        Practice'   172–73
Simply Solar Ltd   26–27
Single Administrative Document
        (SAD)   202
small and medium-sized enterprises
        (SMEs)   14, 248, 252
SMART objectives   85
South Africa   19, 241–42
    Department of Trade and Industry
        (DTI)   43, 241–42
    Export Marketing and Investment
        Assistance (EMIA)
        scheme   242
South African Development Community
        (SADC)   36
South America   7
Southern Common Market
        (MERCOSUR)   35
spot dealing   210
Springboard magazine   252
Standard Shipping Note (SSN)   194
Stella Artois   138
strategy   87, 89 see also export strategy
support services   2, 7
    government   17, 56–57, 239–42, 243,
        247–52
    market research   67–68

tactics   87, 89–91 see also example
        export plan
tariff numbers 61, 204
    see also Harmonized Commodity
        Description and Coding
        System (HS)
Trade Association Forum   59
trade associations   58–59, 120, 245
trade blocs   33–36
trade directories   60, 245
trade exhibitions/shows   146–47
Trade Facilitation Office Canada
        (TFO Canada)   241
trade missions   148–50
trademarks   218–19
TradeShow Access Programme   147
transport insurance   191–92
    basic shipping insurance (limited
        liability)   192

documents   195–96
general cargo   192
goods-in-transit   192
Turkey   37

UK (United Kingdom)   5, 228–29, 243
    Department for Business Innovation
        & Skills (BIS)   160, 174
    Department of Commerce   21, 28, 42
    exports   7
    government support
        organizations   239–42
    government support services   247–52
UK Exporters Ltd   121
UK India Business Council (UKIBC)   59,
        121, 236
UK Trade & Investment (UKTI)   2, 16, 17,
        21, 26, 43, 55, 67, 139, 149, 226,
        239–40
    Business Opportunities Service   251
    country guides reports   56, 238, 247
    'Exporting – an overview'   16
    High Value Opportunities
        Programme   252
    individual services   248–49
    online peer self-help   252
    Overseas Security Information for
        Business (OSIB)   207
    'sector in country' reports   57
    Springboard magazine   252
    trade teams   121, 249
    website   8, 56, 57, 247–48, 252
unfair competition legislation   127
'unit load device' (ULD)   184
United Nations (UN)   61, 184
    Central Product Classification (CPC)   61
    Harmonized Commodity Description
        and Coding System (HS)   61
USA (United States of America)   3, 5, 42,
        231–32
    AESDirect   203
    CAN-SPAM Act 2008   163
    Census Bureau   200, 203
    classifying export goods   199–200

Commercial Service   56, 57, 150, 226
country guides/reports   56–57, 238
Department of Commerce and
        International Trade   67, 97,
        240
Export Assistance Center   200
exports   7
Federal Trade Commission   163
reporting procedures for
        exporters   203
trade missions   150

value added tax (VAT)   159, 201

Water Valves and Fittings Pty Ltd   29
websites   1, 140–41
    domain names   154–55
    financial data   245
    government statistics   244
    government support organizations
        243–44
    industry   59
    intellectual property rights   246
    international e-commerce   152–53
    market and sector reports   245
    market research organizations   245
    ordinary or e-commerce   153–55
    search engines   154, 157
    trade associations   245
    web hosting service   155–56
World Chambers Network   59
World Customs Organization (WCO)
        197–98
world trade   6, 31
    regional trading agreements   33–36
    top economies   32, 42
    top exporters of commercial
        services   4
    top merchandise exporters   4
    total value of exports   3
World Trade Organization (WTO)   3, 33
    website   42

Yellow Pages   120